THE GNOME COMPENDIUM

The Gnome Manuscript Part III

The
GNOME COMPENDIUM

Excerpts of the works of J.H.W. Eldermans

By

Wilmar Taal

TROY BOOKS

Published by Troy Books
www.troybooks.co.uk

Troy Books Publishing
BM Box 8003
London WC1N 3XX

Cover design: Gemma Gary
Artwork: JHW Eldermans

Contents

PREFACE

In this final tome on the Gnome manuscript of J.H.W. Eldermans, we will look into the non-magical and non-behavioural aspects of the research Eldermans did on this type of Little People. We will be looking into the folklore and mythology, as most of his work in this field was based on folkloric writers and the mythologists who wrote down the aspects of the gnome presence in our world. In this part of the manuscript, we are dealing with the purported Germanic origins of the gnomes and the way in which these creatures found their way into our folklore. These two subjects are knitted together into one chapter. The *Edda* plays an important part in these studies. Written by Snorri Sturluson in the twelfth century, it was a mainly unknown work during the Middle Ages and later Renaissance. The Edda was translated into Latin and then later, into German and Dutch. During the nineteenth century, when nationalism began to take a hold of most countries in Europe, these writings were important in establishing a national identity. Many folklorists went into the country to note down the stories people were still telling each other and the work of the Brothers Grimm was very important, to that note. Their work was later transformed into what we now call *Fairy Tales*. Dutch folkloric writers like Jan de Vries, J.R.W. Sinninghe and Gustav van de Wal Perné were also very important to Eldermans.

Eldermans also met with a great number of people who told him about gnomes. We can split these people into two categories: people who told stories about gnomes which they had learned second or third hand and those people who were witness to the existence of gnomes. The latter category will cover chapter three of this book. Some of these stories have been subject of study in *The Silent Listener. The Life and Works of J.H.W. Eldermans*. This chapter will be additionally supplemented with the field studies, which had been performed in Twente and on De Veluwe. There will be no commentaries, since these stories are the personal experiences of people. The second chapter will deal with the people who provided information to Eldermans about gnome folklore. Eldermans could be quite ambivalent to these people. He did not hesitate to call them liars if he suspected them to be such persons.

A final category are the entries in the manuscript that are hard to categorize and these make up the fourth chapter of this book, the so-called *miscellanous writings*. These writings conclude the studies into Eldermans' gnome folklore and at the end of this book, you will find a closing chapter and the acknowledgments, which are meant to cover all three tomes in this trilogy. The people mentioned in them have contributed to the books or provided help in manifold ways. *The Gnome Compendium* should not be considered as a leftover tome, as the information provided in this book is as important as it was in *The Gnome Manuscript* and *The Gnome Grimoire* - especially the chapter concerning the witnesses might provide information on where to find gnomes in The Netherlands and you can use the other books to learn how to make contact with these beings.

If you have questions concerning these books, I am willing to answer them for you. You can contact me through Facebook: https://www.facebook.com/wilmarbjtaal. You can drop me a line through a Personal Message or simply ask me on the page.

I hope that *The Gnome Compendium* will live up to your expectations.

Wilmar Taal
Koog aan de Zaan, 27th December 2017

CHAPTER ONE

GNOME FOLKLORE
AND MYTHOLOGY

As we have seen in the previous instalments, The Netherlands has a rich gnome folklore, especially in the southern parts of the country. These gnome folkloric aspects still live on in certain names of places, like the *Alverberg*. 'Alf' is a different name for gnome, and in the Peel regions of The Netherlands, there are many places that refer to the Alves as once being part of the Brabant and Limburg landscape. But not only there do we find names that tie into a past associated with gnomes. The Dutch word for gnome, *kabouter*, can be found inside some forests named *kabouterbos*, gnome-forest, which ties in tightly with the fairy tale aspect of the gnomes. Mostly these woods or forests are filled with statues of gnomes and directed towards children. In Voorthuizen, a flamboyant citizen of that town, Bep Welters, created a gnome-forest of her own. When the gamekeeper of the forest accidentally destroyed the first gnome village that she had established there, she rallied people to bring small statues of gnomes and to restore the gnome village. Just outside of Nunspeet there is another gnome-forest, with wooden statues of gnomes and all kinds of little stories concerning gnomes.

Most of the gnome folklore seems to originate in mythology - and not only in Dutch mythology but Germanic mythology, Norse mythology and even Greek mythology. As we learned in *The Gnome Manuscript*, there are 'historic' elements at work in this mythology, which is also stated in the *Encyclopedia of Magic & Superstition* - the so-called Pygmy-theory. In the Pygmy theory, we see that gnomes might descend from a small race of people which once lived on Crete and moved north once their mines were depleted. The Pygmy theory is further explained in the books by Martin Koomen, *Kingdom of the Night* and *The Icy Seed of the Devil*. Because these Little People lived on their own and didn't have much contact with the locals, they developed into myths concerning little people with red pointy hats who live in the woods or the mountains. In this chapter, we will study what Eldermans collected throughout the years concerning the tales of gnome creation and how folklore dealt with these little folk.

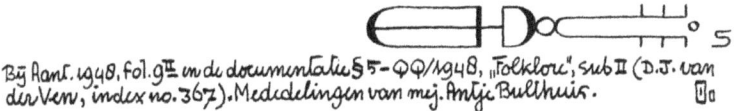

Bij Aant. 1948, fol. 9^{II} in de documentatie §5-QQ/1948, "Folklore", sub II (D.J. van der Ven, index no. 367). Mededelingen van mej. Antje Bulthuis.

At Note 1948, fol. 9II and the documentation §5-QQ/1948, "Folklore", sub II (D.J. van der Ven, index no. 367). Gleanings from miss Antje Bulthuis. O.

Here we recognize the symbol of Nopa Padous from *The Greater Key of Solomon* but, more interesting, is the name of Antje Bulthuis. Eldermans was acquainted with the Dutch journalist and author Rico Bulthuis, who lived in Bezuidenhout, a district in The Hague, just around the corner of where Eldermans lived. They met on the tram 6, which Eldermans took to work. Is this Antje Bulthuis related to Rico Bulthuis? Or is it pure coincidence that these two people share the same surname?

[Below]: *Documentation §46-II/1942: "Viskedieken"= Visschedijk Almelo. (Report no. XII). In the beginning of the 19th century, at the end of the French occupation, a transport guided by Cossacks spend the night on the Visschedijk [dijk is a dyke, this would roughly translate as 'fish-dyke']. On one of the heavily burdened wagons -the wheels sunk deep into the bank of the road-*

were a small number of little kegs, which according to the curious bystanders must have been very heavy.

p.505.

Documentatie §46-II/1942: „Viskedieken": Visschedijk, Almelo. (Verslag no. XII). In het begin van de 19e eeuw, het einde van de Franse overheersing, overnachtte een transport, begeleid door kozakken, op de Visschedijk. Op een der zwaar beladen wagens —de wielen zakten diep in de berm van de weg— stond een gering aantal kleine vaatjes, die dus, zo meenden de nieuwsgierige omstanders, zeer zwaar moesten zijn. Dit trok ook de aandacht van een nabij wonende boer en diens zoon, die het geval in het oog hielden. Toen de schildwacht zich 's nachts even had verwijderd, namen vader en zoon een vaatje van de wagen teneinde zich dat toe te eigenen. De schildwacht keerde echter onverwachts terug en ontdekte de diefstal. Hij achtervolgde in het duister en tussen de houtwallen de vader, die het vaatje op zijn schouder droeg —de zoon was in een andere richting gevlucht. De schildwacht schoot tijdens de achtervolging op de vader en doodde de man, die het vaatje inmiddels had weggeworpen. De zoon had, evenals enkele buren, een en ander zo nauwkeurig mogelijk gevolgd toen hij meende in veiligheid te zijn. Hij, én de buren waren er van overtuigd dat het vaatje door de kozakken niet was teruggevonden. Later vernam men, dat zulke vaatjes veelal waren gevuld met zilvergeld, soms zelfs met goudgeld, zodat men in de omgeving bleef zoeken naar de plaats waar het vaatje kon zijn gebleven. Echter zonder resultaat…. Tot een veertigtal jaren later de zoon een boerenknecht aannam, die van Manderveen kwam, een vreemde, eenzelvige knaap. Toen deze knecht het verhaal over het waardevolle vaatje vernam, vroeg hij enige dagen vrij en vertrok naar zijn geboortestreek, waar hij met toverij het contact vernieuwde met daar verblijvende aardgeesten, kabouters. De knecht wist aldus een van deze kabouters mee te lokken naar de Visschedijk waar het aardmannetje hem op een geheimzinnige wijze en zonder woorden of gebaren duidelijk maakte waar het vaatje —dat in een kolk diep in de veenderij was geraakt— zich bevond…. [Zo groot was in die jaren de trouw en de eerlijkheid van het personeel, dat de knecht het vaatje, dat gevuld bleek te zijn met zilverstukken, triomfantelijk naar zijn 'patroon bracht….]. Documentatie §46-IV/1942 bevat meer topografische details en personalia.— ♀o

It drew the attention of a farmer and his son, who lived nearby and kept a close eye on the case. When the guard took his leave that night, father and son took a keg from the wagon in order to steal it. The guard returned unexpectedly and discovered the theft. He pursued the father, who carried the keg on his shoulder, into the dark, through the wooded banks - the son had fled in the other direction. The guard shot and killed the father, who had, during the pursuit, thrown the keg away. The son had closely watched, as did the neighbours, when he thought he was in safety. He, and the neighbours, were convinced the Cossacks didn't retrieve the keg. Later, they learned that these kegs were mostly filled with silver coins, sometimes with gold coins which caused many people to search the area where the keg could have been hidden. Alas without success.... Until around forty years later, the son hired a farmhand coming from Manderveen - a strange, solitary fellow. When this farmhand learned the story about the valuable keg, he asked for a few days off and returned to his birthplace, where he renewed contact through magic with nature spirits residing there - gnomes. The farmhand managed to lure one of these gnomes to the Visschedijk, where it was able to make clear where the keg was, in a secretive manner without words or gestures - sunk into a gully in the peat bog.... [Loyalty was so great in those years that the farmhand returned triumphant to his master with the keg, filled with silver coins....]. Documentation §46-IV/1942 contains more topographic and personal details.- S.

Mr. G.J. ter Kuile wrote an entire chapter about the French occupation of The Netherlands from 1799 until 1815, also known as the Napoleonic time. Although Ter Kuile does not mention the Visschedijk at all, he does mention something else:

In Amsterdam, I was told that a vanguard of 60 Cossacks had arrived in Almelo on November 6th.[1]

The information appeared to be wrong. The first Cossacks came across the border near Ootmarsum on November 9th and they had come with the intention of liberating The Netherlands from the French occupation. They were commanded by Prince Naritschkin. Although Ter Kuile indeed confirms the presence of the Cossacks, the story about the silver-theft did not appear to stick in the memories of the people of Almelo. It is not known where Eldermans heard this story.

---

1. Mr. G.J. ter Kuile, *Twentsche Eigenheimers. Historische schetsen*, Almelo, 1936, pp 85

Anm. 1957, fol. 210D: bedoeld wordt: „Denn da hielten auch im lande/Noch die guten zwerglein Haus;/Kleingestalt, doch hochbegabet,/Und so hülfreich überaus!"— (Müller, zie onder „Switzerland".) E

Fol. 210D, bij F4: „Alpenrosen for 1824, ap. Grimm, Introd. to Irish Fairy Legends".

Note 1957, fol. 210D: Meaning is: [from German] *"And out in the country / the good dwarfs had their home / small of stature but very gifted / and so helpful overall"*- (Müller, *see under "Switzerland".*) E.

Fol. 210D, at F4: *"Alp-roses for 1824, by Grimm, introduction to Irish Fairy Legends".*

Bij §1d: cluricaun = kabouter (Ierland), zie)5 (Crofton Croker). E

At §1d: Cluricaun = gnome (Ireland), see)5 (Crofton Croker). **S.**

Thomas Crofton Croker has been detailed in an earlier installment but what some of you might not know, is that his works on fairy legends of Ireland had been translated into German. The German edition of Crofton Croker's book had a preface by the Brothers Grimm. This preface has sometimes been translated into English to serve as the preface for the English edition. In Crofton Croker's book, there is an entire chapter of tales concerning the *Cluricaun* but he does not actually explain what a Cluricaun is! Brian Froud and Alan Lee do have an explanation for the Cluricaun:

> *When the Leprechaun has a wild night after his daily work, he is called a Cluricaun. He goes on a predatory raid through wine cellars, then makes drunken rides on the backs of sheep or shepherd dogs.*[2]

According to Thomas Keightley, the Cluricaun is a typical Irish fairy but he does not make the connection with the Leprechaun, which is considered to be a very rich, shoe-making fairy which lives in the bushes. Irish people try to catch Leprechauns to seize their riches but the Leprechaun

---

2. Brian Froud & Alan Lee, *De elfen*, Bussum, 1979, no pagination

has been known to be a trickster - the riches you seek may become worthless once you set the Leprechaun free. As we will see, Eldermans had limited interest in these Little People from Ireland, although it has been reported on many occasions that the respect the Irish feel for the Little People is very much alive today!

Toevoegen aan §2ª, Aant. 1947, sub 38-III: „De Veluwenaar Gust. van de Wall Perné verzamelde zijn Veluwsche Sagen (2 delen, 1911-1912) uit de volksmond, maar gaf ze weer in eigen bewerkingen die een naïef plattelandsexpressionisme vertonen. Een enkele keer heeft zijn stijl een zekere charme, minstens even vaak echter verwalt hij in een wollige brei van woorden zonder betekenis". =)2.

Add to §2a, Note 1947, sub 38-III: "Gust van de Wall Perné, living on De Veluwe, collected his Sagas from De Veluwe (2 tomes, 1911-1912) from the common people, but re-worked them into stories which reflect a naïve country-expressionism. Sometimes his style has a certain charm, but as often he falls into a fuzzy mess of words without meaning".=)2. **H.**

   Gustaaf Frederik van de Wall Perné (1877-1911) was a Dutch artist, born in Apeldoorn - a mere distance from Hoog Soeren, where most of his collected tales had taken place. He worked as an artist in the style of the English 'Arts and Crafts' movement and also for various Dutch publishing houses. He owned a house in Hoog Soeren, stylized with wolf-heads carved in wood and the house was called 'Mjölnir', after the hammer of Thor, in The Netherlands known as *Donar*, in German *Thunar*. Van de Wal Perné started to take up painting in Hoog Soeren and he was a prominent artist in The Netherlands during the years 1900-1910. During these years, before he died of a lead-poisoning in 1911, he collected local sagas and filled in the voids in these tales with local tradition or even with fragments from the Edda. Eldermans' harsh criticism isn't even his own, but Martin Koomen's, who uttered these words in his book *Kingdom of the night.* (pp 221)

Bij §2C: „*Een van de ijverigste Nederlandse verzamelaars van volks-verhalen is Jacques R.W. Sinninghe, geboren in 1904. Zijn hele volwassen leven heeft hij verzameld, niet alleen door oude archieven, volksboeken en almanakken door te werken, maar vooral ook door de boer op te gaan, het hele land door. Hij placht eerst de pastoor of de dominee te bezoeken, want van de plaatselijke zielenherder mocht worden verwacht dat hij de mensen kende die graag mooie verhalen vertelden. Al zijn vondsten zijn op fiches gezet, en deze verzameling van ca. 45 000 verhalen is in 1977 door het rijk aangekocht ten behoeve van het provinciaal genootschap voor kunsten en weten-schappen te 's-Hertogenbosch".* - S.

At §2C: "One of the most diligent Dutch collectors of folktales is Jacques R.W. Sinninghe, born in 1904. His entire adult life he collected his tales, not only from old archives, folk-books and almanacks, but mainly of going out into the country, throughout the entire land. He first consulted the pastor or the reverend, because the local soul shepherd knew the people who told the beautiful stories. All his work is copied onto micro-chips and the entire collection of around 45 000 stories is bought by the government in 1977 for the Provincial Society for Arts and Sciences in 's Hertogenbosch".- S.[3]

Sinninghe, born in the same year as Eldermans, worked as a journalist until he published his first book on local sagas in 1933. He wrote about ten books about local sagas, before he started to work on more national tales. During World War II Sinninghe was a member of the 'Kultuurkamer', an institution brought to life by the National Socialist government. They awarded Sinninghe with a *Folkloristic Price* in 1942. After World War II, Sinninghe fell from grace. In 1955, he founded his own Institute for Folk Tales in Breda and in 1974, he donated a part of his collection to the regional Archives in Zeeland. Nowadays, part of his collection is kept at the University library of Tilburg and another part is being kept in the Meertens Institute in Amsterdam. It appears that Eldermans often admired people with a shady political

---

3. Martin Koomen, Het Koninkrijk van de Nacht, Amsterdam, 1978, pp 222

preference, because next to Sinninghe, we see the name of Frederik Willem van Heemskerck-Düker in his collection - an engineer and photographer with a keen interest in old motives and signs found in old Dutch architecture. Van Heemskerck – Düker was a well-known national socialist.

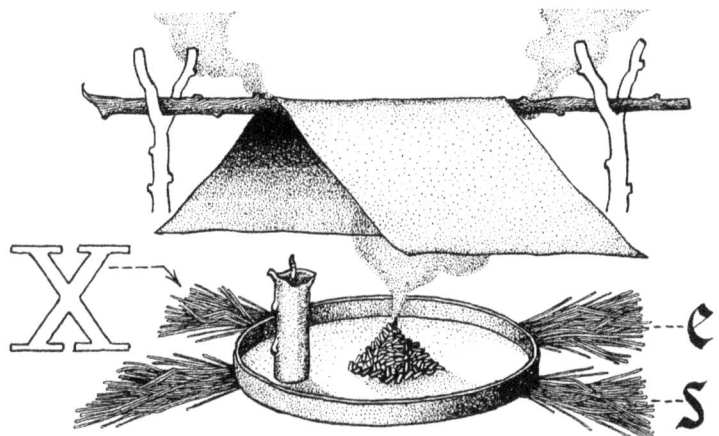

By Aant 1948, fol. 332B, „Gnomes", &c., „Throughout most of history most people have believed that beside its human and animal population the world is thronged by multitudes of spirits", &c.. Idem: documentatie §43-p/1948, F6 en F8.

At Note 1948, fol. 332B: "Gnomes"&c., "Throughout most of history most people have believed that beside its human and animal population the world is thronged by multitudes of spirits", &c.. Idem: documentation §43-p/1948, F6 and F8. **E.**

Aanvulling II by Aant. 1956, fol. 219A: „In 1968 men building a new road in County Donegal in Ireland downed tools and refused to fell a tree which stood in the road's path, because it was known to belong to „the little people". Attempts to persuade another contractor to cut the tree down failed for the same reason and in the end the local council decided to leave the tree alone and re-route the road".—

Addition II at Note 1956, fol. 219A: "In 1968, men building a new road in County Donegal in Ireland downed tools and refused to fell a tree which stood in the road's path, because it was known to belong to "The Little people". Attempts to persuade another contractor to cut the tree down failed for the same reason and in the end, the local council decided to leave the tree alone and re-route the road".- **E.**

This is a prime example of how folk-beliefs can interfere with modern planning. There is a great story concerning the Dutch artist, Marten Toonder, well known for his Ollie B. Bommel cartoons. Toonder moved to Ireland and became a firm believer in Little People. When some journalists visited him in 1977, they wanted to film a 'fairy-ring'. The director asked Toonder if fairies were friendly, to which Toonder replied that we just say that to propitiate them. Then, all kinds of accidents started to happen: sound tapes that started slithering across the field in an inexplicable way and car keys that suddenly disappeared.[4] This type of mingling of folk-beliefs is unheard of in The Netherlands, even during the time that Eldermans recorded this entry.

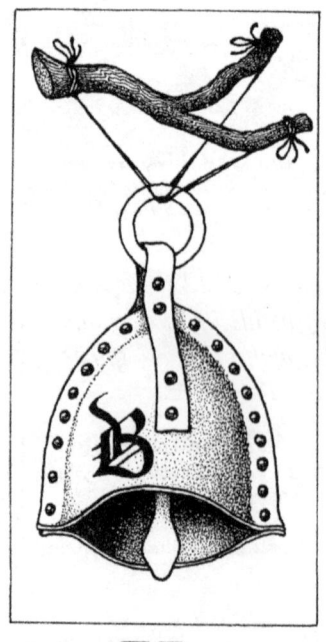

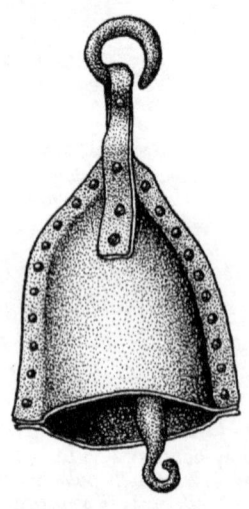

SA

SB

Bij §2ª, Aant. 1952, fol. 14½, volgens opgave van mevr. B.M. Raaymaker-van Strien: Bodleian Library, CIV-i-240. [Idem: The Tools and Methods of Magic: Aant. 1943, fol. 401½]. Toevoegen: F2. Kabouters mijden de klank van kerkklokken, maar schuwen niet het geluid van andere klokken of bellen. —

---

4. Martin Koomen, *Het Koninkrijk van de nacht*, Amsterdam, 1978, pp 14

At §2d, Note 1952, fol. 141, according to a report by Mrs. B.M. Raaymaker-van Strien: Bodleian Library, CIV-i-240. [Idem: The Tools and Methods of Magic: Note 1943, fol. 401a]. Add: F2. Gnomes avoid the sound of church bells, but don't shun the sound of other bells.- **S.**

[Below] *Add like "figure 4" to §3a, Note 1948, fol. 392II. See also under: Gust. Van de Wall-Perné, §3c, and (anonymous) "A very peculiar gnome-history": §3e.-* **E.**

The object in the following drawing is an oil-lamp, which burns at the spout. If both Van de Wall-Perné and the anonymous gnome-history are connected, it should take place on De Veluwe. The only tale Van de Wall-Perné ever recorded concerning gnomes, is the goblin of the "Aardmansberg" (Goblin Mountain), which is quite close to Hoog Soeren, where Van de Wall-Perné lived. This goblin lived inside the mountain and was in love with the daughter of Earth and Air, called Echo. He married Echo and she became quite miserable. If you stand on the top of the hill, and ask questions, Echo still might answer. There is in the whole tale, however, no mention of an oil-lamp. If you ask her four questions, she answers: who is your father you fled in despair (**air**), who was your mother who gave you birth (**earth**), how was the goblin you married so bold (**old**), do you love him or not (**not**).

Als „Fig.4" Toevoegen aan §3ᵉ, Aant. 1948, fol. 392ᴵᴵ. Zie ook onder: Gust. van de Wall-Perné, §3ᵉ, en (anoniem) „Een zeer merkwaardige kabouterhistorie": §3ᵉ. —

Toevoegen aan §2, Aant. 1950, sub 145ᶜ -III: „Bij Bussum is een Aardjesberg waar, volgens een overlevering, door de Germanen jonge maagden werden geofferd aan een aardman.
Misschien is op dezelfde manier het aardmannetje dat in de Veluwse Aardmansberg huisde aan zijn echtgenote gekomen. Die echtgenote het Echo, en wie bij de Aardmansberg komt kan met haar spreken, zoals Gust. van de Wall Perné vertelt in Veluwse sage:
Hoe heette uw vader, die ge zijt ontvlucht? _____ Lucht.
Hoe heette de moeder die je baarde? _____ Aarde.
Hoe was de aardman toen ge met hem zijt getrouwd? _____ Oud.
Houd je van hem ja of neen? _____ Neen!"

Add to §2, Note 1950, sub 145C -III: "Near Bussum is an "Aardjesberg" [Earth Mountain] where, according to tradition, young virgins were sacrificed by Germanic people to a goblin. Maybe the goblin in the Aardmansberg on De Veluwe got his wife in the same manner. This wife is called Echo, and who arrives at the Aardmansberg can speak with her, like Gust. Van de Wall-Perné tells in his Saga from De Veluwe: What was your father's name you fled in despair – Air. Who was your mother who gave you birth – Earth. How was the goblin you married so bold – Old. Did you love him or not – Not." **S.**

This citation has been taken from the book by Martin Koomen, *Kingdom of the Night* (pp 44), which was published in 1978.

[Below] *Add to §3 and 3a, Note 1955, sub-68-III: "The dwarfs left some trails in The Netherlands in the shape of names of places. In the woods of Soeren on De Veluwe there is a place called "Aardmanshegge"* [Goblin-bushes]. **H.**

"Many of these places have a saga connected to them: the Kabouterberg [gnome mountain] in the village Gelrode on De Kempen has cavities which were once occupied by very helpful gnomes. When the village miller had worn out his millstones, he only needed to lay them outside with a sandwich and a glass of ale to get them sharpened again. He could do the same when the linen needed washing." **S.**

At §1, Note 1955, sub 70C-III: "Near Vught was also a Kabouterberg, [gnome mountain] which was excavated".- At F2: "The name of the island Urk has something to do with Urks or Hurks, an old name for goblins".

"In Nunen, North Brabant, there is a neighbourhood called Alvershool. Also in Brabant, lies in Casterlé near Eersel the Alvenberg, a place infamous for the hauntings that are recorded there. The North Brabant town Alfen was originally called Alfheim. In Limburg one can find Averputten [gnome pits], pits in which the Avermenkes (South Limburgian for goblins) lived. In the lonely, soggy area near Bunde is such a pit, as well.

Toevoegen aan §3 en 3², Aant. 1955, sub 68-III: „De dwergen hebben in de Nederlanden ettelijke sporen nagelaten in de vorm van plaatsnamen. Zo is er in het Soerense bos op de Veluwe een plek die de Aardmanshegge heet." **H.**

„Aan veel van zulke plaatsnamen is een sage verbonden: de Kabouterberg in het Kempense dorp Gelrode bevat holen die ooit bewoond heten te zijn door hoogst hulpvaardige kabouters. Als de dorpsmolenaar zijn molenstenen had afgesleten hoefde hij ze maar buiten te leggen, met een boterham en een glas bier ernaast, om ze geslepen te krijgen. Hetzelfde kon hij met zijn linnen doen als dit moest worden gewassen." **S.**

Bij §1, Aant. 1955, sub 70E-III: „Bij Vught was eveneens een Kabouterberg, deze is later afgegraven". — Bij F2: „De naam van het eiland Urk heeft misschien te maken met urken of hurken, een oude naam voor aardmannetjes."

„In het Noordbrabantse Nunen is een buurt genaamd Alvershool. Eveneens in Brabant ligt in Casterlé bij Eersel de Alvenberg, een plek berucht om de spookverschijnselen die er worden waargenomen. Het Noordbrabantse Alfen heette oorspronkelijk Alfheim. In Limburg vindt men averputten, kuilen waarin de avermenkes (Zuidlimburgs voor aardmannetjes) wonen. In de eenzame, drassige streek bij Bunde ligt ook zo'n put."

This entire epistle is copied from the book, *Kingdom of the Night*, by Martin Koomen (pp 47). Eldermans actually cuts off the citation at a crucial point: the Averput in the swamp of Bunde holds another secret:

> *As the story goes, a long time ago, a fierce knight, in a golden coach with four feisty horses, after a reckless ride through this wild land, sunk in moments into this Averput. The golden coach is now the property of the gnomes who play with it every night, after which they disappear into the pit.*[5]

9.

Aant.1943, §7.fol.289ª; hier het citaat uit „E" (1947) toevoegen:
„Uit de Germaanse mythologie zijn tal van bestanddelen overgegaan in de volksreligie van later tijden en ten dele leven deze nog altijd onder ons voort. Gedeeltelijk liggen ze in de animistische sfeer, voorzover ze betrekking hebben op zielenvering: daarop gaat terug het geloof aan elfen, zielen van afgestorvenen, dienaressen van Vrouw Holle, de doodsgodin. Nauw verwant aan deze geesten zijn de witte wieven of witte juffers en de kaboutermannetjes of kobolden, gedienstige geesten van het huis". —

Note 1943, §7, fol. 289a; here the citation from "E" (1947) Add: "From Germanic mythology, a number of components have transferred into folk-religion of later times and in part these still live on. Partly these are in the animistic sphere, as far as they refer to soul worship: the belief in elves goes back to this, souls of the deceased, servants of Lady Holle, the goddess of death. Closely related to these spirits are the White women or white damsels and the gnomes or kobolds, obliging spirits of the house".- **P**

En bij §7, F1: „Naast de animistische laag kende deze Germaanse mythologie een hogere laag, die van het daemonengeloof, waarin zij gestalte gaf aan haar verering van de natuurkrachten. Deze water-, wind- of lucht- en berggeesten leven eveneens nog altijd voort in het volksgeloof, als meerminnen, waterwolven, nekkers, boomnimfen, als de wilde jacht en als dwergen of aardmannetjes". Overgenomen uit „E" (1947); zie ook Aant.1940, §4, fol.28-

---

5. Martin Koomen, *Het Koninkrijk van de nacht*, Amsterdam, 1978, pp 47

And at §7, F1: "Next to this animistic layer the Germanic mythology knew a higher level, that of the belief in demons, in which it gave shape to the worship of the powers of nature. These spirits of water, wind, air and mountains live on in the folk-beliefs, as do mermaids, waterwolves, nekkers, woodnymphs, as does the Wild Hunt and the dwarves or goblins". Copied from "E" (1947); see also Note 1940, §4, fol. 28. **S.**

Toevoegen aan §4², Aant. 1952, sub 41-III (M.K.): „Op de Britse eilanden worden elfengeschenken zelden ‚zomaar' gegeven, ze gaan dikwijls vergezeld van een taboe. Een boer krijgt bijvoorbeeld een stenen handmolentje, waarmee hij iedere maaltijd die hij maar wil te voorschijn kan draaien. Van het zo gemakkelijk verkregen voedsel mag echter niets worden verkocht. De vrouw van de boer schendt dit taboe, waarna blijkt dat het molentje zijn toverkracht heeft verloren (Killarney)". —   **C.**

§4²: (M.K.) „Een hoogst gevoelig punt in de betrekkingen tussen mensen en de elfenwereld is gelegen in het bestaan van stukken territorium die de elfen als onvervreemdbaar de hunne beschouwen. Vooral in Ierland hoort men hier zeer veel over. In dat land zijn dan ook proefondervindelijk bepaalde methodes in zwang gekomen om te controleren of de elfen wellicht aanspraak maken op de plaats die men wil gaan bebouwen". —   **D.**

Bij §4²: „Ook legt men wel een turfje neer op de plaats waar men wil gaan bouwen: als het er 's morgens nog ligt is alles in orde, maar indien het van die plek is weggemeten, dan zou men er bijzonder onverstandig aan doen zijn domicilie toch daar te kiezen". —   **E.**

Bij §1, Aant. 1952, sub 45 ²-III: Ten aanzien van soortgelijke proefnemingen in de omgeving van Vierhouten meent Derk Pontstein, dat de Kabouters het ten zeerste op prijs stellen door de mensen te zijn geraadpleegd. Zij zullen dan ook alleen negatief reageren wanneer zij daartoe een klemmende reden hebben". (AKWE., Sept. 1939, F2).   **F.**

Add to §4a, Note 1952, sub 41-III (M.K.): "On the British Isles, the gifts of Elves are rarely "just a present" but are always accompanied by a taboo. A farmer gets, for instance, a stone handmill, with which he can churn out every meal he wants. He is not allowed to sell any of this easy given food. The farmer's wife defies this taboo and so it appears the mill has lost its magical power (Killarney)".- **O.**
§4C : (M.K.) "A highly sensitive matter in the relations between mankind and the world of Elves is the existence of pieces of territory which the Elves consider inalienable theirs. Especially in Ireland, one hears much about it. In this country, some experimental methods have

been developed to check if the Elves claim the place where one wants to build".- **A.**

At §4d: "It is customary to lay a slab of peat on the place where one wants to build: if it still lays there in the morning, everything is alright but if it has been cast away from that place, it would be very unwise to choose this area as their domicile".- **S.**

At §1, Note 1952, sub 45b-III: "With respect to similar experiments in the vicinity of Vierhouten, it is the opinion of Derk Pontsteen that gnomes appreciate it highly when humans consult with them. They will only react in a negative manner when they have a stringent reason for it". (JHWE., Sept. 1939, F2). **H.**

The parts with the letters M.K. in parentheses refer to the work of Martin Koomen. The entry of paragraph 4d also comes from the work of Martin Koomen. The final entry appears to be from Eldermans' personal archives. Does it refer to the manuscript "E" of which he copied a few citations? Strangely enough, it oozes the atmosphere of Koomen's book, although I haven't been able to find these citations in his work.

> Aant. 1938, fol. 42: Er staat: „An old woman who lived near Tavistock had in her garden a splendid bed of tulips. To these The Pixies of the neighbourhood loved to resort, and often at midnight might they be heard singing their babes to rest among them. By their magic power they made the tulips more beautiful and more permanent than any other tulips" (&c.-Thomas Keightley, 1878).— ∃□

Note 1938, fol. 42: It says: "An old woman who lived near Tavistock had in her garden a splendid bed of tulips. To, these the Pixies of the neighbourhood loved to resort, and often at midnight might they be heard singing their babes, to rest among them. By their magic power, they made the tulips more beautiful and more permanent than any other tulips"(&c.- Thomas Keightley, 1878).- **E.** *[Sic]*

This story is cited from the book called *The World Guide to Gnomes, Fairies, Elves and other Little People* by Thomas Keightley. Eldermans does not cite the entire story. It appeared the old woman died and the tulips were taken from her garden and replaced by parsley but the power of the Pixies made the parsley wither and die. The Pixies, however, did tend to the grave of the old woman, not allowing a single weed to grow on her tomb and they sang to it in great laments and dirges.[6]

[Below] *At Note 1948, fol. 9IV and the documentation §6-BB/1948, "Magic", &c., see under "Nature Spirits".- F2: "Pieter Emiel Keuchenius (swastika), 1940".* **E**

At Note 1948, fol. 10: "About getting into contact with nature spirits one tends to call gnomes", Miss Bertha de Jong (Rotterdam, 1947). Add to F2: "The rise of the druids among the Celts was an accompanying phenomenon of the decay of the race and also occurred through the rise of magical customs. Magic and the entire priesthood in Germanic people should be considered as strange influence", ("Blood and Myth as the law of Life", P.E. Keuchenius (swastika), June 1940). **E**

Mrs. W.H.D. Ravestein-van Tol speaks of a "D-shaped lantern of pottery": §6-DD/1948, sub 2. **H**

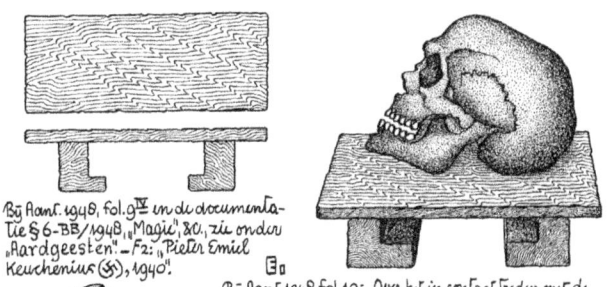

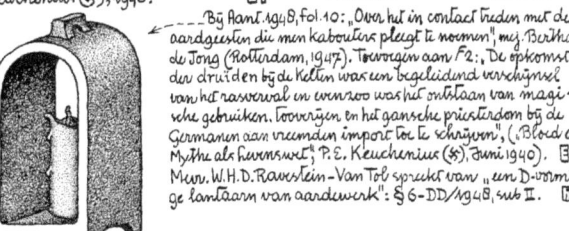

---

6. Thomas Keightley, *The World Guide to Gnomes, Fairies, Elves and other Little People*, New York, 1978, pp 304

The small swastikas in this entry are mainly for the source of the information: Pieter Emiel Keuchenius, who held national-socialist sympathies, which indeed speaks from the citations that Eldermans collected here. Keuchenius (1886-1950) was a biologist and virulent antisemite. The mentioned book, *Bloed en Mythe als Levenswet*, [Blood and Myth as a Law of Life] is considered his 'greatest work' and even considered equal to Alfred Rosenberg's *Der Mythus des 20. Jahrhunderts* [The myth of the twentieth century]. In what manner the drawing relates to the citations given here, is uncertain. The skull motive has been connected with an immortality cult in another framed work of Eldermans.[7] The book by Keuchenius can be considered 'neo-Germanic', in the sense that his work holds no historic value and is only based on the romantic views of the Germans, in particular, the Nazis, on their purported forefathers. In more recent years, research has brought to light that the historic Germanic people were nothing like the Germanic tribes portrayed in national socialist 'historic' works, which were based on the *Germanica* by Tacitus and on clairvoyant visions of shady people, like Karl Maria Wiligut. The greatest myth is talking about 'the Germanic race', as the Germanic people were a conglomerate of tribes who fought more among each other, than that they resisted against a 'common enemy' like the Romans. Although united tribes did fight wars against the Roman legions, the unity did not last, as the national socialist thinkers would have us to believe.

---

7. For more details see my book *The Silent Listener. The Life and Works of J.H.W. Eldermans.*

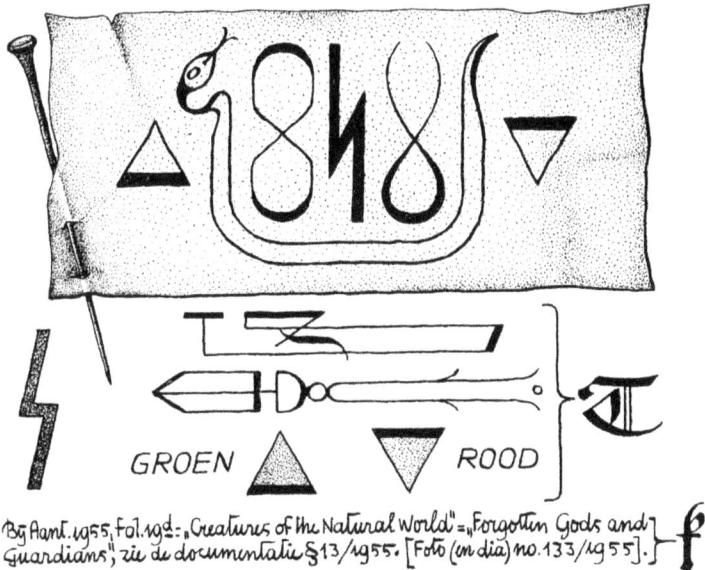

Bij Aant. 1955, Fol. 19ᵈ: „Creatures of the Natural World" = „Forgotten Gods and Guardians", zie de documentatie §13/1955. [Foto (en dia) no. 133/1955].

At Note 1955, fol. 19d: "Creatures of the natural World"=
"Forgotten Gods and Guardians", see the documentation §13/1955.
[Photo (and slide) no. 133/1955].

Although the justification refers to *Encyclopedia of Magic & Superstition* (from 1970 at earliest), the drawing appears to mingle magical traditions again: at the bottom we see symbolism from *The Greater Key of Solomon* but above, we see a more runic and Germanic tradition (hence the serpent). The two triangles are the principle of Hermes Trismegistus' 'as above, so below'.

§14/1955: „Pre-Christian figures such as giants and gnomes, once part of pagan mythology, appear and so do magicians and witches," &c.. Idem: Fig. 271-II, „La Fabrication du Talisman".

§14/1955: "Pre-Christian figures such as giants and gnomes, once part of pagan mythology, appear and so do magicians and witches", &c.. Idem: fig. 271-II, "La Fabrication du Talisman". **H.**

[Below] *At fol. 47e: "The Germanic people thought horses' heads were meant to ward off evil"- "The skulls of sacrificed horses were put on stakes", &c., see §21/1957. [Ootmarsum, Mr. G.J. ter Kuile Senior, Almelo].* **H.**

It is commonly accepted in Twente that these horsehead ornaments, mostly found on barns, are symbols to ward off evil and that they originated from the first century before Christ. In later times, these ornaments were christened, by adding a small cross to the head.[8]

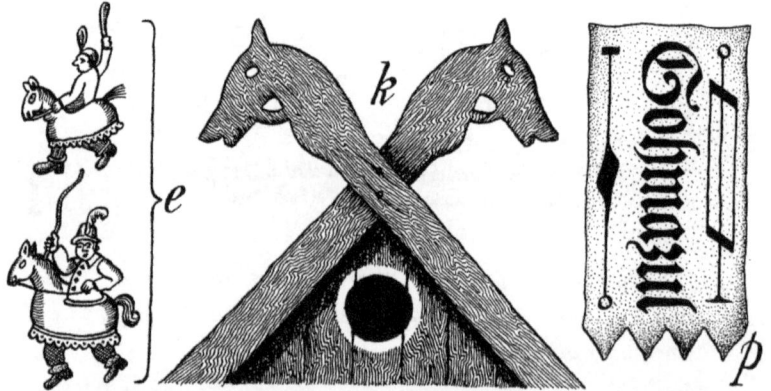

Bij fol. 47e: „De Germanen kenden aan paardekoppen een onheil afwerende betekenis toe"– „de schedels der geofferde paarden werden op staken gestoken", &c., zie §21/1957. [Ootmarsum, Mr. G.J. ter Kuile Sen., Almelo].

The name Gohmazul does turn up a couple of times in Eldermans' work and it is probably something he copied from an obscure manuscript or grimoire. Unfortunately, I have been unable to trace the name back to its original work.

---

8.   https://web.archive.org/web/20080413013430/http://www.geocities.com/twentschgenootschap/geveltekens.htm

Bij §1, Aant. 1955, sub 85ᵃ-III: „De haardstee, het centrale punt in de boerenhoeve van de Noordwesteuropese landen, levert via de schoorsteen de verbinding met onbekende duistere machten buiten. Onze voorouders plachten afgevallen broodkruimels en andere etens-resten in de open haard te schuiven en te verbranden, alsof deze aan iets of iemand geofferd moesten worden." – H₀

§1c: „De haardstee een heilige plek en een verbinding met de hogere machten: Wie goed luistert hoort door de schoorsteen misschien de luchtelfen — zeker is dat er, vooral 's nachts, veel te horen valt in de schoorsteen van een open haard". – [Zie „Bronnen" no. 601.] E₀

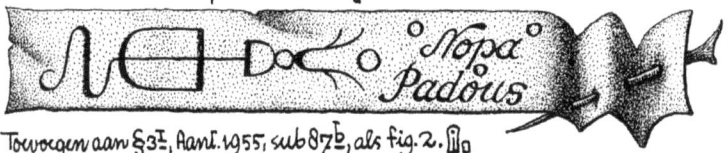

Toevoegen aan §31, Aant. 1955, sub 87b, als fig. 2. A₀

At §1, Note 1955, sub 85a-III: "The fireplace, the central point in the farms of the North-European countries, offers a connection through the chimney with the unknown dark forces outside. Our ancestors shoved fallen breadcrumbs and other leftovers of dinner in the fireplace and burned it, like it should be sacrificed to something or someone".- **H.**

§1c: "The fireplace is a holy place and a connection with higher powers: who listens carefully through the chimney might hear the air elves – it is certain that, especially at night, there is much to hear in the chimney of a fireplace".- [See "Sources"no. 601] **E.**
Add to §31, Note 1955, sub 87b, as figure 2. **A.**

Both entries are from Martin Koomens book *Kingdom of the Night*, first published in 1978. These Notes could not possibly refer to the year, 1955. It appears that this book is "Source no. 601".[9] Why would Eldermans attribute a citation from a book published in 1978 to the year 1955? Does it remind him of something he heard in 1955, or is he working on building a 'fake' tradition?

---

9. Martin Koomen, *Het Koninkrijk van de nacht*, Amsterdam, 1978, pp 59-60

By Aant. 1952, fol. 28ᴱ ["Saga and Myth", "Gnomes" III] "leder van een hinde", zie documentatie §14-II/1952. E₀

At Note 1952, fol. 28E ["Saga and Myth", "Gnomes", III]
"Leather of a doe", see documentation §14-II/1952. **S.**

By Aant. 1942, fol. 41ᵃ, aanvulling IV: „And all around the visitor to Ireland are the artifacts that retain the legends – the thousands of raths, or „earthworks", that traditionally have been, and in many cases still are called „fairy forts"". Fol. 41ᶜ, toevoegen: „F3. Fairies seem to have been prevalent in the whole region. In a field near the road between Champeix and Ludesse is a fourteen-foot menhir known as Pierre des Fées, or fairy stone; nearer to Ludesse is a logan stone and some early Roman remains known as cabanes des fées, or fairy huts". – E₀

At Notee 1942, fol. 41a, addition IV: "And all around the
visitor to Ireland, are the artifacts that retain the legends – The
thousands of raths or "earthworks" that traditionally have been,
and in many cases still are called, "fairy forts". Fol. 41c, add: F3.
Fairies seem to have been prevalent in the whole region in a field near
the road between Champeix and Ludesse is a fourteen-foot menhir
known as Pierre des Fées, or fairy stone; nearer to Ludesse is a logan
stone and some early Roman remains known as cabanes des fées, or
fairy huts".- **E.**

Although this entry breathes the spirit of Thomas
Keightley, it appears not to be from his fairy-publications.
Even Martin Koomen wrote about the *raths* in Ireland.
Presumably Eldermans came across another source which he
failed to mention.

[Below] *At Note 1952, fol. 27F: documentation §14/1952. ["Saga and Myth": "Gnomes", III]. Add to F6: Lenihan, M., "History of Limerick", Dublin, 1884. (J. Duffy).* **E.**

The book *History of Limerick* by Maurice Lenihan or correctly titled *Limerick, its history and antiquities; ecclesiastical, civil, and military, from the earliest ages*, is quite peculiar in Eldermans' gnome manuscript, since the book has only one single entry concerning *fairies*, and it is not even that informative to Eldermans himself. Yet on page 747 of this copious book, we read the following:

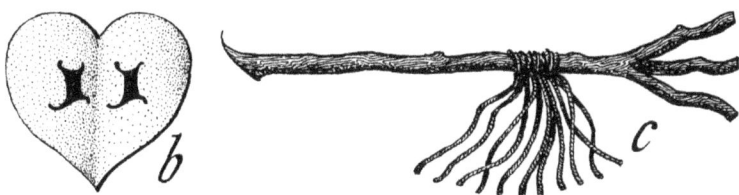

Bij Aant. 1952, fol. 27E: documentatie §14/1952. ["Saga and Myth":, Gnomes", III]. Toevoegen aan F6: lenihan, M., "History of limerick", Dublin, 1884. (J.Duffy). E.

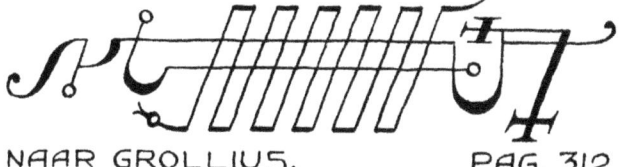

NAAR GROLLIUS,   PAG. 312.

THE SO-CALLED DANISH FORTS AND TOMBS OF THE EARLY IRISH. Sir W. Wilde, in his interesting lecture on "Ireland, Past and Present", remarks that if the Danes had erected these curious mounds, the popular belief would not ascribe them to the Fairies or "Good People"; more probably they were constructed by the Tuatha de Danaans, whose name they preserve. These were "globular-headed, intellectual, and refined specimens of humanity", as compared with the "long-headed, thick-skulled 'Firbolgs'".[10]

---

10. Maurice Lenihan, *Limerick, its history and antiquities; ecclesiastical, civil, and military, from the earliest ages*, Dublin, 1884, pp 747

Interestingly, Lenihan mentions the *Tuatha de Danaans*, which are mentioned in the works of Martin Koomen and Brian Froud, as being a *Divine people*, followers of the Goddess Dana. The Tuatha de Danann were the people who invaded Ireland before the current Irish people came to the island, and they appeared to 'come from the sky'. They used an intricate form of magic; they brought all kinds of strange relics like the Sword of Nuada, the spear of Lugh, the kettle of Dagda that could feed a hundred people without getting empty and more importantly, the Stone of Fal. This stone, apparently, had been taken to London, where it became part of the Coronation Seat. It is said that if the stone remains silent during the coronation, it might have serious consequences for the Monarchy. Another word that stands out is "Firbolgs". These Firbolgs lived in Ireland before the invasions of the Tuatha de Danann and the current Irish population. They waged war on the Thuatha de Danann, causing the Firbolgs to retreat to the West of Ireland. There are still people who claim to count Firbolgs among their ancestors. The Tuatha de Danann were considered 'other people' by the Irish ancestors like the Celts, not as 'divine' or 'supernatural', although they are compared to fairies in later times, presumably the nineteenth century.

CHAPTER TWO

PEOPLE ASSOCIATED
WITH GNOMES

Concerning the subject of gnomes, there were two types of people Eldermans came into contact with and these people I have divided in two categories: people who *witnessed* gnomes for themselves and those who knew something about gnomes. These categories are not absolute and some of the people may fit into both of them. In this chapter, we will look at the latter category. Eldermans mentioned these people as being some sort of 'expert' on one side, or as a fraud and liar on the other. Some of these people are not mentioned by their full name but abbreviated by their initials - which is strange, when you consider that this manuscript was not meant for publication. I have already conveyed my thoughts about this ambivalence in Eldermans' work: I deem it possible that this was a work Eldermans intended to leave behind, presumably as a special manuscript collection for the Royal Library - an institute he was a member of, in the time when memberships were obligatory. Nowadays, a membership is not obligatory, you can visit the Royal Library any time and you are allowed to use the reading room free of charge. Eldermans might have met some of the people he mentions in his works, through his visits to the Royal Library but he could also have met these people through his travels in The Netherlands. In an article about gnomes, in the Dutch magazine, Panorama, issued in September 1980, Eldermans was interviewed by Arnold Jan Scheer and he is cited as saying the following:

Eldermans about his conversations with gnome-witnesses on De Veluwe, in De Peel, Drenthe and North-east Twente: "at night you are talking and when the others are gone, it comes: mister, you will not believe... You see, among each other they know it. They know damned well what they should hide for the vicar.[11]

Eldermans commented on this interview with the words 'a strange report', apparently, he was interviewed for an hour and this was everything he could read back of what he had said. Arnold Jan Scheer was quite interested in gnomes, as he already written an article about Annie Gerding-Le Comte, in the magazine, *Nieuwe Revu,* and had also made a television item about this remarkable woman in the television show, Showroom, which was broadcasted in 1978.

See the documentation §16/1939: "Gnomes", "Mrs. W. Groothengel – Kemperink, Note 1939, at fol. 96.

There is not much known about this particular lady, but the year of reference might suggest that Eldermans had spoken with her, somewhere in Twente. What this conversation had been about was not recorded, unfortunately.

---

11. Arnold Jan Scheer, *Kijk, daar gaat een kabouter* in Panorama no. 39, 26 September 1980

Aant. 1952, fol. 5Ⅳ: Hier wederom de verwikkelingen omtrent de naamgeving! Waren de waargenomen „dwergen", die ook nog individueel in grootte variëerden, en vaak zó „warig" waren, „aardgeesten" en „dus kabouters", of zou een ander hen „gnooms" hebben genoemd? In de door „B.J.J." aangehaalde „observaties" is terzake ook geen uitsluitsel te vinden. Er wordt daarin geschreven over „gnomes" en „dwarfs", „Heinzelmänchen" en er is ook sprake van een „Kobold" en een kennelijk mannelijke „Fairy", van „Pixies" en „Pucks".... Ik vraag mij af of „B.J.J." en deze informanten zelf wel wisten waarover ze spraken in of ze een sluitende definitie zouden hebben kunnen geven voor elk van deze fenomenen. (JHWE.)

Note 1952, fol. 5IV: Again, there are problems with the naming! Were the observed "dwarves", who individually varied in size, and so often were "fuzzy", "nature spirits" and thus "gnomes", or would anyone else have called them "goblins"? In the "observations" mentioned by "B.J.J." there is no answer to this. In there is spoken about "gnomes" and "dwarfs", "Heinzelmänchen" [German for gnomes] and there is also spoken of a "Cobold" and apparently a male "Fairy", of "Pixies" and "Pucks"... I ask myself if "B.J.J." and these informants knew what they were talking about and if they could give a definitive definition for each of these phenomena. (JHWE.) **H.**

We do know two things: Eldermans is sceptical here and B.J.J. is apparently not native-Dutch. He speaks of "gnomes" and "Fairy" and one single German word (which Eldermans had spelled incorrectly - it should be Heinzelmännchen), so the report Eldermans refers to, must be written in a language other than Dutch, probably English. But without knowing what is said in this document, it is hard to judge if Eldermans' criticism was justified.

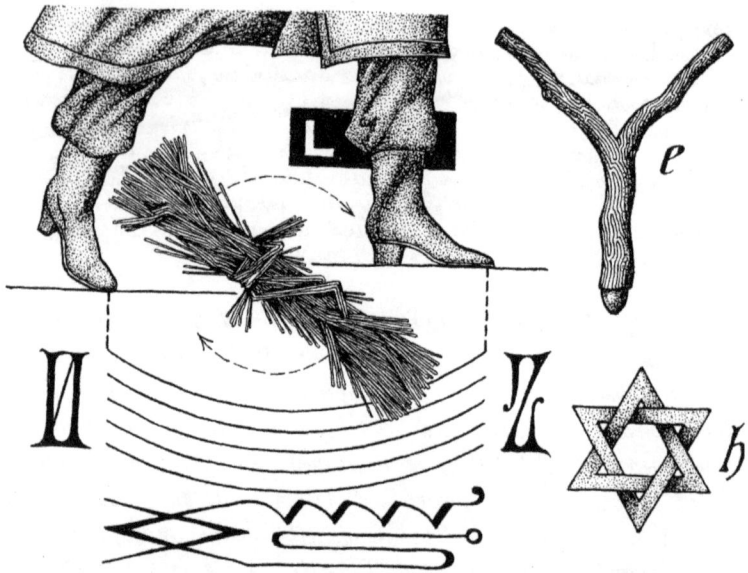

Bÿ Aant. 1939, fol. 12F: „Aardgeesten". Toevoegen: F4. Porta, Giambattista della, Magia naturalis oder Haus-, Kunst- und Wunderbuch, Nürnberg, 1680." Bÿ e: „Die Wünschelrute", 17e eeuw, documentatie VII sub D „Entschleier-te Magie". [Mevr. Hilda Janssens-Dijkstra lijkt mÿ een onbetrouwbare en leugenachtige getuige, die zichzelf als interessant wil doen kennen. JHWE.] H.

At Note 1939, fol. 12F: "Nature Spirits". Add: F4. Porta, Giambattista della, Magia Naturalis oder Haus-, Kunst- und Wunderbuch, Nürnberg, 1680". At e: "Die Wünschelrute", [the Divining rod], 17th Century, documentation VII sub D, "Entschleierte Magie" [Unveiled Magic]. [Mrs. Hilda Janssens-Dijkstra appears to be an unreliable and lying witness, who wants to be considered interesting. JHWE.] **H.**

This is a peculiar entry, since it refers to *Natural Magick* by John Baptista Porta, published in London in 1658 - a book in which Gnomes are not spoken about. Is that what Mrs. Hilda Janssens-Dijkstra is 'lying' about? The divining rod can indeed be found in the drawing, but what does the rest refer to?

Aant. 1948, fol. 399C: "Though dwarfs' fictional habits might differ from country to country, all were probably the distant relatives of the dark, little men who lived thousands of years ago", &c.. – Bij F14 "Mevr. Hilda Janssens spreekt zichzelf herhaaldelijk tegen en doet zich kennen als een weinig betrouwbare, leugenachtige vrouw. (JHWE.) **H.**

Note 1948, fol. 399C: "Though dwarfs' fictional habits might differ from country to country, all were probably the distant relatives of the dark, little men who lived thousands of years ago", &c.- At F14 "Mrs. Hilda Janssens repeatedly contradicts herself and makes herself known as a little reliable, lying woman. (JHWE.) **H.**

The citation is from the *Encyclopedia of Magic & Superstition* (p. 65) but again, the connection to Mrs. Hilda Janssens is really obscure.

Bij Aant. 1957, fol. 48C: "Gnomes", &c.- Idem: documentatie §21-H/1957, "Aardgeesten", &c. - §21, F5, toevoegen: "Cecil H. Williamson, who had founded a witchcraft museum", enz., de tekst van)12. Zie ook onder: "Jack L. Bracelin". **H.**

At Note 1957, fol. 48C: "Gnomes", &c.- Idem: documentation §21-H/1957, "Nature spirits", &c.- §21, F5, add: "Cecil H. Williamson, who had founded a witchcraft museum", etc., the text of)12. See also under: "Jack L. Bracelin". **H.**

The citation about Cecil H. Williamson is literally from the book *Modern Witchcraft* by Frank Smyth.[12] There is another

---

12. Frank Smyth, *Modern Witchcraft. The fascinating story of the rebirth of paganism and magic*, London, 1970, pp 29

name mentioned and again, the book by Smyth provides us with the answer:

> *The rest of Gardner's money went to a few remaining relatives and to several of the 'witches' initiated by him, including Jack L. Bracelin, co-founder with Gardner of a nudist colony in St. Alban's and the biographer of the 'chief witch'.*[13]

Bracelin appears to be the biographer of Gardner, his book *Gerald Gardner: Witch*, published in 1960 was, according to Smyth, more a hagiography than a biography. According to Bracelin's wikipedia page, it was Sayed Idries Shah who wrote the biography of Gardner and used Bracelin's name as a pseudonym. Bracelin was initiated into the Bricket Wood Coven, in 1956. Later on, he became an ambivalent figure in the Wicca-movement and he seriously doubted if Wicca satisfied his religious needs, which it did not.

By §4, Aant. 1940, sub 133-IV: Derk Mulder zegt regelmatig kabouters te zien en ook wel „gedachtencontact" met deze „dwergjes" te hebben. Al „sinds zijn volwassenheid". Zie het verslag: §3, Aant. 1939, sub 351-III (JHWE.)—

At §4, Note 1940, sub 133-IV: Derk Mulder says to see gnomes on a regular basis and to be in 'telepathic contact' with these dwarfs. Already since his adulthood". See the report: §3, Note 1939, sub 351-III (JHWE.)- **H.**

One annoying detail in Eldermans' works is the incomplete nature of it. He refers to a report, from which he had already cited some information, so why not reproduce the entire report?

---

13. Ibid

See documentation §19/1939, "Goblins", F4, Miss Berna van Heek. Note 1939, fol. 216a. [Twente: 1919-1938] **E.**

Another mysterious entry, concerning a pentacle, a name (Berna van Heek), an area (Twente) and a timeframe (1919-1938, nineteen years). What do all these variables have in common? Because we lack information in this entry, there is nothing to say here, that would make any sense. It should not refer to Eldermans' time in Twente: he moved there in 1936, and we don't know what he was doing in 1919, when he was fifteen years old.

Note 1953, fol. 478e: Mrs. M.S. van der Stelt – De Beer is not willing to provide more information. Speaking about this subject would make her lose "the power". See the attached correspondence with miss Jo Manasse. **E.**

Apparently, this entry is not as weird as it would appear. The Little People are hard to bargain with and what is given by them, can be easily taken away. In a lot of sagas, we see that any gifts given by the Little People, in many cases the Elves, come with the condition that they should not be spoken about, otherwise the receiver would lose it. A man who received a shilling a day from the Elves was not allowed to tell his own wife. His wife was disgruntled and blamed her husband for having secrets. When he blurted out that the Elves gave him money, his shilling turned into worthless

wood and he never received any money from the Elves
again. It would be the same with Mrs. Van der Stelt: her
given power could have been taken away, if she had spoken
about it with Eldermans.

Mej. Grada Steenhagen, die zichzelf „herborist" noemt en in haar omgeving bekend staat als „knokenzetster", vervaardigt een pentakel, dat de drager in staat zou stellen zich te verstaan met kabouters. Zie de documentatie § 27/1948. Grada Steenhagen, een pientere, wonderlijke, ongehuwde en zeer zelfstandige, „geëmancipeerde" vrouw, is, naar zij vertelt, een volgelinge en bewonderaarster van Eliphas Levy. Zij heeft in het verleden als textielarbeidster in het zuiden van België gewoond en gewerkt en geeft blijk de werken van Levy onvertaald te kunnen lezen. — Zie Aant. 1948, fol. 432a.

*Miss Grada Steenhagen, who calls herself a 'herborist' and is
known in her surroundings as "knokenzetster" [a difficult term,
it would be translated as 'bone setter']* manufactured a pentacle,
which allows the wearer to understand gnomes. See the documentation
§27/1948. Grada Steenhagen, a bright, wonderly, unmarried and
very independent, "emancipated" woman, is, as she tells, a follower and
admirer of Eliphas Levy. She worked and lived as a textile-worker in
the south of Belgium and appears to be able to read the works of Levy
in the original language.- See Note 1948, fol. 432a.* **H.**

Again, we see a name appear resembling the name of
someone in Eldermans' own family: his mother's name was
Grada. He calls her an independent "emancipated" woman,
which actually applies to his mother, as well. Does Grada
Steenhagen exist? Or did Eldermans base her on his mother
and invented a 'witness'? The name Grada Steenhagen does
appear in another place, in the manuscript, with the pentacle
that Eldermans describes.

Documentatie § 63/1940: „Albert van 't Grote Jong", Albert Willemsen (Windslaan 1a) te Almelo, geboren aldaar 15-11-1872, geneest „verstuikte ledematen en kneuzingen" door „strijken". Hij vertelde twee kaboutermanhalen, die zich omtrent 1935 afspeelden in de omgeving van De Pook te Almelo. Hij weet uit eigen waarneming dat kabouters bestaan ; zeggen dat zoiets niet kán bestaan, is twijfelen aan God's macht....

*Documentation §63/1940: "Albert van 't Grote Jong", "Albert
Willemsen (Windslaan 1a) in Almelo, born there 15 November 1872,*

heals "sprained limbs and bruises" by "rubbing". He told the two gnome-stories which played around 1935 in the surroundings of De Pook in Almelo. He knows from his own observations that gnomes exist; saying that such a thing can't exist, is doubting God's might…. **E.**

Albert Willemsen was indeed living at the Windslaan 1a in Almelo but he lived at Windslaan 1 until 26th March 1953. During the time Eldermans lived in Almelo, Willemsen did not move into the neighbouring house 1a. The entry could not have been from 1940! He was indeed born on 15th November 1872 in Ambt Almelo, a small neighbourhood near Almelo, which has since been absorbed by the city of Almelo. Willemsen passed away on 1st May 1966, in Almelo and worked during his life as a factory worker. Apparently, Eldermans did keep in contact with people from Almelo after he moved to The Hague in 1949.

[Below] *At §1d, Note 1948, fol. 394, mention: "No. 17. Annie Gerding – Le Comte, "Kabouters/Gnomen & Fantomen/ Ontmoetingen met natuurwezens", Lemniscaat, Rotterdam, 1979".-* **E.** *[*Gnomes/Goblins & Phantoms. Meetings with nature beings".*]*

At §3*, Note 1948, fol. 399: Annie Gerding (F2) writes: "Gnomes can't be touched. They rather don't come too close to us, presumably because our emanation is different. It is too heavy, too rude and bothers them. They are ethereal beings. They radiate a faint light that surrounds them as if it were like a lighting glow, a sort of aura, which is present with us as well, though less subtle and refined". See page 13.

Bij §1ᵈ, Aant.1948, fol.394, vermelden: „No.17. Annie Gerding-Ie Comte, „Kabouters/ Gnomen & Fantomen/ Ontmoetingen met natuurwezens" Iemniscaat, Rotterdam, 1979."— ⊟ₒ

Bij §3*, Aant.1948, fol.399: Annie Gerding (F2) schrijft: „Kabouters kun je eigenlijk niet aanraken. Zij komen ook liever niet te dicht bij ons in de buurt, vermoedelijk omdat onze uitstraling anders is. Die is te zwaar, te grof en hindert hen. Het zijn etherische wezens. Zij stralen een zwak licht uit dat hen als het ware omgeeft als een lichtend waas, een soort aura, die bij ons overigens ook aanwezig is doch minder subtiel en verfijnd". Zie pag.13.

Eldermans knew Annie Gerding-Le Comte. He wrote to her in 1976 and she mentioned Eldermans in her television appearance, in 1978. Eldermans sent her a couple of his drawings but it is not known what she did with these drawings but knowing that the letter made it to the Museum of Witchcraft and Magic, the drawings might be in that collection as well.

[handwritten:] ᗰ = Annie Gerding–Le Comte, „Kabouters Gnomen & Fantomen" [Lemniscaat R-dam, 1979]. „Ontmoetingen met natuurwezens". —   JHWE.

M = *Annie Gerding – Le Comte, "Kabouters, gnomen & fantomen" [Lemniscaat R-dam, 1979]. "Meetings with natural beings".- JHWE*

This book has caused some confusion with certain "researchers" of Eldermans. In 2015, Frans van Noppen published an online article, which can be found on the website https://rondehuis.nl in both English and Dutch. In this article, Van Noppen briefly refers to Annie Gerding and her acquaintance with Eldermans:

> *In the mid-70's, he met Annie Gerding-Le Comte, the wife of Professor Gerding. [...] She subsequently received some manuscripts from Eldermans. These manuscripts inspired Henriëtte Gorter, a member of the family that runs the farm 'Welna', to use the work of Eldermans in her second book about gnomes. She was given a folder with approximately 400 freely usable manuscripts by Richel (Eldermans had already passed away at the time). The folder was labeled 'Elves, Gnomes & Phantoms', probably not coincidentally the same title as the book by Gerding-Le Comte.*[14]

First of all, it is not at all certain that Eldermans met with Annie Gerding. He wrote her a letter and she confirmed on national television that she received the

---

14. Frans van Noppen, *J.H.W. Eldermans in Nunspeet*, on the website http://rondehuis.nl/?page_id=287, p. 20

letter but she never said that she had met Eldermans. Then, Van Noppen makes a mistake: he states that the folder Henriëtte Gorter received was titled *'Elves, Gnomes & Phantoms'*. It was not. It was called *Aardgeesten, gnomen, kabouters etc...* or another variant on this is *Kabouters, gnomen, aardgeesten* [Nature spirits, goblins, gnomes etc... or Gnomes, goblins, nature spirits]. It had nothing to do with the title of Annie Gerding's book at all...

The book by Gerding has been translated into various foreign languages. There is a German translation called *Zwerge, Gnome und Fantome* (Dwarfs, Goblins and Phantoms). There is no known English translation.

41

CHAPTER THREE

GNOME WITNESSES

Eldermans interviewed about seventy people about their experiences with gnomes. Some people had actually met with gnomes; others had only seen the gnomes in the distance – either gnomes who did not care at all that they were being watched or were unaware that they were being observed. Some people are said to have a paranormal ability which allows them to see the gnomes - others don't but accidentally meet with a gnome, because they are, apparently, in the 'right emotional state'. These stories speak for themselves, so I will withdraw from making any commentaries. There are a few witness reports which mention various areas on De Veluwe or in Twente, which demand some explanation. This explanation will come in the shape of a terrain-study and some anecdotes.

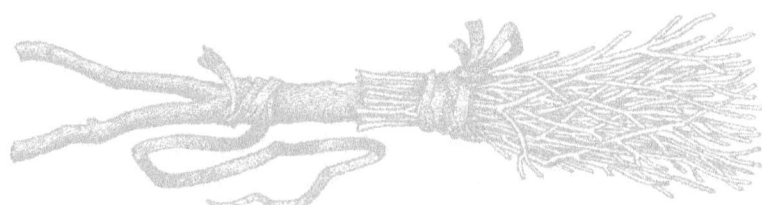

Reconstructie van het beschadigde deel van de prent: zie Aant. 1951, fol. 2ᴰ, bijl. III. De kabouter is getekend naar de serie afbeeldingen, gebaseerd op „De Waarnemingen van Harmke Postma", zie §2-DD/1951. **H.** Ter vergelijking bij Aant. 1951, fol. 3, enkele punten, die betrekking hebben op de mededelingen van José Walburgh — waarnemingen in De Peel. „De aardgeesten (kabouters) vertonen zich veelal vanuit een wazig begin en verdwijnen ook vaak alsof ze zich oplossen in de lucht. De duidelijkheid en de helderheid van hun verschijning hangt ook af van de aandacht, de concentratie van de waarnemer. De aardgeesten vertonen zich aanvankelijk wazig, in een weinig sprekende kleur, grijzig, in een grijs dat zweemt naar tabaksbruin of bronsgroen. Bewegen de aardgeesten zich opgewekt, vrolijk, dan verhelderen de kleuren en worden de kleuren meer sprekend, eveneens vrolijk. Een en ander geldt ook voor de kleur van het gelaat, de handen, enz.. Even variabel is de lengte – de grootte – van de zich manifesterende aardgeesten. Bij het verschijnen lijken zij meestal niet meer dan ca. 30 cm. hoog, maar later, in een vloeiende, onmerkbare overgang, blijken zij wel 60 à 70 cm. lang te zijn. Vaak schijnt het, dat de aardgeesten zich niet aanpassen in het perspectief van hun omgeving. José Walburgh – 53 jaar oud, boekbindster van beroep – zegt geen verbaal, geestelijk contact met de aardgeesten te hebben. Wel meent zij vaak dat deze haar door mimiek en gebaren iets duidelijk willen maken, maar zij begrijpt dat niet, lacht dan vriendelijk en wuift hen vriendelijk toe...."(zie Aant. 1950, fol. 349ᴵᴵᴵ.) **E.**

Aant. 1951, fol. 3ᴰ: bij f2. „Kobolds and Knocking-spirits (Polter Geister): They are the Devil's spectres, and I do not belong to them". Zie „Hinzelmann". **H.**

Reconstruction of the damaged part of the drawing: See Note 1951, fol. 2D, appendix III. The gnome is drawn according to a series of drawings, based on the "observations of Harmke Postma", see §2-DD/1951. **H.**

In comparison at Note 1951, fol. 3, some points that relate to the gleanings of José Walburgh – observations in De Peel. "The Nature Spirits (gnomes) show themselves mostly from a hazy start and vanish also like they dissolve in the air. The clarity and brightness of their appearance depends on the attention, the concentration of the observer. The nature spirits appear fuzzy, in a stale colour, greyish, *a grey that buzzes to tobacco-brown or bronze-green. Do the nature spirits move with delight, happy, then the colours become more bright, more speaking and even happy. One or the other applies to the colour of the face, the hands etc. Evenly variable is the length -the size- of the manifesting nature spirits. When they appear, they are not larger than 30 centimeters but later, in a fluent, unnoticed transition, they appear to be 60 to 70 centimeters tall. Quite often, it appears that nature spirits do not adapt to the perspective of their environment. José Walburgh -53 years old, bookbinder by profession — says she has no verbal, spiritual contact with the nature spirits. She does think that they try to make things clear through mimics and gestures but she does not understand, laughs and waves friendly....." (See Note 1950, fol. 349*III.) **E.**

Note 1951, fol. 3D: at F2. "Kobolds and Knocking-spirits (PolterGeister): They are the Devil's spectres, and I do not belong to them". See "Hinzelmann".- **H.**

Ter vergelijking bij Aant. 1951, fol. 14ᴿ: Het verhaal van „vrouw Klaasje Duursma" [zie de documentatie §77-YY/1950] luidt, ontdaan van de minder terzake doende mededelingen, als volgt: Bij de wandeling van haar huis naar het dorp, of van het dorp naar haar woning, volgde zij bij goed weer vaak een iets langer, maar mooier en rustiger pad, lopend door een heuvelachtig terrein en begroeid met hei, brem, jonge dennen en jeneverbesstruiken. Waar dit pad door een laagte voert, werd zij veelvuldig begeleid door een kabouter, steeds dezelfde, al was hij soms maar een voet lang en even later wel een el. De kabouter was dikwijls vrij wazig en meestal somber van kleur, maar nabij een bepaald punt gekomen, werd hij steeds meer helder en duidelijk, kleurryker en, vooral, beweeglijker. Hij bewoog zich dan sneller, druk en zenuwachtig, maakte nadrukkelijke gebaren en trok de meest vreemde gezichten. Klaasje kon niet met de kabouter spreken en begreep er niets van. Zij heeft hem wel eens toegeroepen: „Wat wil je toch", en gevraagd: „Kan ik je helpen?", maar op haar roepen reageerde de kabouter slechts met vreemde grimassen en rare sprongen. Met zijn armen maakte hij dan bewegingen, alsof hij wilde, dat de vrouw op die bepaalde plek bleef staan, hetgeen zij ook wel eens voor korte tijd deed. Dan bleef de kabouter stil, ingespannen staan toekijken, gebogen naar de grond starend. Vervolgde de vrouw dan weer haar tocht, dan keek de kabouter bedroefd, met afhangende schouders en armen.... Zo werd hij dan weer minder kleurig, waziger, en verdween....

Bovenstaand verhaal was bekend aan diverse bekenden en verwanten van Klaasje Duursma. Enige jaren later, de vrouw was inmiddels overleden, werd op de omschreven plaats een buitenhuis gebouwd. Bij de grondwerkzaamheden werd op de plek waarvoor de kabouter aandacht vroeg, een restant van een oude fundering gevonden, alsmede een oude stenen kruik, inhoudende 29 gouden en 47 zilveren munten.— **H.**

In comparison with Note 1951, fol. 14D: The story of "Miss Klaasje Duursma" [see the documentation §77-YY/1950] goes, stripped of the less relevant gleanings, as follows: During the walk from her home to the village, or from the village to her home, during good weather, she followed a slightly longer but more beautiful and silent trail, running through hilly terrain and overgrown with heath, dyer's broom, young pines and juniper bushes. This trail goes through a small valley where she often was accompanied by a gnome, always the same, although he was only a foot tall and later an ell. The gnome was often very fuzzy and sometimes dreary coloured but coming to a certain point he became clearer, colourful and, especially, more mobile. He moved faster, busily and nervous, made emphatic gestures and pulled the strangest faces. Klaasje was not able to speak with the gnome and didn't understand. She shouted at him: "What do you want?" and asked "Can I help you?" but in response to her calling, he only made stranger faces and weird jumps. With his arms, he made movements, like he wanted her to stay put in a certain place, which she sometimes did for a short while. The gnome then stood still, intensely watching, bent over, staring at the ground. When the woman went on her way, the gnome looked sad, with hanging arms and shoulders.... He became less colourful, fuzzy and disappeared.... The story above was known to certain acquaintances and family members of Klaasje Duursma. Some years later, the woman already had passed away, an outdoor building was built on the described place. During the ground work on the particular spot, the foundations of an older building were found, as well as an old stone jar, containing 29 gold and 47 silver coins.- **H.**

Aanvulling bij Aant. 1958, fol. 29ᴮ: „F2. Het spontaan waarnemen van kabouters is een gave die men heeft of niet heeft. Heeft men deze, dan is het voor be-
oefenaars van de Grote Kunst mogelijk de kabouters met magische mid-
delen meer of minder zichtbaar te maken. In alle gevallen is het uttermate
moeilijk met deze aardgeesten in (geestelijk) contact te treden". Zie ook fol. 31ᴰ
onder: „Mededelingen van mevr. M.F.A. van Raalte-Rijks". –

Addition at Note 1958, fol. 29B: "F2. The spontaneous observation of gnomes is a gift one has, or has not. Does one have the gift, then practitioners of the Great Art are able to make the gnomes more or less visible with magical aids. In all cases, it is very hard to get into (mental) contact with these nature spirits". See also fol. 31D under: "Gleanings of Mrs. M.F.A. van Raalte-Rijks".- **O.**

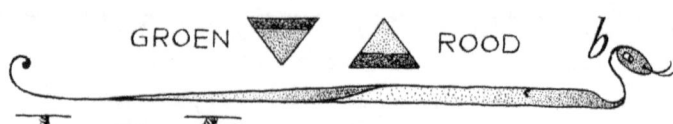

GROEN ▼ ▲ ROOD *b*

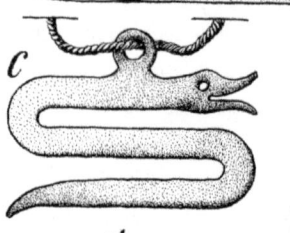

c

Idem: Aant. 1947, fol. 344d: Mededelingen over Margot Rijnbout, die in de jaren 1930-1942, in en om haar woonplaats, regelmatig „Kabouterkens" zou hebben ontmoet, niet doordat zij een „vreemde begaving" had, maar doordat zij met een van haar grootmoeder ontvangen Talisman om haar hals in de vrije natuur, waar die aardgeesten wel voorkwamen, bepaalde „vreemde handelingen" verrichtte. De „kabouterkens" waren haar zeer goed gezind en hielpen haar ernstige problemen en moeilijkheden oplossen. Aan deze hulp van de „aardmannen" zou het dan ook te danken zijn geweest, dat Margot —die in 1942 op 68-jarige leeftijd (ongehuwd) overleed— beoordeeld werd als een „zeer wijze" vrouw, niet slechts in haar eenvoudige milieu, maar ook door „de notabelen". In de bezettingstijd zou zij door haar goede inzichten en haar „bijna voorspellende geest" veel Nederlanders hebben behoed voor bestialiteiten van de zijde der bezetter. Enz., enz., zie de documentatie §22-III/1947, met een in dialect gesteld verslag. **S.**

Idem: Note 1947, fol. 344d: Gleanings about Margot Rijnbout, who during the years 1930-1942 in and around her abode, met with gnomes, not because she had a "strange gift" but because she received a talisman from her grandmother, which she wore around her neck when in wild country, where nature spirits frequently appeared, to perform some "strange proceedings". The "gnomes" were favourable to her and helped her solve all serious problems and difficulties. Through the help of these "goblins", Margot — who passed away, unmarried, aged 68, in 1942! - was considered a "very wise" woman, not only in her own simple surroundings, but also by "the notables". During the occupation, her good insights and almost "clairvoyant mind" saved many Dutch from the bestialities performed by the Germans. Etc., Etc., see the documentation §22-III/1947, with a report written in dialect. **S.**

[Below] At Note 1937, fol. 283III, documentation §26/1937: [Add to F3: "Evans Wentz, "The Fairy Faith in Celtic Countries"= "There seems never to have been an uncivilized tribe

or a race or nation of civilized men who have not had some form of belief in an unseen world", &c.]. The figure to the left has been compiled from six, unclear drawings by José van Kalmthout, drawn by her around 1915: gnomes, according to her observations and contact occurred in the Peel-area. Miss Van Kalmthout approved of this sketch in 1937. See further: Note 1937, fol. 296III, in which more will be mentioned about the conditions one has to live up to, to get into contact with these little-forthcoming gnomes and to gain their help.+ S.

With respect to Note 1937, fol. 287a ["Gnomes on the North-Veluwe"] she mentions incidental contact in the years 1924-1927, certainly in Nunspeet, with the far from youthful "Mister Goudswaard" - a retired education specialist, probably a teacher or schoolmaster, who spent his holidays in Guesthouse Denneheuvel in Nunspeet- and Miss Toos Frenks -resident of Rotterdam and working as the head of a Kindergarten, a very well-read and travelled old spinster, who spent her summer vacations in those years in Nunspeet-. H.

Note 1937, fol. 283III: see also under "▲ Nunhem – Haelen – Heythuisen", [Jean Roeimans]. F8: "The "Peel-gnomes of Miss José van Kalmthout"- also mentioned and observed by others: see fol. 285 and further - they move "as easy through the earth as through the air" [This must be understood as "over the earth"; they don't fly, that's Drs. K. Razenberg's misunderstanding]. E.

This entry begs for commentary, and because of this sketch of a well-proportioned, muscular looking gnome from De Peel. This gnome contradicts everything that has been written by other authors about gnomes in De Peel. The best known is Ton van Reen, who wrote several books about gnomes in De Peel and provides us with very different descriptions. Van Reen describes gnomes as being 'flesh and blood' creatures, who were cast out of their societies - sometimes because they were deformed in some way, or had a growth disorder and in some cases, because they suffered from Down's Syndrome. These people lived out in the forests and moors of De Peel and when they needed clothing or food, they offered their services at farms, which were furthest away from the populated villages. Gnomes detested the church bells and they have been reported as saying that "the blackskirts (pastors) needed a good whipping". They hated everything associated with Christianity. Gnomes received their rewards through special small doors, so the farmers or their wives did not have to look at them, since they were convinced that gnomes were descendants of the Devil. Gnomes were mostly dressed in rags and not in a loincloth with a pointy hat. Contrary to Van Reens observations, Eldermans' reports do not include 'flesh and blood' gnomes, but rather aethereal beings which obviously belong to 'another reality' and who can be seen by people who have a 'special ability'. It is possible that there are various kinds of gnomes: ones called gnomes because of their 'abnormality' from the local folks, and others considered as gnomes due to their supernatural nature. Ton van Reen had already published a book on gnomes in the 1970's, so it is quite peculiar that Eldermans had never heard from him or had never read his work. On the other hand: Eldermans might have disagreed with Van Reen and for that reason, not included his publications.

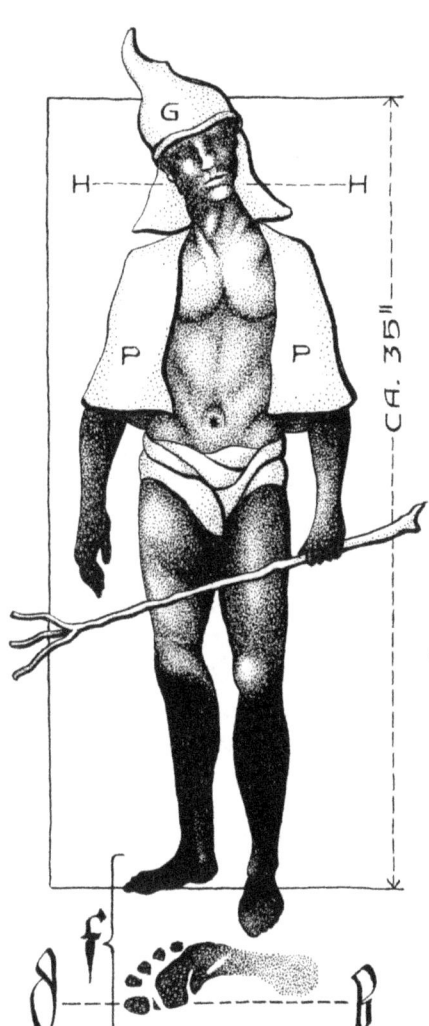

Bij Aant. 1937, fol. 283ᵛ, documentatie § 26/1937: [Toevoegen aan F3: „Evans Wentz, „The Fairy Faith in Celtic Countries". „There seems never to have been an uncivilized tribe, or a race or nation of civilized men who have not had some form of belief in an unseen world", &c.]. De figuur links is samengesteld uit de zes onduidelijke tekeningen van José van Kalmthout, door haar omstreeks 1915 getekend: Kabouters, zoals die volgens haar waarnemingen en contacten voorkomen in het Peelgebied. Mej. Van Kalmthout keurde deze schets in 1937 goed. Zie verder: Aant. 1937, fol. 296ᵛ, waarbij meer wordt vermeld over de voorwaarden waaraan men moet voldoen om contact met deze weinig toeschietelijke kabouters te krijgen en hen tot hulp te bewegen⁺.

Ten aanzien van Aant. 1937, fol. 287ᵛ [„Kabouters op de Noord-Veluwe"] zij vermeld, dat er in de jaren 1924-1927 zeker te Nunspeet incidentele contacten zijn geweest tussen de verre van jeugdige „Heer Goudswaard" — een gepensionneerd onderwijsman, waarschijnlijk leraar, misschien onderwijzer, die zijn vacantie's regelmatig doorbracht in Pension Dennehevvel te Nunspeet — en mej. Toos Frenks — woonachtig te Rotterdam en daar werkzaam als hoofd van een Kleuterschool, één zéér belezen en bereisde oude vrijster, die in die jaren vaak haar zomervacantie's te Nunspeet doorbracht —.

Aant. 1937, fol. 283ᵛ: zie ook onder „Δ Nunhem-Haelen-Heythuisen", [Jean Roeimans]. F8: „De Peelkabouters van mej. José van Kalmthout⁺ ook door anderen genoemd en waargenomen: zie fol. 285 ev. — bewegen zich „even gemakkelijk door de aarde als door de lucht⁺ [dient te worden verstaan als „over de aarde"; zij vliegen niet, dat is een misverstand van Dr. K. Razenberg]."

Bij)⁸ :„De jachtopziener —tevens „onbezoldigd rijksveldwachter"— M.v.d.S., kwam, samen met zijn collega H.F.R., in de vroege morgen terug van een surveillance in het Biesterveld, waar in die dagen de stropers zeer actief waren. Het was nog niet geheel licht toen zij de nietige en zeer afgelegen woning van vrouw J.B. wilden passeren. Zij kenden de bejaarde, zichzelf en haar omgeving verwaarlozende, vieze vrouw als een vreemde vogel, die zich vooral bezig hield met het verzamelen van kruiden en die bij ziekte wel door de keuterboeren en boerenknechts werd geraadpleegd. Zo waren de mannen hoogst verbaasd toen zij zagen dat de vrouw in het halfduister met emmers putwater doende was haar kleine ruiten aan de buitenzijde te reinigen…, te ontdoen, zo zagen zij nabijgekomen, van een witte, slijmerige substantie. De vrouw, daarover vriendelijk ondervraagd, verklaarde op mopperende toon, dat dit alles een gevolg was van het onheuse en sikkeneurige gedrag van de kabouters die zich ophielden in de omgeving van haar stulp. Af en toe tracteerde zij deze baloriige kereltjes namelijk op lammetjespap met basterdsuiker, teneinde hen te vriend te houden. Echter: wanneer de pap —'s avonds in een schaal gedaan en op een omgekeerd kistje buiten gezet— hen niet beviel, smeten zij de tractatie tegen de deur of tegen de kleine ramen van het huisje. Zo was het ook die nacht weer geschied en de vrouw wilde deze sporen van plaagzucht verwijderen vóór eventuele voorbijgangers de verontreiniging zouden zien…. De jachtop-

ziener H.F.R. had tijdens het gesprek met de vrouw ongezien een hoeveelheid van de witte substantie in zijn lege tabaksdoos weten te verzamelen en bracht dit nog de zelfde dag bij de apotheker in de nabijgelegen stad, met het verzoek een analyse te maken. Verbaasd verklaarde de pillendraaier later, dat het lammetjespap met veel suiker en veel „ongare klonten" was, maar geen andere bestanddelen bevatte"….

Nadere gegevens: Aant. 1939, fol. 425 ᵈ (ZHWE., sub IV). Zo

At)8: "The gamekeeper — and also "unpaid patrolman"-M.v.d.S., came, together with his colleague H.F.R., back from their surveillance in the early morning in Biesterveld[15], where poachers

---

15. There are three places where Biesterveld could have been located, all three are in the Province of Gelderland near the German border. The first is in Vorden, between Zutphen and the German border, the second is near Kleve in Germany (but still inside the Dutch border) and the third is more south, in the vicinity of Nijmegen. The location near Kleve looks most promising.

were very active in those days. It still wasn't light yet when they passed the small abode of a woman J.B.. They knew the elderly dirty woman, who neglected her surroundings and herself, a strange 'bird', who occupied herself with collecting herbs and who was consulted by small farmers and farmhands in cases of sickness. They saw the woman filling buckets with well-water in the twilight to clean her windows..., as they approached it looked more like removing a white, slimy substance. The woman, who was interrogated in a friendly way, explained grumpily this was caused by discourteous and grouchy behaviour of the gnomes who resided near her abode. Now and then, she treated these peevish fellows to porridge[16] with caster sugar, to keep them friendly. However, when they did not like the porridge - served at night in a bowl on a turned-over chest - they hurled the treat against the door or the small windows of the cottage. This had occurred the night before and the woman wanted to remove these traces of their teasings before eventual passers-by saw the mess. The gamekeeper H.F.R. collected an amount of the white substance during their conversation in his empty tobacco-box and took this to an apothecary in a nearby city, with the request to make an analysis. The surprised 'pill-roller' later explained it was porridge with lots of sugar and many "uncooked lumps" but did not contain any other ingredients.... Further information: Note 1939, fol. 425d (JHWE., sub IV). **S.**

Bij §4, Aant. 1951, fol. 466ᴵ: „Mevr. N.v.E.-S." wil niet dat haar naam — die mij volledig bekend is — voluit wordt genoteerd. Zij wil niet de kans lopen zichzelf terzijnertijd in een tijdschrift of boek tegen te komen, als dat gekke vrouwmens, als een volwassene die gelooft dat kindervertellingen echt waar zijn! — Ja, dát mag ik best weten: zij gelooft in het bestaan van kabouters, zij ziet en ontmoet deze natuurgeesten en heeft af en toe ook geestelijk contact met hen. — En — vriendelijk, maar gedecideerd —: méér wil zij daarover niet zeggen. Even goede vrienden en tot allerlei diensten bereid, maar over dát onderwerp wordt door

—haar—

---

16. The Dutch word used is 'Lammetjespap', which does not really translate into English, so here the word porridge is used.

haar niet gepraat! Soit! —   JHWE.

K Toevoegen aan §4, fol. 466 II (1951): Harmen van Eck
— 31 jaar oud, fotograaf, gehuwd, 2 kinderen — is de
jongste van de twee zoons, geboren uit het huwelijk van
„Mevr. N.v.E.–S". De verhouding tussen hem en zijn moeder wordt
uitstekend genoemd, hartelijk en vertrouwelijk. Zijn vader, die
een antiquariaat bezat en dreef, is omstreeks zes jaar geleden ge-
storven. — De heer Van Eck vertelt dat zijn ouders, en later zijn
moeder alleen, „bezeten" waren van „de vrije natuur". Een groot
deel van de vrije tijd werd wandelend of fietsend doorgebracht, hetgeen voor de twee zoons „opvoedend en vormend" werd gevonden.
De heer Van Eck, volwassen gerakend, waardeerde die wandel- en
fietstochten niet in het minst, en zelfstandig geworden „kon hij
geen boom meer zien", zoals dat ook met zijn broer het geval is. —
Tijdens die „natuurexpedities" praatte zijn vader graag met „de
plattelanders", van welke hij ook nog wel eens wat inkocht voor
zijn zaak. Moeder zocht en verzamelde stenen, veldkeiën, e.d.
Zij las ook veel over dat onderwerp en heeft op zolder een uitge-
breide, zéér goed onderhouden verzameling stenen en fossielen, die
zij zelf bijeenbracht en die regelmatig en bewonderend werd bezich-
tigd door belangstellenden. — De heer Van Eck herinnert zich
niet dat zijn moeder hem in zijn jeugd ooit „kabouterverhalen" vertelde. Gesprekken met zijn moeder over kabouters begonnen pas, zo
meent hij, toe hij „een jaar of twintig" was. Wonderlijke gesprekken,
die hij eerst niet goed begreep, maar waaruit hij allengs conclu-
deerde dat zijn moeder geloofde in het bestaan van aardgeesten,
van kabouters! En dat zij die „in de natuur" ontmoette en op een
wonderlijke „psychische manier" contact met hen had.... Aanvankelijk verontrustte hem dat in ernstige mate, en dacht: „zou
dat een symptoom van verkalking zijn". Maar moeder bleef
dezelfde pientere, intelligente vrouw en „zo sleet de angst weer". —
In tegenstelling tot zijn broer heeft zegsman zijn moeder terzake
van „haar kabouters" nimmer tegengesproken, hetgeen hij ook niet
zou hebben gedaan wanneer zij „christelijk gelovend" zou zijn
geworden of als lid zou zijn toegetreden tot „een of andere politieke
partij". Evenmin deed hij duidelijk blijken niet in die wonderlijke
verhalen te kunnen geloven, waardoor er terzake van de kabouterverhalen een zeker vertrouwen bleef en zijn moeder hem wel
een enkele keer over haar ontmoetingen met de kabouters ver-

telde. —

telde. Dat begon eigenlijk nadat hij haar eens had gevraagd:
spreken die kereltjes Nederlands? Ze verklaarde toen dat je met
kabouters niet op de voor ons gewone wijze een gesprek kunt voeren,
maar dat er een „vreemd geestelijk contact" is, waardoor je
„geestelijk, inwendig converseert", maar zulks uitsluitend wanneer je de „goede geestelijke instelling" hebt. — De heer Van Eck
deelt op grond van diverse gesprekken met zijn moeder mee, dat
kabouters „klein zijn", meestal „kleiner dan tuinkabouters". Zij
dragen een rode, niet zo grote puntmuts, die alleen het gezicht
vrijlaat en verbonden is met een soort kraag, een „korte pelerine".
De kleur van de kleding is in het algemeen „van bruin tot groen" en
kan zich wijzigen terwijl je naar ze kijkt. Om hun middel dragen de kabouters een riem, „naar het lijkt van leder". Zo ook
„op leer gelijkende" „lage laarsjes" van een „plomp model".— Lang
niet alle kabouters dragen een baard. Van hun hoofdhaar
— evenals de baarden: blond — is nooit veel te zien. — De kabouter
verschijnt vaak vanuit „een nevelige figuur", vanuit een
„vaagheid met wazige contouren", en verdwijnt ook weer op die
wijze. Hun „trillingsgetal is anders" en daardoor is het ook
mogelijk dat zij zich kunnen bewegen „door vaste stoffen heen", ook
„door de aarde". — Kabouters zijn „vriendelijk", maar ook
„gauw aangebrand", vaak om „redenen die je als mens niet kunt
doorzien". Over hun taak, de zin van hun bestaan op ónze wereld,
heeft de heer Van Eck van zijn moeder nooit iets vernomen. De
kabouters „reizen". Zij „komen van ver en hebben nog ver te gaan",
maar zij „nemen voor dat reizen alle tijd" en verblijven soms
„vele jaren" in één streek. — De „kabouterwaarnemingen" van
zijn moeder — die zich in de loop der jaren een bromfiets kocht —
liggen, voor zover de heer Van Eck dat kan beoordelen, binnen
een gebied dat, ruwweg, wordt begrensd door:

Weert — Heunde — Mierlo — Deurne — Westerbroek — Overloon —
Wanssum — Grubbenvorst — Baarlo — Buggenum —
Heythuysen — Weert.

*At §4, Note 1951, fol. 466I: "Mrs. N.v.E.-S." does not want
her name - fully known by me - written in full. She doesn't want
to risk reading about herself in a magazine or book as the crazy
woman, who as an adult still believes in children's tales! Yes, I am
allowed to know: she believes in the existence of gnomes and she sees
and meets these nature spirits and, once in a while, has mental contact
with them.- And -friendly but decisive-: she does not want to say more
about it. Good friends and willing to do all kinds of services, but she
does not talk about that subject. Soit!- JHWE*

K *Add to §4, fol. 466II (1951): Harmen van Eck -31 years old,
photographer, married, 2 children- is the youngest of two sons born*

from the marriage of "Mrs. N. v. E.-S.". The relationship between him and his mother is excellent, warm and confidential. His father, who owned and managed an antique store, passed away six years prior. Mister Van Eck recounted that his parents, and later his mother alone, were obsessed with "free nature". A large amount of spare time was spent wandering or bicycling, which both sons experienced as "educative and forming". Mister Van Eck, once an adult, could not appreciate the wanderings and bike rides, and once on his own "he could not stand the trees anymore", as does his brother. During these "expeditions with nature", his father loved to talk with the rustic people, from whom he bought some things for his business. Mother searched for and collected rocks, boulders and such like. She reads a lot about the subject and has a very well-maintained collection of stones and fossils in the attic, which she collected herself and was admired by interested people. Mister Van Eck does not remember his mother telling him gnome-stories in his childhood. Conversations about gnomes with his mother started, he thinks, when he was "around twenty years old". Wondrous conversations, which he didn't understand at first, but from which he gradually concluded his mother believed in the existence of nature spirits, of gnomes! And that she met them "in nature" and was in contact with them in a remarkable psychic way…. Eventually he was seriously worried and thought: "would this be a symptom of calcination".[17] But his mother remained the same bright, intelligent woman and "the fear went away". Contrary to his brother, the spokesperson never contradicted his mother on the matter of "her gnomes", just like he wouldn't have done if she "became a Christian" or a member of "one or another political party". Nonetheless, he made clear he could not believe these amazing stories, so the gnome-stories remained a sense of confidentiality and his mother told him sometimes about her meetings with gnomes. It started when he asked her: do these fellows speak Dutch? She explained that you can't converse in a normal way with gnomes, but that there is a "strange, internal conversation" and only if you have "the right mindset". Mister Van Eck mentions, based on many conversations with his mother, that gnomes "are small", mostly "smaller than garden gnomes". They wear

---

17. In earlier times it was believed the brain could suffer 'calcination', which nowadays would be explained as dementia.

*a red, not large pointy hat, which only shows the face and is connected
to some sort of collar, a "short pelerine". The colour of the clothing is
in general from "brown to green" and can adjust while you are looking
at them. Around their waist the gnomes wear a belt, "it appears to
be leather". Their "low boots" of a cumbersome model "appear to be
made of leather". Not all the gnomes have a beard. Their hair, like
their beards: blonde- can't be seen much. The gnome appears from a
"hazy figure", from a "vagueness with fuzzy contours" and disappears
the same way. They have "a different frequency" and because of that it
is possible for them to move "through solid matters", also "through the
earth". Gnomes are "friendly", but also "quickly disgruntled", quite
often for "reasons a human cannot fathom". Mister Van Eck never
heard his mother speak about their task, the meaning of their existence
in our world. Gnomes "travel". They "come from far and have far to
go", but "they take their time for those travels" and stay sometimes "in
the same region for years". The "gnome-sightings" of his mother – who
bought a moped in recent years- are, as far as Mister Van Eck can
estimate, within the borders of this area: Weert – Leende – Mierlo
– Deurne – Westerbroek – Overloon – Wanssum – Grubbenvorst –
Baarlo – Buggenum – Heythuysen – Weert.* **F**

By §2c, Aant.1951, fol.468* (en Aant.1948, fol.27bis): De mededelingen van de heer B.C. van Breda omtrent zijn ontmoetingen met "aardgeesten" zijn gesitueerd in een gebied dat wordt begrensd door: Deurne/ Ysselsteyn/ Maasbree/ Meijel/ Liessel/ Deurne.
Toevoegen aan §1a, Aant.1951, fol.468II: Grote Peel/ Heijdse Peel/ [Griendtsveen] Helena Peel. – Ala

At §2C, Note 1951, fol. 468 (and Note 1948, fol. 27bis): The
gleanings of mister B.C. van Breda about his meetings with "nature
spirits" which occur in an area bordered by: Deurne / Ijsselsteyn /
Maasbree / Meijel / Liessel / Deurne.*

*Add to §1a, Note 1951 fol. 468II: Grote Peel / Heijdse Peel /
[Griendtsveen] Helena Peel.-* **A.**

DE PEEL

De Peel is a region in the south of The Netherlands, in
earlier times much larger than it is nowadays. Today, it is a

small region on the border of the provinces North Brabant and Limburg, roughly between Eindhoven and Weert. From all regions in The Netherlands, it appears that De Peel has the richest gnome-folklore and as we have seen, there are a large number of ways in which people see the gnomes. Up until the twentieth century and even the twenty-first, there are still people who remember seeing gnomes, or who know someone who, on occasion, witnesses a gnome. The Peel area is slightly hilly, mostly rural in character, and has some stretched forests in which one can find mounds, castles and small streams that connect these stretches of woods. To the east, De Peel borders on to Germany.

As the entire region is too large to cover in a few days, I have selected some areas where gnome folklore seems to exist today.

In the centre of the town of Horst, there is a statue of a gnome called *Eigenwijs* [Smart Pants], surrounded by all kinds of fairy figures. The gnome of Horst appeared to be an invented tradition; the story was concocted by the mayor. It does express how much the gnome-folklore still exists in De Peel.

Fairy tale figures around the central figure of a gnome, depicting a sleeping toad, the small gnome houses and working gnomes inside a little house (Photographs: Wilmar Taal)

Next to this invented tradition, there is the real gnome tradition, which I documented, on directions of the book by Ton van Reen, in the small town of Helden, in northern Limburg. There are still some locations where gnomes have been sighted and, most peculiar - near a crucifix. Limburg is a Catholic part of The Netherlands and votives are quite common on cross-sections in the road, or as we see below, in a curve towards the town of Baarlo. Along the Baarlose Weg (a large road with several farms along the way), there are a number of locations where gnomes have been seen working, passing by or even fishing. In a small stretch of forest which can be seen in the distance, there are even remnants of gnome-houses, which already have been discussed in *The Gnome Grimoire*. The photographs don't do the location

any justice. The stretched rectangular holes are barely made out on the photograph and the holes are actually all that is left of the gnome-abodes. Gnomes apparently lived *underground*, not only was it quite cool in the summers but it also retained some warmth in the winter. The following photographs have been made just outside of Helden. These show us various locations where gnomes supposedly lived and worked.

To the left: the crucifix on the curve in the road leading from Helden to Baarlo. Frits Engels, a local elderly person, witnessed a couple of gnomes crossing the road here. The gnomes came from behind the crucifix and walked towards the viewer. Above left: the now ruinous remains of the farm of widow Lormans. On the opposite side is a gnome-monument. Widow Lormans provided food to gnomes through a small door in her kitchen. It allowed her to feed them without looking at them, as she believed the gnomes were followers of the Devil. Above right: the woods outside of Helden where the gnome houses are located. (Photographs: Wilmar Taal)

To the left: an old overgrown tree which might have attracted gnomes. It stands near a small creek, which can be seen in the centre photograph. This creek was a big lake about a hundred years ago, where the gnomes fished for eels and carp. Above centre, a rural road, next to the crucifix, looking out over the forest where the gnome-houses are located. (Photographs: Wilmar Taal)

Bij §2ᵈ. Aanf. 1940, fol. 17ᴵᴵ [„Guernsey", &c., JHWE.]
Miss Evely Queripel, 28 jaar oud, vertelt dat men op Guernsy
— regelmatig —

regelmatig kabouters —„gnomes"— waarneemt. Ten aanzien van vreemdelingen praat men daar niet, althans niet graag over. Zij zegt zelf nimmer een kabouter te hebben gezien: niet iedereen heeft de gave die aardgeesten te kunnen waarnemen. Haar grootmoeder van vader's kant bezat dat vermogen wel. Zij zette 's avonds versnaperingen voor dat kleine volk in haar achtertuin. Evely's moeder heeft eveneens de gave kabouters te kunnen zien, maar is van mening dat mensen niet moeten trachten met die kabouters in contact te komen: dat zou heel gemakkelijk tot misverstanden kunnen leiden die dan voor de mens onaangenaamheden met zich meebrengen en zelfs onheil, ongeluk, kunnen veroorzaken. Kabouters zijn snel geïrriteerd en reageren dan kwaadaardig. Evely's grootmoeder zou dat wel hebben ondervonden. Heeft men de gave wel op de juiste wijze in contact te treden met het kleine volkje, dan kunnen de kabouters ook onheil voor de mens afwenden en materieel gewin brengen. — De kabouters zijn niet permanent op Guernsey: zij trekken vanuit Schotland, en vooral vanuit Ierland, via Wales en de Kanaaleilanden naar het vasteland, met als einddoel Noorwegen. Gedurende die grote reis verblijven de kabouters van jarenlang op één plaats: een plek waar het rustig is, waar de mensen hen niet hinderen en waar niet al te nabij kerkklokken luiden. JHWE.

At §2d, Note 1940, fol. 17II ["Guernsey", &c., JHWE] Miss Evely Queripel, 28 years old, tells that on Guernsey, "gnomes" are regularly sighted. She isn't eager to talk about it, at least to strangers. She has never seen a gnome: not everyone has the ability to observe nature spirits. Her grandmother on her father's side had this ability. At night, she placed refreshments in her backyard for the Little People. Evely's mother has the ability as well although she believes that people should not try to contact gnomes: it could easily lead to misunderstandings which could get uncomfortable for humans and even cause disaster and misfortune. Gnomes are easily irritated and react in a malevolent way. Evely's grandmother experienced that. If one uses the ability to contact the Little People in a right way, gnomes can avert doom for humans and bring fortune. The gnomes don't stay permanently on Guernsey: they travel from Scotland, and especially Ireland, through Wales and the Channel Islands to the mainland, with the final destination Norway. During this large trek, they can stay in one place for years: a place where it is quiet, where they are not bothered by people and where church-bells are not close by. JHWE.

[Below] *At §2e, Note 1940, fol. 18I: "Miss Mary"- Maria Rooyakker-, of Dutch nationality, married to a Welshman, travel guide and living in St. Peter Port for about seven years, says that the belief in gnomes on Guernsey is quite common. One does not speak about it, or barely, especially with strangers, with outsiders. They are convinced that gnomes are just passing through Guernsey on their way to Scandinavia. However, there are stories about gnomes who reside in one area for many years. "Miss Mary" never talks with tourists about gnomes and she is never asked about the subject. When she is critical or sceptical about the belief in gnomes, her husband tells her that she talks about things she doesn't understand and knows nothing about, and: - teasing- gnomes in clogs don't exist.... A.*

Bij §2e, Aant. 1940, fol. 18I̱: „Miss Mary"
—Maria Rooyakker—, van Nederland-
se nationaliteit, gehuwd met een Welshman,
reisleidster en omstreeks zeven jaar wo-
nend te St. Peter Port, zegt dat het geloof in
kabouters op Guernsey vrij algemeen is.
Men spreekt er echter niet of nauwelijks
over en zeker niet met vreemdelingen, met
buitenstaanders. Men meent dat de kabouters Guernsey slechts passeren op hun weg
naar Scandinavie, hoewel er verhalen
zijn over kabouters die vele jaren in één
bepaald gebied bleven. „Miss Mary" spreekt nimmer met haar toe-
risten over kabouters en haar worden terzake ook nimmer vragen
gesteld. — Wanneer zij zich kritisch of ongelovig uitlaat over dit
—kaboutergeloof—

kaboutergeloof, zegt haar man: je praat over dingen die je niet begrijpt en waar je niets van afweet, en: —plagend— kabouters
op klompen, die bestaan niet....

A photograph taken by Diek Eldermans – Callenbach during a holiday
on Guernsey. The subject of the photograph can be seen in between
the bush and the corner of the house. It is a toadstool like shape, which
Eldermans considered to be a hiding place for gnomes. Actually, this is a
staddle stone, used as a foundation for all kinds of sheds. (Photograph:
Museum of Witchcraft and Magic)

§9ᶜ, bij F4: Govert Stam is van mening dat de storende invloed van aardgeesten zich niet alleen doet gelden bij het zoeken naar schatten, maar vooral ook bij archaeologische nasporingen, bij het botaniseren, het zoeken naar bepaalde geologische objecten, en wat dies meer zij. De aardgeesten kunnen daarbij de zoeker op een dwaalspoor brengen en zelfs het gezochte tijdelijk onzichtbaar maken. Buitendien kunnen de aardgeesten, wanneer zij menen dat de mens het onder hun toezicht en beheer vallend terrein verstoort, deze mens onheil toebrengen, onheil dat hij pas later ervaart.—

—§9ᶜ: Govert Stam—

§9ᶜ: Govert Stam [geïntroduceerd door de heer D.E. van Strien (agent van politie-rechercheur)] is 67 jaar oud, gepensionneerd typograaf. Hij is al 21 jaar weduwnaar en woont alleen. Hij is, vertelt hij en doet hij blijken, overtuigd van het bestaan van aardgeesten. „Kabouters" vindt hij een verkeerde benaming: die staan in de tuin", „van gips", en „daarover vertellen de mensen flauwe kindervertellingen". Zijn grootmoeder van moeder's kant, met wie hij als klein kind al veel in de natuur —het Peelgebied— wandelde, had „het vermogen" aardgeesten te kunnen zien en met hen „in geestelijk contact" te komen. Hij, Stam, kan de aardgeesten helaas niet zien, maar heeft, in de natuur zwervend, wel vaak ervaren dat de aardgeesten hem „geestelijk hielpen", bijvoorbeeld bij het zoeken naar, en vinden van een zeer zeldzame plant. Zo heeft hij eens een stenen bijl en een andere keer twee gave urnen gevonden op een plaats waar hij die zaken nooit zou hebben gezocht, maar waar hij „een dringende ingeving kreeg dáár te gaan graven." Toen hij een schop had gehaald en terugkeerde op die plek, dacht hij: „ik lijk wel gek", maar „twijfel aan die ingeving zou veel gekker zijn geweest...!" — Van zijn „opoe", die „de (R.K.) kerk had afgezworen", leerde hij veel „over de natuur en de natuurkrachten", ook over de aardgeesten, die „in het Al" evenzeer een plaats hebben als de mens, de dieren en de planten, en „wie weet wat nog meer". — Evenals zijn grootmoeder dat was, is Stam vegetariër, hij rookt niet en gebruikt geen alcohol. 't Liefst gaat hij wandelen, „zwerven in de natuur"; thuis leest hij veel, „rijp en groen", „studieboeken". Hij leest graag „toverboeken", „oude boeken over magie", waaruit hij gegevens, in het bijzonder over amuletten en talismans, overneemt, „natekent en naschildert": zijn „no+tities", maar die wil hij niet tonen! Zijn „opoe" was „een wijze en belezen vrouw", en ook zij maakte notities, die hij zorgvuldig heeft bewaard en „nog vaak naleest." — Hoe aardgeesten er uitzien zegt hij niet precies te weten; van „opoe" heeft hij begrepen dat ze „klein" zijn, „zo omtrent een halve meter". Ze dragen altijd een rode, „enigszins puntige" muts. Hun kleding wisselt van van kleur, zelfs „terwijl je er naar kijkt", „daar heb je weer zo'n kameleon", zei „opoe" dan wel.... De aardgeesten verschijnen „vaak wazig en onduidelijk" aan de mens, ze „kunnen oplossen in de lucht" en „dwars door de dingen in de natuur heenlopen", „of door muren van huizen en tuinen", en zij

—„verdwijnen—

"verdwijnen ook dikwijls in wazigheid"... De aardgeesten spreken niet, in ieder geval niet met of tegen mensen. Dat is, zo vertelde "opoe", ook "niet noodig": de aardgeesten "verstaan wat in 't hoofd van de mens omgaat", en zij kunnen hun gedachten, waarschuwingen of bevelen "in 't hoofd van de mens overbrengen", zelfs zonder dat deze zulks bemerkt"... — Om het verhaal, dat aardgeesten voor bepaalde lieden werk, arbeid, zouden verrichten, moest "opoe" altijd lachen, en dat vindt ook Govert Stam een dwaze gedachte. — Hij zegt ook niet te weten of de aardgeesten in een bepaalde streek thuis horen, dan wel op reis zijn. — ◻

Bij §9f, F3: Govert Stam, een beleefd en ietwat onderdanig mannetje, liet zich niet gemakkelijk overhalen tot het geven van inlichtingen over aardgeesten. Hij vond het bezoek kennelijk wel gezellig, was kwistig met de koffie, maar meed uitspraken over het thema dat mij het meest interesseerde zo veel mogelijk. Eén keer liet hij zich —lachend— ontvallen: "ik laat me de tong niet schrapen"! — ◻

F *§9C, at F4: Govert Stam has the opinion that the disturbing influence of nature spirits not only occurs during search for treasure, but also during archaeological excavations, during botanizing, the search for certain geological objects and more of that matter. The nature spirits can lead the searcher astray and even make the desired object temporarily invisible. Apart from that, the nature spirits can bring disaster to a human, when he disrupts a terrain which they manage and oversee, disaster he will experience later on.-* **A.**

§9e: Govert Stam [Introduced by mister D.E. van Strien (officer of the police – investigator)] is a 67 years old, retired typographer. He is a widower of 21 years and lives alone. As he tells and makes clear, he is convinced of the existence of nature spirits. "Gnomes" he considers a misnomer: "those stand in the garden", "made of gypsum" and "of which people tell bland children's stories". His maternal grandmother, with whom he wandered through nature as a small child -the Peel area- had "the ability" to see nature spirits and to get "into mental contact" with them. He, Stam, can't unfortunately see nature spirits, but experienced, wandering through nature, that the nature spirits "helped him in a spiritual way", for example with looking for and finding a very rare plant.[18] In this way, he once found a stone

---

18. This is actually alike to a story Annie Gerding – Le Comte told in her book about gnomes, that she managed to find the quite rare Sundew plant with the aid of the gnome Jodocus.

axe and two urns in good order, in a place where he would never think to look for those things, but where he got an urgent intuition to dig there. When he got a spade and returned to the place, he thought: "I must be mad", but "doubting the intuition would be much crazier"…!" – From his "grandma", "who denounced the (Roman Catholic) church", he learned a lot "about nature and the powers of nature", also about the nature spirits, who have their place "in everything", just like humans, the animals and the plants and "who knows what more".- Just like his grandmother, Stam is a vegetarian, he doesn't smoke and doesn't drink alcohol. He loves to go walking, "wandering through nature"; at home he reads a lot, "ripe and green", "study books". He loves to read "grimoires", "old books about magic", from which he copies information, especially about amulets and talismans, "he traces and paints them": his "notes", but he does not want to show them! His "grandma" was a "wise and well-read woman", and she made notes as well, which he kept carefully and "often re-reads them".- What nature spirits look like, he is not sure; from "grandma" he understood they are "small", "approximately half a metre". They always wear a red "somewhat pointed" cap. Their garment changes colour, "even when you look at it", "there is another chameleon", "grandma" used to say…. The nature spirits appear "often fuzzy and unclear" to humans, they can "dissolve in the air" and "move right through objects in nature", "or through walls of houses and gardens", and they "disappear, often in fuzziness"… The nature spirits do not speak, not with or to humans. "Grandma" said that it is "not necessary": nature spirits "understand what goes on in the head of a human", and they can transfer their thoughts, warnings or orders "into the head of a human", even without one noticing"…- "Grandma" always had to laugh out loud when she heard the story that nature spirits performed tasks or labour for certain people, and Govert Stam thinks it is a foolish thought. – He does not know if nature spirits belong to a certain area, or that they are travelling.- **A**.

At §9f, F3: Govert Stam, a polite and somewhat subservient fellow, wasn't easy to persuade to provide information on nature spirits. He appreciated the visit, was very generous with coffee, but avoided the theme which interested me most, at all cost. One time he -laughing- let slip: "you can't scrape my tongue"!- **E**.

[Handwritten note:] Bij §2b, Aant. 1939, fol. 380 II: „Mijn ervaring is dat veel „vertellers", veelal met jeugdige personen, vaak argwanend en met tegenzin reageren. Zij blijken dikwijls bang zich belachelijk te maken met die kaboutervirhalen, zulks in de wetenschap dat de gemiddelde mens niet in kabouters gelooft en de kabouter slechts kent als tuinattribuut met een kruiwagentje of een hengeltje, dan wel vanuit kinderverhalen". JHWE.

d *At §2b, Note 1939, fol. 380II: "In my experience most "storytellers", mostly not very youthful persons, are suspicious and respond with reluctance. They are often scared to be ridiculed about their gnome stories, such with the knowledge that the average person doesn't believe in gnomes and only know the gnome as a garden-attribute with a wheelbarrow or a fishing rod, as well as from children's tales." JHWE*

Although Eldermans was quite negative about garden gnomes in the previous entry, he did collect some specimens for himself. This one is in the garden of Jeannet Richel in her abode in Benest, France. (Photograph: Wilmar Taal)

[Handwritten note:] Aant. 1942, fol. 119 II, bijlage no. III: „W" = [dertig jaar oud, huisvrouw, moeder van twee kinderen, vóór haar huwelijk met een accountant werkzaam als bibliothecaresse (Haar naam en adres zijn mij bekend. JHWE.)] wil onder geen beding dat haar

— naam —

naam in verband met deze mededelingen wordt genoemd. Zij be-
sprak de onderwerpelijke ervaringen met haar zéér nuchtere
echtgenoot, die er geen geloof aan hecht, haar er wel gekscherend
mee plaagt en zegt: je dróómde, en met een goede huisvriend, die
er —met haar toestemming— met mij over sprak. JHWE. —
   „W" vertelt dat zij sinds haar twintigste jaar —zij was
eerst kort geleden gehuwd— zes keer een kabouter zag en, naar
zij meent te mogen zeggen, „ontmoette". Dat geschiedde alle keren
ten noorden van het Kanaal van Almelo naar Nordhorn, in de
omgeving van de z.g.n. Hunenborg in het Voltherbroek nabij Ootmarsum. — Zij had tevoren nimmer iets gehoord of gelezen over het
al of niet bestaan van „echte kabouters". Zou dat wel het geval zijn
geweest, dan zou zij zo'n „kabouterverhaal" ongeloofwaardig
hebben gevonden en hebben afgewezen als een vreemd bijgeloof. Ze
zou er waarschijnlijk om hebben gelachen, zoals je ook wel spot
met mensen die bang zijn van geesten, of die zeggen „spoken" of
„witte wieven" te hebben gezien. — „W" groeide op in de binnen-
stad van Rotterdam, waar haar vader een kleine, maar goede
boekhandel dreef; het gezin woonde achter de zaak. Door de boekhandel gingen de ouders zelden met vacantie, en gebeurde dat
wel, dan bezocht men Brussel, Parijs of Londen. Het „echt buiten zijn" ontbrak in haar jeugd totaal. — Zo was Twente, waar
zij gehuwd kwam te wonen, „een openbaring"! In haar vrije
tijd deed —en doet— zij niets liever dan wandelen en fietsen in
dat zo gevarieerde, fraaie landschap, soms met haar echtgenoot,
of met kennissen, maar eigenlijk 't liefst alleen, „dan geniet
je intenser". Dat ontspant haar, regt ze, ook „wanneer ze eens
niet zo in d'r hum is". —
Aldus trok zij er in Juni 1932 met de fiets op uit, nadat zij tele-
fonisch had vernomen dat de ernstige ziekte, waaraan haar nog
te Rotterdam wonende vader al een tijd leed, ongeneeslijk was
en de goede man nog slechts enkele maanden zou leven....
Ze was, fietsend, zéér verdrietig en had weinig belangstelling
voor haar omgeving. Piekerend, in de put en van streek zocht
zij een rustplaats, ergens in 't Voltherbroek, waar zij op de ver-
hoogde berm van een smal pad ging zitten, de ellebogen op de
knieën en het hoofd in de handen. Zij huilde en was totaal van
streek, „radeloos-ontredderd".... Totdat plotseling en onverwacht
„een klaarte over haar kwam", „een gevoel van rust" en „berusting", van „acceptatie". 't Was of het licht werd", „in en om haar".
Zij droogde haar tranen, snoot haar neus en keek op met een

                                                    gevoel—

„gevoel van herborenheid". Toen, opkijkend, zag zij „een goede
vier meter vóór zich", tegen een bremstruik en vóór een gagel, een
heel klein en baardig mannetje staan, een kabouter. Die vriendelijk naar haar keek en wat aarzelend, groetend een hand
optilde. Wat nerveus-beweeglijk bleef hij gedurende korte tijd naar
haar staan kijken en verdween toen, alsof hij „langzaam in
de lucht werd opgelost...."

Achteraf, zo vertelt „W", heeft het haar „hooglijk verbaasd" dat zij
van die toch wonderlijk te noemen verschijning niet in het minst
geschrokken was — zo'n heldin is ze niet! Vreemd ook dat zij
nimmer twijfelde ten aanzien van haar waarneming, en dat
zij zonder bedenken of overwegen, als een realiteit verband
legde tussen haar „berusting", „de ontvangen vertroosting" en
de „vriendelijk-medelijdend kijkende" kabouter. —

Zij heeft gedurende maanden met niemand over deze ontmoeting
gesproken. Had daar, vreemd genoeg, ook geen behoefte aan, nog
afgezien van haar vrees zich belachelijk te maken.... Eerst na
het overlijden van haar vader heeft zij het verhaal verteld aan
haar echtgenoot, die haar „kennelijk geschrokken bezag" en „niet
wist hoe hij 't had". Hij ontkende de mogelijkheid van „zoiets".
Dat „middeleeuwse boeren" zich „zoiets konden verbeelden" was
„al gek genoeg", maar een intelligente, goed geschoolde vrouw in
negentienhonderdzoveel"..., „dat slaat alles"! „W" heeft, naar zij
zegt, nóg de gedachte, dat haar man haar verdenkt van het op
hem toepassen van een door hem niet begrepen practical joke....

Heel voorzichtig en altijd „onderzoekend kijkend" plaagt hij haar
wel eens met „haar kabouter", en als er in de tuin — inmiddels
versierd met twee tuinkabouters — een werkje te doen valt dat
hem niet aanstaat, vraagt hij haar wel of zij „haar kabouter" niet
te hulp kan roepen.... Ook met hun getrouwe huisvriend, een
66-jarige weduwnaar [Pim Stork. JHWE.], sprak zij over „haar
kabouter". Die had altijd „meer geduld om te luisteren en was meer
bereid te argumenteren, maar „daar bleef het bij".... —

Sinds de hiervoor omschreven ontmoeting heeft „W", naar zij zegt,
in de loop der jaren nog vijf keer een kabouter — misschien steeds
dezelfde? — gezien. Altijd wanneer zij alleen was en totaal onverwacht, steeds op een afstand van vier of vijf meter, vriendelijk naar
haar kijkend. Langer dan „een of twee minuten" duurde dat
nooit, dan verdween de kleine man, zich „wazig oplossend", haar

— altijd

altijd achterlatend „met een gelukkig, blij gevoel", „blijmoedig", „of
de wereld beter was dan zij in feite deed blijken"....

„W" zegt het moeilijk te vinden het uiterlijk van „haar kabouter" te
beschrijven. Het meest opvallend vindt zij de rode puntmuts, die
lang niet zo hoog is als men dat bij de tuinkabouters en in de
kinderboeken ziet. Die muts omsluit aan de voorzijde het zon-
verbrande „wind-en-weer-gezicht van de kabouter en gaat aan
de onderzijde over in een brede, van voren openstaande kraag —of
heel korte schoudermantel?—, nauwsluitend om de hals. Daar-
onder droeg de kabouter een nauwsluitend pak met lange
mouwen, dat wel uit één stuk leek te zijn geweven, een „soort
tricot-pak" van een „wat onbestemd bruin", dat „soms groenig
werd", „of leek", „een soort changeant-effect", „maar dan over
het hele pak", „of het geheel van kleur veranderde". Om zijn middel
droeg de kabouter een ceintuur, een riem, „waarschijnlijk van
leer, en aan de voeten vrij grove, plompe laarzen, wel „gelij-
kend op bergschoenen". De lichaamslengte van de kabouter
wordt door „W" geschat op „een centimeter of zeventig, hooguit
tachtig", „net boven een gewone tafel uit." —

*Note 1942, fol. 119II, appendix no. III: "W"= [thirty years
old, housewife, mother of two children, before her marriage with an
accountant working as a librarian (her name and address are known
to me. JHWE.)] absolutely doesn't want her name mentioned in
connection to these announcements. She spoke about her experiences
with her very down-to-earth husband, who doesn't believe it, and
jokingly teases her with it and said: you dreamt it, and with a good
friend who -with her permission- spoke about it with me. JHWE.-*

*"W" told that she saw a gnome six times and actually met with
him when she was twenty years old – and recently married before that-
. It happened all times north of the Canal from Almelo to Nordhorn,
in the vicinity of the so-called Hunenborg in the Voltherbroek
near Ootmarsum.- She had never heard or read anything about the
existence of "real gnomes" before. Was that the case, she would
have considered such a "gnome story" unbelievable and rejected it as
strange superstition. She would have laughed about it, like you mock
people who are afraid of spirits, or who say to have seen "ghosts" or
"white women". "W" grew up in the inner city of Rotterdam, where
her father ran a small but good bookstore; the family lived behind the
store. Because of the bookstore her parents rarely took a vacation,
and when it did happen, they visited Brussels, Paris or London. The*

"real outdoors" she never experienced during her youth.- Twente, where she came to live after her marriage, was "a revelation"! In her spare time, she did -and does- nothing more than walk and ride through the varied, beautiful landscape, sometimes with her husband, or with acquaintances, but mostly rather alone, as "you enjoy it more intensely". It relaxes her, she says, also "when she sometimes is in a bad mood".-

Thus, she went out in June 1932 on her bicycle, after she had received a phone call about the serious disease her father, who still lived in Rotterdam, had been suffering from for a while, had turned out to be incurable and the good man had only but months to live...

She was riding, very sad and had little attention for her surroundings. Worrying, down in the dumps and upset she looked for a place to rest, somewhere in the Voltherbroek, where she sat down on the bank of a heightened path, her elbows on her knees and her head in her hands. She cried and was totally upset, "distraught-upset".... Until she experienced "feeling clear", "a sense of rest", of "acceptance". "It was like it turned light", "in and around her". She dried her tears, blew her nose and looked up with a sense "of being reborn". Then, looking up, she saw "a good four meters in front of her", against a broom bush and before a myrtle, a very small, bearded man, a gnome, who looked at her friendly and somewhat hesitating, and lifted a hand to greet her. He kept looking at her for a short while, nervously moving and disappeared, like he "slowly dissolved in the air...."

In hindsight, "W" tells, she was "highly surprised" she wasn't startled by this highly wondrous apparition – "she is no hero"-. Strange that she never doubted her sighting and made a connection between her "acquiescence", "the received comfort" and the "friendly-compassionate looking" gnome.-

She didn't speak for months to anyone about this meeting. She felt, strangely enough, no urge to, apart from the fear of being ridiculed... First, after her father passed away, she told the story to her husband, who looked at her "visibly startled" and "was shaken to the core". He denied the possibility of "such". If "Medieval farmers" could "imagine something like that" was "crazy enough", but an intelligent, well-educated woman in "nineteenhundredandsomething"..., "that beats everything"! "W" still has, as she said, the impression her husband suspects her of playing a practical joke on him.... Very cautious and always "investigative looking" he teases her with "her gnomes" when a job needs to be done in the garden that he doesn't like -in the meantime adorned with two garden gnomes- if "her gnome" can't come to help.... She also spoke to her loyal friend, a 66-year-old widower [Pim Stork. JHWE], about "her gnome". He had more time and patience to listen and was willing to reason about it, but "that's it"....-

Since the meeting described above "W" has, according to herself, met with a gnome five times -maybe still the same one? Always when she was alone and totally unexpected, on a distance of four or five meters, looking friendly upon her. These meetings lasted no longer "than one or two minutes", the little man disappeared, "dissolving fuzzily", always leaving her with "a blissful, happy feeling", "cheerful", "like the world was a better place than it appeared to be"....

"W" says she finds it hard to describe the appearance of "her gnome". The most outstanding feature is the red pointy hat, which isn't nearly as high as one sees with garden gnomes and in children's books. The cap closes to the front of the weathered, sunburnt face of the gnome and connects below into a collar which is opened to the front -or a short shoulder cape?- closing around the neck. Underneath the gnome wore a tight-fitting suit with long sleeves, which appeared to be woven into one piece, a "kind of tricot-suit" of "an undefinable brown", which sometimes "turned greenish", "or appeared to be", "a sort of changing effect", "but concerning the entire suit", "like it changed colour overall". Around the waist, the gnome wore a waistband, a belt, "presumably of leather, and on the feet very rough and plump-looking boots, "resembling mountain shoes". The length of the gnome is estimated by "W" on "around 70 centimetres, at most 80", "just reaching above a normal table".

The place where "W" presumably met "her gnome" for the first time. This is a heightened path, the bank is now hidden in the foliage, and 'De Hunenborg' is to the left. The picture is taken in 2017. The situation in 1932 was different. (Photograph: Wilmar Taal)

Bij §1ᴵᴵ, Aanf.1942, fol.151ᵈ: Volledigheidshalve vermeld ik hier het met de pen getekende en „1822" gedateerde kaartje van „Oost-Twenthe", dat in het bezit is van de wed. B.J. Hedeman (ootm.str.82, Almelo) en eigendom zou zijn geweest van haar echtgenoot. Dit kaartje ─ zo zegt mevr. Hedeman ─ zou de strook aangeven waarin kabouters verblijven

─ en ─

F *At §1II, Note 1942, fol. 151d: For the sake of completeness I mention here that the pen drawing and dated "1822" map of "East-Twente" was the property of the widow B.J. Hedeman (Ootmarsumse Straat 82, Almelo) and belonged to her husband. This map -so says Mrs. Hedeman- would indicate the area where gnomes reside and also travel in a northeastern direction, with final destination, Norway. I was not allowed to make a (photographic) reproduction of the map (37,5 centimeters wide and 50 centimeters high) (Mrs. Hedeman was annoyed because I wondered if this map really was connected to gnomes). I have,*

en ook verder trekken in noordoostelijke richting, met als einddoel Noorwegen. Het werd mij niet toegestaan een (Fotogr.) reproductie van het kaartje (37,5 cm. breed en 50 cm. hoog) te maken (mevr. Hedeman was gepikeerd omdat ik mij afvroeg of dit kaartje werkelijk verband houdt met kabouters). Ik heb, beginnend in het zuiden, de plaatsnamen genoteerd die in de —vrij brede— strook vermeld zijn: 't Hof te Boekelo en Osselo / Twickelo / Lonneker en Lintezijde / De Denneboom / Arnikhoven / Duringen / Hondemot en Leemselo / De Nieuwstad / Stift Weerselo / Gr. Agelo / Reutum / Haarle / Old Ootmarsum / Nutter / De Molens / Gr. Heesingen / Manden / Getelo. =

De heer P.M. Rogmans —rentmeester— zegde toe het onderwerpelijke kaartje nader te bestuderen en daarvan verslag te doen. [Vermeld zij dat de overleden echtgenoot van mevr. Hedeman bij leven wel beweerde gedurende de jacht meermalen kabouters te hebben gezien.]

starting in the south, noted the names of places mentioned in the – very broad- area: 't Hof te Boekelo and Osselo / Twickelo / Lonneker and Lintezijde / De Denneboom / Arnikhoven / Duringen / Hondemot and Leemselo / De Nieuwstad / Stift Weerselo / Gr. Agelo / Reutum / Haarle / Old Ootmarsum / Nutter / De Molens / Gr. Heesingen / Manden / Getelo.=
Mister P.M. Rogmans -steward- promised to study the map in question and to report about it. [It should be said that the departed husband of Mrs. Hedeman during his life stated that he saw gnomes on many occasions while hunting.][19]

Bij §1, Aant.1946, fol. 9²: Mevr. H.S. van de Pol-Veldstra zegt er van overtuigd te zijn dat kabouters werkelijk bestaan, zulks op grond van „het feit", dat haar —inmiddels overleden— moeder „de gave had" deze aardgeesten op bepaalde plaatsen te zien, en zelfs contact met hen te hebben. Moeder vertelde daar wel over, zij het alleen wanneer zeer vertrouwde relaties daarop aandrongen. Moeder zag die kabouters uitsluitend in een natuurgebied te

—Nunspeet—

---

19. Liberta (B.J.) Hedeman – Wolf, born on 30th October 1878, indeed lived at the Ootmarsumsestraat 82 and passed away on 26th June 1949. She had no profession during her life.

Nunspeet. Een gebied, liggende „om en tussen":

RC | het Mosterdveen — Saxenheim (toen nog geen kampeerterrein) —
| de Ossenkolk — de Witte Klap — (Mosterdveen). —

Haar echtgenoot, de heer J. van de Pol — automonteur — gaf
later een enigszins andere opsomming:

| de Witte Klap — de Mythstee, de Roo Stee, langs het Eibertjes-
| pad — de Ossenkolk — het Mosterdveen — (de Witte Klap). —
RD | hater voegde hij daar — tussen de Witte Klap en de Mythstee —
| het — toenmalige — Ronde Huis nog aan toe. —

De moeder van mevr. H.S. van de Pol-Veldstra was Nederlands-Hervormd,
een „gelovige vrouw", kerkelijk meelevend. Het waarnemen van kabouters bracht haar ten aanzien van haar „kerkelijke opvattingen" in
een conflictsituatie, haar mening was namelijk „dat kabouters iets
heidens zijn". Een terzake daarvan door moeder geraadpleegde predi-
kant „hield zich op de vlakte" en „nam dat kabouterverhaal niet
serieus", iets waarover moeder zeer verontwaardigd en boos was! Toch,
ondanks deze innerlijke conflicten, meed moeder het genoemde gebied
niet: zij ging daar veelvuldig — en bij voorkeur alleen — wandelen,
en in later jaren fietsen: „een mooier stuk land vind je nergens"!
Moeder woonde tevoren in Friesland en in Noord-Holland, tot „reizen"
was zij — arbeidersvrouw met vier kinderen — nooit gekomen.
Moeder zegde de kabouters te zien wanneer ze geen gezelschap had.
Eén keer wandelde in de omgeving van de Mythstee met een toen omtrent veertien jaar oud nichtje. Moeder zag twee kabouters staan en
zei tegen het nichtje: dáár, bij die lariks, zie jij daar niets bijzonders? Maar „het nichtje zag niets" en de kabouters („aangewezen",
„wat nooit mag") verdwenen heel snel. — Wanneer moeder wandelde
en „uitkeek naar kabouters", zag zij er nooit een: zij vertoonden
zich altijd onverwacht, zo dat zij er altijd een beetje van schrok.
Maar de kabouters — altijd op een afstand van „een meter of vier,
vijf" — zeiden nooit wat, maar „straalden een sfeer uit" die je
geruststelde en „waardoor kommer en zorg" (die zij in haar
gezin wel kende) „verdwenen". Na zo'n ontmoeting met een kabouter
„voelde je je altijd beter", „meer opgewassen tegen moeilijkheden"….
Hoe vaak moeder kabouters zag, zegt mevr. Van de Pol niet te
weten, „niet te kunnen benaderen"; „waarschijnlijk niet zo vaak",
„een keer of vier in een jaar", zowel 's zomers als 's winters. Moeder
beschreef de kabouters altijd zeer summier. Vele mededelingen
samenvattend: „klein, maar wel volwassen", „lang haar en
vaak een baard", „ een puntmutsje op en om het hoofd, „ een kleine

— cape —

cape, meestal vast aan de muts", „ eenvoudige kleding, net werkkleren"
en „schoenen die puntig lijken, maar van voren veel ruimte hebben".
De „muts soms bruin, maar vaker rood", „de schoentjes bruin", de
ruim zittende kleding, met een bruine ceintuur om het middel,
vaal bruin, grijs, en ook wel flets groen", en „soms veranderden
die kleuren terwijl je naar ze keek", „je zag ze trouwens lang niet
altijd scherp", „soms leken ze doorzichtig te worden", „vooral wanneer ze verdwenen". —

t *At §1, Note 1946, fol. 9b: Mrs. H.S. van de Pol-Veldstra says to be convinced that gnomes really exist, even based on "the fact" that her -already deceased- mother had "the ability" to see these nature spirits in certain places and even had contact with them. Mother told about it when very trusted relations urged her to. Mother only saw the gnomes exclusively in a nature reserve in Nunspeet. An area lying "around and between": (RC) Mosterdveen – Saxenheim (Not a camping terrain then) – Ossenkolk – Witte Klap – (Mosterdveen).-*

Her husband, Mister J. van de Pol -car mechanic- gave slightly different details:

(RD) Witte Klap – Mijthstee, RooStee, along the Eibertjespad – Ossenkolk – Mosterdveen – (Witte Klap) – Later he added – between Witte Klap and the Mijthstee – the -former- Round House.-[20]

The mother of Mrs. H.S. van de Pol-Veldstra was Dutch Reformed, a "woman of faith", religiously sympathetic. Observing gnomes brought her into conflict regarding her "religious views", as she was opinionated that "gnomes are a pagan phenomenon". A preacher whom she consulted about the matter "kept aloof" and "didn't take the gnome-story too seriously", about which she was very indignant and angry! Yet, despite all these inner conflicts, mother did not avoid the area: she walked there – by preference alone- and in later years she rode a bike: you can't find a more beautiful stretch of land anywhere! Mother lived in Friesland and North Holland before, she never "amounted to travel", being a –'labour' woman with four children-. Mother said she saw gnomes when she had no company. One time she was walking in the surroundings of the Mijthstee with a niece who was around fourteen years old. Mother saw two gnomes standing and said to the niece: "there, next to the larch, do you see something extraordinary?" But "the niece saw nothing" and the gnomes ("pointed at", "which was not allowed") vanished rapidly.- When mother walked and "was on the lookout for gnomes", she never saw one: they appeared always unexpectedly, in a way that

---

20. This indicates that the report has been made not in 1946, but after 1967 or 1968, when the Round House was demolished. After that people in Nunspeet started to speak of the 'former' Round House.

startled her. But the gnomes — always on a distance of "about four or five meters"- never said anything, but "radiated a mood" which comforted you and "made all "grief and worry" (which she had with her family) disappear. After a meeting with a gnome "you always felt better", "more ready to cope with difficulties".... How often mother saw gnomes, Mrs. Van de Pol doesn't know, "no estimation", "presumably not too often", "possibly four times a year", during the summer as well as in the winter. Mother rarely described the gnomes. Summarizing many gleanings: "small, but adult", "long hair and often a beard", "a small pointy hat on the head", "a small cape, mostly attached to the cap", "simple clothing, resembling working clothes" and "shoes that appear pointy, but appear to have a lot of space in the front". The "cap, sometimes brown, but more often red", "the shoes brown", the spacious fitting clothes, with a brown waistband around the waist, rusty brown, grey and sometimes pale green", and "sometimes these colours changed while you watched them", "you didn't see them very sharp", "sometimes they appeared transparent", "especially when they vanished".- **E.**

De heer J. van de Pol vertelt —buiten de aanwezigheid van zijn echtgenote, mevr. H.S. van de Pol-Veldstra— dat zijn schoonmoeder, die haar laatste jaren bij hen inwonend was, tijdens haar leven „een strenge, rechtlijnige vrouw" was, strikt eerlijk en rechtvaardig, „op het harde af", en met zeer persoonlijke inzichten over goed en kwaad. Zij was „op haar manier zeer gods-dienstig". Zij bezocht maar enkele jaren de lagere school, „ergens in Friesland", „kon wel goed leren", maar moest al op jeugdige leeftijd helpen het gezinsinkomen van haar ouders te vermeerderen. Zij kon „moeizaam lezen" en haar schrijven was „beroerd slecht". Toch was zij in veel opzichten „een wijze vrouw", die door haar recht-lijnige eerlijkheid vaak de indruk wekte over weinig tact te beschikken. Ze leek soms „een vrouwelijke aartsvader". Fantasie bezat ze niet". — De heer Van de Pol zegt een ieder die met zo'n verhaal over kabouters was gekomen, „voor gek te hebben verklaard", maar zijn schoonmoeder, met haar simpele, onopgesmukte verhalen, geloofde hij, en in de loop der jaren steeds meer...! — **E**

t *Mister J. van de Pol tells -when his wife is not present, Mrs. H.S. van de Pol – Veldstra – that his mother-in-law, who lived with them in her final years, was a "strict, rectilinear woman", very honest and righteous, "lacking nuance" and with very personal views on* *good and evil. She was "in her own way very religious". She attended primary school for some years, "somewhere in Friesland", "was a good learner", but had to help raise the family income at a very young age. She was a "laborious reader" and her writing was "really bad". In many ways, she appeared to be "a wise woman", who through her rectilinear honesty gave the impression that she lacked tact. She resembled "a female arch-father". "She lacked imagination".- Mister Van de Pol says he would consider anyone who told a story about gnomes "a fool", but his mother-in-law with her simple, unadorned stories, he believed, and as the years went on, he believed her even more....!-* **E.**

A trail leading to the Mythstee, where the mother of Mrs. Van de Pol – Veldstra may have observed gnomes. The Mythstee is straight ahead to the left. (Photograph: Wilmar Taal)

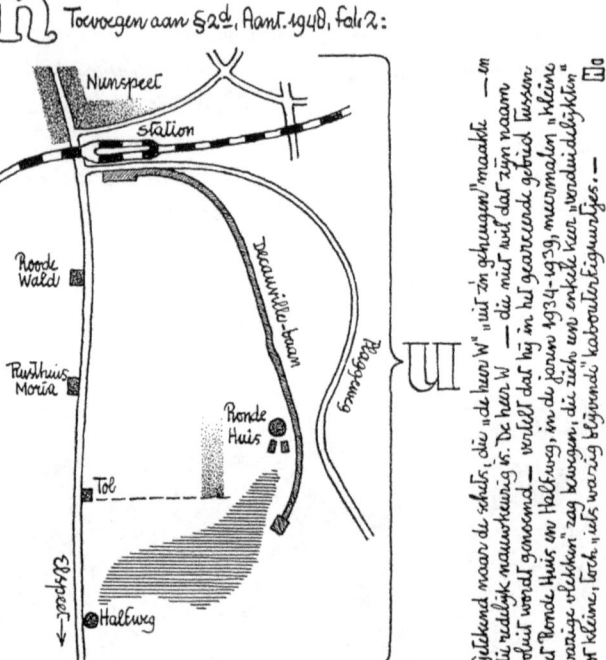

n Toevoegen aan §2ᵈ, Aant. 1948, fol. 2:

   n *Add to §2d, Note 1948, fol. 2: Drawn according to a sketch,
which Mister "W" made "from memory"- and is rather accurate. Mister
W – who does not want his name mentioned in full- tells that in the
shaded area, between the Round House and Halfweg, during the years
1934-1939, he saw "small hazy spots" move on multiple occasions,
which "cleared up" sometimes to small, yet "still fuzzy remaining"
gnome-figures.* **H.**

§2ᵉ, fol. 2ᵃ: Een dochter van „de heer W.", werkzaam bij het Ministerie
van Justitie te Den Haag, vertelde mij dat haar vader, wanneer „het
occulte" ter sprake komt, altijd zegt: „ wij weten niets, of hoogstens
maar héél weinig van die duistere dingen". Bestaat het gezelschap uit
„erg vertrouwde relaties", dan vertelt hij wel eens, dat hij vóór de oorlog
in het bos bij Nunspeet enige keren een kabouter heeft gezien.—

Op grond van die mededeling heb ik —zonder mijn contact met zijn
dochter te noemen— met hem een afspraak weten te maken voor een
ontmoeting in de stationsrestauratie te Heiden. Met moeite bracht ik
hem daar op het Thema „kabouters". Nadat hij had ontkend iets over

—kabouters—

kabouters te weten, werd hij toch meer toeschietelijk en vertrouwelijk, en wilde hij mij „zijn verhaal" wel vertellen, mits zijn naam niet zou worden genoteerd.... Hij was, vertelde hij, werkzaam bij de Nederl. Spoorwegen, „ploegbaas bij weg en werken" en kwam daardoor gedurende „een jaar of vijf voor de oorlog" vaak in Nunspeet. Hij „houdt van de natuur" en in zijn rusttijd of na de dienst ging hij daar graag in de bossen wandelen, veelal vanaf het station in de richting van het Ronde Huis, „een prachtig bosgebied". Wanneer hij aldus „een eind had gestapt", ging hij veelal „op de Elspeterweg af" en zo terug naar het station. — Op die terugweg, tussen het Ronde Huis en Halfweg, ontdekte hij op zekere dag in het bos „wonderlijke, nevelige vlekjes", die „soms stil stonden, soms bewogen". Hij dacht eerst, dat „'t iets aan z'n ogen" was, maar tijdens een volgende wandeling zag hij duidelijk dat die „vlekken in 't bos stonden of bewogen" en „er naar turend" —ze waren altijd „minstens vijf meter van hem af"— ontdekte hij dat die „vlekken", „zo'n goeie halve meter hoog", een „min of meer gelijke vorm" hadden. En op een van zijn volgende wandelingen zag hij „die vage, warige vorm" duidelijker worden en zag hij, „eerlijk gezegd met schrik en verbazing", dat het kabouters waren, „soms zelfs héél duidelijk". Hij had er tevoren nooit over nagedacht —of over gelezen— dat kabouters, die hij wel uit kinderverttellingen kende, „echt konden bestaan", en „zou dat ook nooit geloofd hebben wanneer een ander hem dat zou hebben verteld". Hij durfde zijn wonderlijke ervaring dan ook niet aan anderen te vertellen, „ze zouden hem voor gek hebben verklaard"! Later, na de oorlog —hij was toen in jaren niet meer in Nunspeet geweest— heeft hij er wel „met heel goede bekenden" over gepraat, altijd eigenlijk „in de hoop dat iemand hem een verklaring kon geven", maar hij ontmoette steeds „een vriendelijk of een onbeleefd ongeloof". Daar heeft hij „zich nu bij neergelegd". Je „hoort en leest wel meer van die vreemde verhalen" en „'t zal wel zo zijn dat er meer bestaat dan eigenwijze mensen kunnen geloven".... Wanneer hij nu iets over kabouters zegt, en de mensen kijken ongelovig, dan denkt hij: „je hebt gelijk", „als jij 't vertelde geloofde ik jou ook niet".... JHW2.

§2e, fol. 2a: *A daughter of "Mister W.", working at the Department of Justice in The Hague, told me that her father, when "the occult" was discussed, always says: "We know nothing, or at least very little of these dark subjects". When in "trusted company", he might tell on occasion, that before the war he saw sometimes gnomes in the forest near Nunspeet.-*

Based on this announcement, I have -without mentioning his daughter as my contact- made an appointment with him for a meeting in the Stationbuffet of Leiden. With a little effort I steered the conversation to the theme of "gnomes". After he had denied to know anything about gnomes, he became more willing and trusting, and wanted to tell me "his story", under the condition his name was not written down.... He was, as he told me, working with the Dutch Railways, "foreman with Road and Works" and came "a year or five before the War" quite often in Nunspeet. He "loves nature" and during his break or after his work ended, he walked in the forest, mostly from the station in the direction of the Round House, "a magnificent forest area". When he thus "walked for a while", he mostly went "to the Elspeterweg" and back to the station.- On the way back, between the Round House and Halfweg, he discovered on a certain day in the woods "wondrous, hazy spots", which "sometimes stood still, sometimes moved". At first, he thought "something was the matter with his eyes", but during a next walk he saw clearly that these "spots stood in the forest or moved" and "gazing at it"- they were mostly "on a distance of five metres"- he discovered that these spots, "a good half metre high", had "a more or less similar shape". And, on one of his next walks, he saw "the vague, hazy shape" became clearer and he saw, "honestly with fright and surprise", that these were gnomes, "sometimes even very clear". He never had given it any thought before - or read about it- that gnomes, which he knew from children's tales, "really could exist", and "would have never believed if somebody else had told him". He never dared to tell his wondrous experience to others, "they would have told he was crazy"! Later, after the war -he hasn't been to Nunspeet for years- he spoke "with very good acquaintances" about it, always "hoping someone could provide him an explanation", but he always encountered "a friendly or unpolite disbelief". He has "accepted the situation". You "hear and read more of these strange stories" and "it probably is true that there is more than these stubborn people can believe".... When he says something about gnomes, people look at him in disbelief, and he thinks: "you are right", "If you told me, I would not believe you as well".... JHWE.

NUNSPEET

We already discussed the Mythstee in The Gnome Manuscript, but Nunspeet has a strange connection with gnomes and probably that has something to do with its surroundings. Nunspeet will be mentioned even further in this chapter but according to the announcements of Mister "W", we might take a look at the areas he described. Roughly, these areas correspond with an area surrounding the Mythstee. During the field-research for this book, I visited the Mythstee to take some photographs, during which, I encountered a strange phenomenon. When standing next to the pond of the Mythstee, its view obscured by a large rhododendron bush, I was taking a few shots of the area where "W" might have seen the 'spots', when I heard a huge splash next to me in the pond, which broke my concentration and startled me quite a bit! I ran around the bushes to a clearing so that I could see the pond but there was no sign that the waters had been disturbed, and in the surroundings, I did not see any wet animals that might have jumped into the pond. I do think it was probably a large animal but why was there no trace of the water being disturbed? Were these the gnomes that "W" had seen and who were giving me "a warning"? I would love to believe that this was the case but without any physical evidence (let's say a gnome that I actually, see?), I will go for the best explanation ... a deer.

The area shaded on the map by "W" is mostly forest, with very few buildings. The first building is roughly a mile from the Mythstee, on an estate called Roostee. Nunspeet is actually surrounded by forest. Between Nunspeet and Hulshorst is the Belvédère forest. To the southwest, there are the forests of Leuvenum, which could be counted among the most beautiful woods of De Veluwe; to the east we have a number of forests and moors with small towns littered over the landscape like Doornspijk, Epe and 't Harde, whilst further south near Vierhouten, there is even more forest and moors to be found. Both Nunspeet and Vierhouten have their gnome-tales but Nunspeet has had someone who had seen gnomes during the Twentieth Century.

What causes people to see gnomes in Nunspeet, is something we can only guess about. Is it something in the soil? Is it something in the air? Or, is it because Nunspeet is quite an orthodox town, with a strong belief in God and an equally strong belief in the Devil and the supernatural? I dare to state that areas where the church has a firm hold over the people, the belief in the supernatural is just as common, and mostly considered 'evil'. As we saw in the entry concerning the mother of Mrs. Van der Pol-Veldstra: she was very religious and very conflicted about the gnomes she encountered. But it is not only Nunspeet that has a strong belief in the supernatural. It is also in towns like Putten, roughly 25 miles from Nunspeet, where there are pastors who perform exorcisms and claim to cure homosexuality, which, in my opinion, is quite insane (especially the latter!). Maybe the supernatural does tend to oppose Christian beliefs, which might offer an explanation as to why these phenomena appear to be experienced more near Nunspeet than elsewhere. It is also an area where nature still appears to be 'rough' and wild, although the landscape is also cultivated.

The Mythstee, where mister "W" saw his gnomes. We are looking at the Mythstee itself. We do not know exactly where he saw them, but this is well inside the shaded area. (Photograph: Wilmar Taal)

On the 'wall' of the Mythstee. These fallen trees are kept lying on the ground, for entomological research. In the centre above, you see a 'hunting chair'. Underneath the fallen tree is a mysterious hole (Photograph: Wilmar Taal)

The Mythstee in the direction of Halfweg, where Mister "W" saw his gnomes. (Photograph: Wilmar Taal)

The Mythstee with the Eibertjespad (Eibertjes trail) in the distance, which got its name from the poor Eibertje, who went begging in Nunspeet while living in Vierhouten. The trail she walked became known as the Eibertjespad. The current trail carries this name, but is not the exact trail Eibertje walked (Photograph Wilmar Taal)

K Aanf. 1951, fol. 455, en toevoegen aan §4, fol. 466 (1951):
"Harmen van Eck", &c. —
Op zijn verzoek heb ik 22-12-1951 in de stationswachtkamer
te Zutphen nog een onderhoud gehad met de heer Van Eck. Hij wilde
graag "nog enkele zaken benadrukken", en, nu hij over een en
ander had nagedacht, nader toelichten. —
De heer Van Eck noemt zijn moeder een zeer intelligente vrouw. Zij
genoot voor haar huwelijk middelbaar onderwijs, maar had toen
al contact met haar latere echtgenoot en wilde er niet voor verder
te studeren, wat door allerlei relaties werd betreurd, want zij was
"een weetgierige, vlotte leerlinge". Die "weetgierigheid" bleef gedurende haar leven, én "studiezin". Zij is, zegt de zoon, wat men
zou kunnen noemen "een erudite vrouw". Zij is nuchter in
haar denken en overwegen, een "realiste", tolerant ten aanzien de medemens. Moeder is — evenals vader — afkomstig
—uit—

uit een niet godsdienstig milieu, zo zegt de heer Van Eck, ook later
"deden zij niet aan godsdienst." Met "bijgeloof" werd in het
gezin "de draak gestoken", de "Wetenschap" werd immer hoog geprezen: "die knapen weten niet alles, maar met elkaar weten en
kunnen ze heel erg veel"... Levensbeschouwelijk was moeder
altijd geneigd tot "de linkse politiek", "op haar manier een
socialiste", echter zonder zich als lid bij enige groep of partij aan
te sluiten. Moeder trok er "heel graag op uit", "liefst alleen", de
"vrije natuur in": "de hort op" zei men in het gezin, en zij had
een grote belangstelling voor wat zij noemt "natuurhistorie",
"natte his". Dat culmineert in haar grote belangstelling voor geo-
logie en haar omvangrijke verzameling stenen en fossielen. Ook
leest zij veel over archaeologie. Alles bijeen, zo oordeelt de heer Van
Eck, is zijn moeder een vrouw waarvan niemand ooit zou
denken of vermoeden dat zij geloof hecht aan het bestaan van
kabouters. Uit haar mededelingen over dat "kaboutergeloof" blijkt
steeds weer dat het haar grote ernst is, en dat "het bestaan" van
die aardgeesten haar "verwondert", ook misschien "een beetje
bang" maakt, of "onzeker". Moeder heeft nimmer getracht dat
"kaboutergeloof" op anderen over te brengen: "Als jullie dat
talent, die bijzondere gave om kabouters te zien en te ontmoeten
hadden, dan was dat wat anders", "daarom is het onzin er
veel over te praten", "te bevechten". "Ik begrijp best dat jullie me
uitlachen en bezorgd en een beetje wantrouwend aankijken..."
"laat mij nou maar gelukkig zijn met mijn kleine, maar heel
wijze vriendjes!" —   JHWE.

k *Note 1951, fol. 475, and add to §4, fol. 466II (1951):*
"Harmen van Eck", &c.-

*On his request I had a conversation on 22 December 1951, in
the anteroom of Station Zutphen with Mister Van Eck. He wanted
eagerly "to emphasize some matters", and, now he had thought one
and another over, clarify things.-*

*Mister Van Eck calls his mother a very intelligent woman. She
had before her marriage some secondary education, but when she had
relations with her later husband, she didn't feel for it to study any
further, which other relations regretted, because she was a "curious
and quick study". This "curiosity" stayed her entire life, and she
remained "studious". She is, according to the son, what one could
call an "erudite woman". She is sober in her thinking and concern, a
"realist", tolerant towards her fellow human. Mother is -like father-
from a non-religious background, thus says Mister Van Eck, and
even later "they never got religious". "Superstition" was always*

"ridiculed" by the family, "Science" was praised highly: "these people do not know everything, but together they know and can do a lot"… Philosophically, mother was inclined to "left politics", "in her own way a socialist" without being a member of a certain group or party. Mother went out "very much by herself", "preferably alone", into "free nature": "out the door" the family said, and she had great interest in what she called "natural history". This culminated in her great interest in geology and her comprehensive collection rocks and fossils. She also read a lot about archaeology. Everything taken together, is the judgment of Mister Van Eck, his mother is a woman of whom no one would think or suspect she had any belief in the existence of gnomes. From her announcements about this "gnome belief", it appears she is very serious about it, and that "the existence" of these nature spirits makes her "wondering" and also "frightens her" or makes her "uncertain". Mother never tried to convey the "gnome belief" to others: "If you had the talent, the special ability to see gnomes and to meet them, it would be something different", "that's why it is nonsense to talk about it a lot", "to bicker". "I do understand you laugh at me, are concerned and look at me with a bit of distrust…" "Let me be happy with my small, but very wise friends!"- JHWE

ⓔ „Harmen van Eck", &c.: „Mevr. N. v. E-S" = zie §4, Aanf. '51, fol. 466⁼:

„Moeder heeft haar ontmoetingen met kabouters, naar zij zegt, in „alle jaargetijden", het goede of slechte weer speelt daarbij geen rol. / Zij ontmoet de kabouters niet op alle tochten die ze „in de vrije natuur" maakt. „hang niet!" Misschien „tien of twaalf keer" per jaar ziet ze zo'n „kleine vriend" en dan nog lang niet altijd even scherp en duidelijk. Meermalen trekken de kabouters zich vrij snel terug in „een verdwijnende nevelvlek". / Het „geestelijk contact" met de kabouters ontstaat ook niet bij iedere ontmoeting, of „misschien is het er wel", maar „merk je het dan niet." Over de inhoud van dat „geestelijk contact" — een soort telepathie" — laat moeder zich nooit uit. / Moeder uitte bij

— herhaling —

herhaling het vermoeden dat zij bij het vinden van byzondere, vaak zeldzame stenen of fossielen, hulp van een kabouter heeft gehad. Haar „mooiste stukken" vond zij op een andere manier en een andere plaats dan zij met háár ervaring" had verwacht, zulks „door een dwaas lijkende ingeving. — Ⓔ□

e *"Harmen van Eck", &c.: "Mrs. N.v.E.-S."= see §4, Note '51, fol. 466I: "Mother always had her meetings with gnomes, as she said, in "all seasons", good or bad weather never plays a part./ She may not meet gnomes on all her treks through the free nature. "Not by a longshot!" Maybe "ten or twelve times a year" she sees such a "small friend" and not every time as sharp and clear. Most times the gnomes retreat very quickly in "a disappearing mist"./ The "mental contact" with gnomes does not occur with every meeting, or "maybe it is there" but "you don't notice". What the "mental contact" is about — "a kind of telepathy"- mother never mentions anything./ Repeatedly, mother suspected that she had help from a gnome when finding her rare rocks or fossils. Her "best pieces" she found in a different way and another place then she would expect based on her experience, by "a seemingly foolish hunch.- S.*

Aant. 1944, fol. 39^{III} (bijlage): De opvatting dat „kabouters zonder baard" „vrouwelijke kabouters" zijn, komt van mevr. D.R. Steinman - Van de Weg. Zij „weet dat", maar kan haar betoog niet met „bewijzen" staven, noch nader toelichten. Het komt mij voor, dat mevr. Steinman een weinig betrouwbare informante is. Het verhaal over haar ontmoetingen met kabouters in het bos te Vierhouten" heb ik haar na omtrent vier weken nog eens laten vertellen. Het was toen een —met evenveel verve voorgedragen— totaal ander verhaal! —   JHWE.

Note 1944, fol. 39III (appendix): The concept that "gnomes without beard" are "female gnomes" comes from Mrs. D.R. Steinman – van de Weg. She "knows that" but can't produce "evidence" for her arguments, nor would she explain herself. It appears to me, that Mrs. Steinman is a little reliable witness. I had her re-tell the story about her meetings with gnomes "in the woods of Vierhouten" after approximately four weeks. It was a totally different story, yet told with as much verve!- JHWE.

Toevoegen aan §2b, Aant. 1937, fol. 306II: Het „kampeerhuisje" te Vierhouten (naar een potloodtekening, gemaakt door de heer F. Schelfhout, en in
het bezit van mevr. Vera Bondam te Den Haag) waar de heer M.R. Verhoog,
naar hij vertelt (1935), alleen vanuit het met R gemerkte raam herhaaldelijk — wel „vijf of zes keer" in de „drie of vier maanden" verblijf aldaar per jaar — kabouters zag. Vanuit het bedoelde raam keek
men uit over een heel smalle met dennenaalden bedekte zandstrook en
eikenhakhout ter breedte van omstreeks vier meter, in een enigszins
verwilderd dennenbosje, waarin die kabouters zich bewogen, soms
„vreemd wazig en nauwelijks zichtbaar", maar vaker „heel scherp en
duidelijk". Gasten hebben er nimmer een kabouter gezien, hoewel de
heer Verhoog hen meestal wel op zijn waarnemingen attendeerde. —
Zelf zag hij — zo vertelt de heer Verhoog — die kabouters „uitsluitend en alleen" vanuit dat — naar het oosten gekeerde — raam. —
Zie bij §3II, bijlage no. 1, de „Mededelingen van de heer M.R. Verhoog", genoteerd in September 1935. —
In Maart 1937 was het slecht onderhouden en nogal vervallen
„kampeerhuisje" gesloopt. Het gelukte mij niet de plaats waar het
stond terug te vinden. JHWE. —

*Add to §2b, Note 1937, fol. 306II: The "camping house" at
Vierhouten (after a pencil drawing, made by Mister F. Schelfhout,
and property of Mrs. Vera Bondam from The Hague) where Mister
M.R. Verhoog, according to him (1935), only from the window
marked with R repeatedly — "five or six times" during a "three or
four months" stay there- saw gnomes. From the supposed window one
looked over a very small strip of sand, littered with pine needles and
oak for the width of four meters in a slightly haggard pine bush, where
the gnomes moved, sometimes "strangely hazy and barely visible", but
more often "very clear and sharp". Guests never have seen a gnome,*

although Mister Verhoog made them aware of his observations.- He saw -according to Mister Verhoog- exclusively from that window -looking out over the east- the gnomes.- See at §3II, appendix no. 1, "The gleanings of Mister M.R. Verhoog" written down in September 1935.- **A.**

In March 1937, the badly maintained and kind of dilapidated "camping house" was torn down. I did not succeed in finding the place where it stood. JHWE.-

Bij §2C: Het genoemde „kampeerhuisje" was gelegen in de driehoek Mosterdveen-Saxenheim-Vierhoutense Heide, het gebied waarin ook mevr. W.S. van Vleuten-Vos de kabouters waarover zij mededelingen deed (zie §3ª Aant. 1936, fol. 28 II) zegt te hebben gezien. — De heer F. Schelfhout te Den Haag (zie F1) duldde mij nog mee, dat de heer M.R. Verhoog ook wel 's winters in het bedoelde huisje verbleef. —   JHWE.

At §2C: The mentioned "camping house" was located in the triangle Mosterdveen-Saxenheim-Moors of Vierhouten, the area about which Mrs. W.S. van Vleuten-Vos made her announcements (see §3a, Note 1936, fol. 28II).- Mister F. Schelfhout from The Hague (see F1) told me that mister M.R. Verhoog also stood in the cabin during winter.- JHWE.

Aant. 1936, §8, fol. 39, Toevoegen: „Sara Velleman (42 j. oud, boekhoudster), zie Aant. 1935, fol. 288, vertelt daarentegen, dat de kabouters die zij op de Veluwe en in het bijzonder in de omgeving van Nunspeet-Vierhouten ontmoette, vaak in 't geheel geen baard droegen. Zij zegt in een boek eens foto's van de Man van Tollund te hebben gezien. De gelaatsuit- drukking van die man vertoont, aldus Sara Velleman, veel overeenkomst met de gezichten van die baardloze kabouters." —   JHWE.

Note 1936, §8, fol. 39, Add: "Sara Velleman (42 years old, bookkeeper), see Note 1935, fol. 288, tells on the other hand that the gnomes which she met on De Veluwe and in particular, in the surroundings of Nunspeet-Vierhouten, most of the time never had a beard. She says to have seen photos of the Man of Tollund in a book.[21] *The facial expression of this man shows, according to Sara Velleman, resemblance to the faces of the beardless gnomes".- JHWE.*

Bij Aant. 1937, fol.330: "F2. Mevr. M. Brummer - Eicholz, tijdelijk verblijvend in het woonwagenkamp te Almelo, ontkent met overdreven nadruk iets te weten over kabouters, "da's iets voor de kinder", "lulpraat"... De heer A.Odding, agent van politie, Ootm. straat 319 te Almelo, houdt staande, dat de vrouw in zijn aanwezigheid aan andere woonwagenbewoners vertelde. meermalen een "echte Kabouter" te hebben gezien." — JHWE.

(c)

At Note 1937, fol. 330: "F2. Mrs. M. Brummer-Eicholz, temporary staying in the caravan camp in Almelo, denied with exaggerated emphasis to know something about gnomes, "that's something for the children", "bullshit"... Mister A. Odding[22], officer of police, Ootmarsumsestraat 319 in Almelo, insists that the woman, even in the company of other caravan-inhabitants, was told to have seen "a real gnome".- JHWE

---

21. Tollund Man is a mummified corpse found in a peat bog in Jutland, Denmark. The Bog body has been preserved so well, that the facial expression of this man, after 2,400 years, still appears as detailed as the day he passed away. The old Germanic tribes sacrificed human beings to plead with the gods for fertility of the lands or to bring prosperity to the tribe. Human sacrifice was also performed when the tribe went off to war, to plead with the war-god (presumably Tyr or Thirwaz, but research has shown that religious convictions could vary from tribe to tribe and that gods could be worshipped on a very local basis) for a quick victory. For what reason the Tollund Man was sacrificed, is unknown, but research showed that he was fed porridge twenty four hours prior to his death, by hanging. Presumably he was a sacrifice for fertile lands, as he presumably ate his porridge in late winter or early spring.

22. A. Odding indeed lived on the Ootmarsumsestraat 319, was born on 3rd February 1887, but no profession was registered in the City Archives of Almelo.

3.

Bij Aant. 1938, §2, fol. 31. Volgens mevr. Dr. H.E. Heimans te Almelo zegt "vrouw Seckel-Reekers, 64 jaar oud, "koopvrouw", "R.K. opgevoed", vaak kabouters te hebben gezien in een strook die verloopt van Volthe, via de Hunenborg, Tilligte, Springendal, Braamberg, (langs de watermolens van Frans en van Bels), Mander, Manderveen, in de richting van Hangeveen. "Vroeger veel meer dan tegenwoordig".

De kabouters, zegt zij, zijn "klein", misschien "tot haar knie". Soms zijn vaag, "of ze in de mist staan", soms zijn ze duidelijk te zien. Ze dragen een "kleine puntmuts" en hun kleding is "eenvoudig", "bruin en groenig" gekleurd, "misschien antieke boerenkleren" en meestal hebben ze een riem om hun kiel. Hun broek is in de laarzen gestoken. Er zijn, zegt de vrouw, "evenveel kabouters zónder als met een baard", en zij dragen "vrij lang haar", maar "allemaal lijken zij nogal oud". Wanneer "vrouw Seckel" de kabouters in het veld ziet staan of lopen, reageren die niet op haar aanwezigheid en zij deed ook nimmer een poging tot toenadering, dat "zou ze niet durven", "je weet 't nooit", "'t zijn toch geen wezens van ónze wereld".... Haar grootmoeder heeft haar in haar kinderjaren wel eens verteld dat kabouters iets van doen hebben met "schatten", en zo heeft zij wel eens gedacht: "ik wou dat zo'n kereltje me uit de brand hielp", maar vragen zou ze niet durven, "zulk geld moet toch iets met de duivel te maken hebben".... ▯□

Bij #: (§2º, fol. 32). Dat er contact zou zijn —of zou zijn geweest— tussen "vrouw Seckel" en "happendina" is niet gebleken en lijkt onwaarschijnlijk. "Vrouw Seckel" zegt het "niet leuk" en "eigenlijk eng" te vinden kabouters te ontmoeten, o een christenmens heeft met zulke dingen niets te maken". Zij zegt er wel eens iets over te hebben gezegd tegen pastoor Waanders te Tubbergen, maar deze "lachte", "of het een grap was" en "praatte er overheen". Aan de "pastoorsmeid" verkocht zij daarna drie aardappelschilmesjes en "dat maakte het weer goed".... "Vrouw Seckel zegt voor 't eerst een kabouter te hebben gezien toen zij "een jaar of zeventien" was. Zij werkte toen bij Spanjaard te Borne en ging dan per rijwiel heen en weer, zulks via het Kanaal Almelo-Nordhorn. Zij zag, vertelt ze, die eerste kabouter heel duidelijk, vlak bij de Hunenborg. — ▯□

At Note 1938, §2, fol. 31. According to Mrs. Dr. H.E.
Heimans from Almelo "Miss Seckel-Reekers, 64 years old,
"merchant woman", "raised a Catholic", has seen gnomes often in
a stretch of land which runs from Volthe, through the Hunenborg,
Tilligte, Springendal, Braamberg (along the mills of Frans and

Bels), Mander, Manderveen in the direction of Langeveen. "In earlier days more often than now." [23]

---

23. Dr. Henriëtte Elisabeth Heimans lived in Almelo and was indeed close with the Eldermans family, although it appeared she was not as close to Jan Eldermans as he would have us believe. In her personal papers, I discovered a letter from Diek Eldermans-Callenbach, from which could be concluded that Diek and Henriëtte (who was called 'Zus' (Sister) by people she had intimate friendships with, and Diek indeed started her letter with 'Dear Zus') were better friends than Jan and 'Zus', and more important: from the letter could be deduced that Henriëtte disapproved of Jan's 'cheating' with other women. If they had a relationship based on friendship, would highly surprise me. Heimans was interesting to Eldermans for another reason: she was a contributing member to the Dutch Society for Psychical Research. Although she published some articles on psychometrics, it is not sure if Heimans ever had any dealings with gnomes. In her personal papers, there are 'parapsychological notes', which are, for the most from the time, before she met the Eldermans family (1936). These papers deal mostly with experiments on spiritualism (Heimans attempted to get into contact with her deceased father Eli Heimans, a famous Dutch biologist) and there were some papers dealing with the phenomenon of "automatic writing", by which the medium holds a pencil or pen, and writes down what the spirit has to say, functioning as a conduit between the spirit-world and our plane of existence. In her notes, there was no single entry on 'elemental beings', or even a 'belief in magic'. Magic was, already in the 1930's, on the fringe of Dutch parapsychology - the Dutch SPR focussed mostly on Extra Sensory Perception and Psychokinesis, simply because these phenomena could be quantified and could be tested in an experimental environment. Although Heimans was a doctor in literature, she didn't work in an academic setting: she was a teacher on a Higher Civilian Academy in Almelo, where she taught Dutch. According to letters from her former students, Heimans was loved as an empathic teacher. Because of her Jewish origins, she was dismissed from the Civil Academy in Almelo and left the city for a short period of time. She returned after the liberation and lived there until her passing in 1975. She and Diek apparently stayed in contact, possibly because of their shared humanistic ideology. The personal papers of Henriëtte have been stored in the Regional Archives of Haarlem, which appears to be 'odd' as she lived in Almelo, but it appears that the papers had gone to a relative who lived in Amsterdam and saw Haarlem as the best repository of these personal papers. Henriëtte Heimans passed away when she was 83 years old.

The gnomes, she says, are "small," maybe as high as "her knee," sometimes they are vague, "like they stand in a mist", sometimes they are clearly visible. They wear a "small pointy hat" and their clothing is "simple," "brown and greenish" coloured, maybe like antique farmer's clothing and most of the times, they wear a belt around their keel. Their pants are stuck into their boots. There are, says the woman, "as many gnomes without beard as those who wear a beard;" they all wear "quite long hair" but "all look very old". When "Miss Seckel" sees the gnomes stand or walk around the field, they don't respond to her presence, and she never made an attempt for rapprochement, she would "not dare", "you never know", "these aren't beings of our world".... Her grandmother told her during her childhood, that gnomes have something to do with "treasures" and she once thought: "I wished such a fellow helped me out there," but she dared not to ask, "such money has something to do with the Devil".... S.

At #: (§2a, fol. 32). It is unlikely and not proven that "Miss Seckel" and "Lappendina" might have been in contact with each other. "Miss Seckel" says she "doesn't like" and is "scared" to meet with gnomes, "A Christian should not have something to do with that." She says she once mentioned it to Pastor Waanders in Tubbergen, but he only "laughed," "like it was a joke" and "changed the subject." She sold three potato peelers to the "Pastor's maid" and "that made it all well".... "Miss Seckel says she first saw a gnome when she was "seventeen years old." She worked at Spanjaard in Borne and rode by bicycle, to and fro, such along the Canal Almelo-Nordhorn. She says she saw the gnome very clearly, near the Hunenborg.- **H.**

Bij Aant. 1938, §2, fol. 392*: De heer B. G. Hulsker (zie de mededelingen van Dr. H. Cohen, §1) meent, naar hij zegt "op grond van eigen waarnemingen", dat de "Kabouter-route A" zich in een soms brede, soms smalle strook beweegt in noordoostelijke richting: Stakenberg—Saxenheim—Het Soerel—Oldenbroekse Heide—de Frijsberg—Ittersum—Dalfsen—Vilsteren—Hemelerberg, en verder langs een hem onbekende weg. De "route B" zegt hij te kennen van Boerskotten (nabij Oldenzaal)—het hutterzand—de Mekkelhorst—Tilligte—de Bergvennen—Hattrop—Springendal—Hezinge—Mander—Manderveen—Hangeveen, en verder...? De heer Hulsker veronderstelt dat deze twee "trekwegen" zich in de richting Wielen—Radewijk zullen verenigen. —

§3, F1: De heer Hulsker, 76 jaar oud, zegt zijn kabouterwaarnemingen voornamelijk te hebben gedaan in de jaren 1902÷1909, en later nog, zij het "minder intensief", in de jaren 1917÷1925. Hij was eigenaar van een kruideniersbedrijf, dat voornamelijk door zijn echtgenote werd gedreven. Zelf legde hij zich toe op het verzamelen van "heilzame kruiden", die hij ook wel kocht van "kruidenzoekers" en kruidenkwekers. De heer Hulsker handelde in die kruiden en noemt zich "herborist".

Bij fol. 393, §1: De heer Hulsker geeft blijk de door hem genoemde gebieden uitstekend te kennen. De "kabouterwaarnemingen" deed hij, naar hij zegt, "van het voorjaar tot in de nazomer" en "altijd in de daguren", "dán zocht hij zijn planten". —

§2*: De heer Hulsker zegt "vrij vaak" kabouters te hebben gezien, "als hij moet schatten: wel een keer of acht à tien per jaar" in de genoemde perioden; daar buiten: "incidenteel". Meestal was het "een enkele kabouter", soms "twee of drie kabouters samen", veelal zag hij de kabouters "gewoon ergens staan"; een enkele keer "wandelden ze". Hij zag ze, zo vertelt de heer Hulsker, dikwijls "vaag, wazig en kleurloos", maar "toch duidelijk herkenbaar". "Vaker" was het beeld "helder en duidelijk", "tot in onderdelen". Nooit waren de kabouters dichterbij dan "een meter of acht". De heer Hulsker zegt het moeilijk te vinden de kleding van die kabouters te beschrijven: "lichtbruine of grijsgroene kleding". Ze droegen "een soort jasje met een liggend kraagje" en "een gordel met een grote koperen gesp om de taille". "Een soort

—puntmutsen—

94

puntmutsen" droegen ze op 't hoofd, en "verder een nogal wijde, vormloze broek", die "van onderen veelal in halfhoge laarsjes was gestopt." "Een enkele keer" zegt de heer Hulsker wel "een kabouter op blote voeten" te hebben gezien. Het haar van de kabouters, zo vertelt de heer Hulsker, was "altijd vrij lang", "een beetje wild en krullerig" en "licht blond of grijs", "dat kon je nooit goed zien". Er waren kabouters met een eveneens "wilde en krullerige baard", maar "zeker evenveel zonder". – Als hij "later eens ging kijken op een plaats waar zo'n kabouter had gestaan of gelopen, dan "waren er nooit voetsporen".-... ▯ₐ

Bij §2ᵉ: De heer Hulsker zegt vaak de indruk te hebben gehad dat de kabouters die hij ontmoette en zág, daarna verdwenen "door zich op te lossen", "in een soort nevel". Andere keren wandelden zij, "wazig wordend", weg in een bepaalde richting, "dwars door aarden heuvels en wallen, dwars door boomstammen" heen". ▯ₐ

Bij §2ᵉ: Bernard Hulsker zegt nimmer contact met zo'n "zichtbare kabouter" te hebben gehad, noch "geestelijk of mentaal", noch anderszins. Hij zegt wel eens "vriendelijk naar zo'n kabouter te hebben gezwaaid" of "een vriendelijke groet te hebben geroepen", maar nimmer werd daarop gereageerd, "ze negeerden hem straal"... ▯ₐ

[T.a.v. mevr. de wed. B.J. Hedeman: De lichaamslengte van de kabouters die de heer Hulsker zegt te hebben gezien, wordt door hem "geschat" op "een zestig tot zeventig centimeter", "zeker niet groter", "gemiddeld eerder iets kleiner".-] JHWE.

At Note 1938, §2, fol. 392*: Mister B.G. Hulsker (see the gleanings of Dr. H. Cohen, §1) says, "based on personal observations", that the "gnome-route A" sometimes in a broad and sometimes in a small stretch, moves in north-eastern direction: Stakenberg – Saxenheim – Het Soerel – Oldenbroekse moor – the Trijsberg – Ittersum – Dalfsen – Vilsteren – Lemelerberg, and further along a road unknown to him. The "route B" he says to know from Boerskotten (near Oldenzaal) – the Lutterzand – the Mekkelhorst – Tilligte – the Bergvennen – Lattrop – Springendal – Hezinge – Mander – Manderveen – Langeveen, and further...? Mister Hulsker suspects that these two "trek-routes" will unite in the direction Wielen – Radewijk.-

§3, F1: Mister Hulsker, 76 years old, says he made his gnome observations mainly in the years 1902 – 1909, and later, be it

"less intensive" in the years *1917 – 1925*. He was the owner of a grocery shop, mainly run by his wife. He himself focused on collecting *"healing herbs,"* which he also bought from *"herb-seekers"* and herbal growers. Mister Hulsker, who traded in these herbs, called himself a *"herborist".*

At fol. 393, §1: Mister Hulsker appears to know the mentioned regions very well. The *"gnome observations"* were made, according to him, from *"spring until the Indian summer"* and *"always during "daily hours"* when he was *"searching for his plants."*

§2* Mister Hulsker said to have seen gnomes *"quite often"*, *"when asked to make an estimation: around eight to ten times a year"* in the mentioned periods; during other times *"incidentally"*. Mostly it was *"a single gnome,"* sometimes *"two or three gnomes together"*, mostly he saw the gnomes *"standing there"*, a single time *"they walked".* He saw them, so says Mister Hulsker, frequently *"vague, fuzzy and colourless"*, but *"clearly visible".* *"Often"* the image was *"clear and manifest,"* *"up to the parts".* The gnomes were never closer than *"about eight meters".* Mister Hulsker says it's hard to describe the clothing of the gnomes: *"light brown or grey-green clothing."* They wore a kind of jacket with a flat collar" and *"a waistband with a large copper belt buckle around the waist."* *"A kind of pointy hat"* was worn on the head and *"further rather wide, shapeless pants,"* which *"were stuck from below into half high boots."* *"A single time,"* says Mister Hulsker, *"he saw a gnome barefoot."* The hair of the gnomes, says Mister Hulsker, was *"always quite long,"* *"a bit wild and curly"* and *"light blonde or grey,"* *"you could never see that clearly".* There were gnomes with a likewise *"wild and curly beard,"* but *"as many without one".- When he *"went back to look at the place where a gnome stood or walked, there *"were never any footprints"…*. **O.**

At §2C: Mister Hulsker says he often had the impression that the gnomes he saw, disappeared afterward *"by dissolving"*, *"into a kind of haze".* Other times, they walked away, *"getting fuzzy,"* in a certain direction, *"straight through earth hills and walls, straight through treetrunks".* **E.**

At §2e: Bernard Hulsker says he never got contact with such a *"visible gnome"*, not *"mental or spiritual"*, nor otherwise. He says he *"waved in a friendly way to a gnome"* or *"shouted a friendly greeting," but he never got a response, "they ignored him completely"… E.*

[To the attention of Mrs. The widow B.J. Hedeman: the body length of the gnomes which Mister Hulsker appears to have seen, was "estimated" by him as "sixty to seventy centimeters," "certainly not taller", "on average a little shorter".-] JHWE.

t *Note 1939, §6, fol. 46d: Mrs. The widow B.J. Hedeman tells that a great-uncle of her deceased husband told, when he was of old age, to his very close of kin, that when he was hunting, he saw gnomes on multiple occasions, "little fellows," "one or one and a half foot high", who "resided in the thicket". Mrs. Hedeman says he must have these "strange meetings" in an area that is "approximately" bordered by: Vriezenveen – De Pollen – Sibculo – along the German border to the Breklenkamp – Tilligte – the Canal Almelo-Nordhorn – Albergen – Vriezenveen. This, she says, was the terrain where he -be it younger of age- regularly hunted in certain areas. "Great-uncle" was "an introvert," "little talkative man" and speaking about these gnomes took some effort. Great-uncle was, according to Mrs.*

97

Hedeman, an "unreligious fellow", a "freethinker" who "mocked heaven and hell". When reaching an older age, he "began to ponder about a Here-after," and based on that he theorized that: "few people believe in the existence of gnomes, but I know they exist; it could be like that with heaven, in which I never believed, but what could be the case.- **S.**

Note 1939, fol. 54: added 3 appendices: IV, V and VI. JHWE.

Bij Aant. 1939, fol. 58^b: Mej. Mia ten Napel vergist zich. Bedoelde „ka-bouterverhalen", medegedeeld door „vrouw Bernardina Dikkers" —eind 19e eeuw— spelen zich niet af op „een zandbelt, midden in het Zendenerbroek", de voorhistorische versterking „ het Homberg", maar op de Hunenborg, gelegen aan het kanaal van Almelo naar Nordhorn.—
E₀

*At Note 1939, fol. 58b: Miss Mia ten Napel is wrong. Meant "gnome stories," mentioned by "Miss Bernardina Dikkers"- end of the 19th century- do not occur on "a sand-hill in the middle of the Zendenerbroek", the prehistoric reinforcement "the Homberg", but on the Hunenborg, situated near the Canal of Almelo to Nordhorn.- **E.***

Aant. 1943, §10, fol. 298*, toevoegen: Derk Tabak, 67 jaar (zie Aant. 1939, fol. 48ª) zegt van zijn grootvader te hebben gehoord, dat kabouters wel gedurende lange tijd in een bepaalde streek kunnen verblijven, maar in feite toch —„op hun gemak en heel rustig"— van het zuiden naar het noorden trekken. Waar zij vandaan komen en waar zij naar toe gaan zegt Derk niet te weten. Zij kiezen voor hun verblijf en voor hun trektocht zoveel mogelijk stille natuurgebieden, zegt Derk —zoals hij dat „zelf ook" doet—, „bos en hei", streken waar weinig moderne, lawaaimakende mensen komen. — Uit familieverhalen weet Derk Tabak dat zijn grootmoeder —al vóór zijn geboorte overleden— vaak kabouters zag, zulks in de omgeving van Vierhouten, het Vierhouterbos en het Hendrik Mouwenveld. Vóór hij deze verhalen over zijn grootmoeder hoorde, had hij zelf al wel kabouters gezien, maar hij vertelde zulks niet aan zijn relaties. Hij zegt zelf sinds zijn 19e of 20ste jaar meermalen een kabouter te hebben

=gezien=

10,

P

gezien, in totaal „misschien wel twintig of dertig keer". Dat was dan steeds in de omgeving van de Ossenkolk, op Saxenheim, bij de Witte Klap, in de omgeving van het Ronde Huis en in het Belvedèrebos (zie bijl. II: „Nunspeet"). Hij zegt daar niet graag over te praten, de mensen zouden denken „dat je kiederwiet bent.... Er is, meent hij, ook niet zo veel over te vertellen. Je fietst of wandelt in zo'n omgeving en dan, altijd plotseling, zie je zo'n kereltje, een vijftig of zestig centimeter lang, staan of lopen...., soms wat warig en vaag, soms duidelijk en scherp. Ze lijken allemaal op elkaar, maar je ziet toch wel verschillen. Sommige kabouters hebben een baard, „de meesten wel". Ze dragen over hun vrij lange haar een niet zo'n hoge puntmuts en een soort kiel, waaromheen ze een leren riem hebben. Een wijde broek dragen ze in halfhoge laarsjes gestoken. Alles „heel simpel".... Felle kleuren dragen ze niet en soms lijkt het of die kleuren — bruin, bronsgroen, grijs en „vaagrood!" — veranderen. Soms ontstaan ze uit een vaag, warig beeld, uit een „mistvlek", uit een „wolkje", soms verdwijnen ze daar ook in. Derk Tabak zegt altijd hevig te schrikken als hij zo'n kaboutermannetje ziet, hij vindt 't „angstig", kijkt wel, maar fietst of wandelt verder. Dat zijn dingen waar je als mens niets mee te maken wil hebben, dat zijn „geheimen van god" of „misschien wel van de duivel".... Derk had altijd de indruk dat de kabouters hém niet zagen. Hij deed ook nooit een poging de aandacht van zo'n kabouter te trekken, zou „dat niet durven". Hij zegt wel eens te hebben „gehoord of gelezen" dat zulke kabouters iets van doen hebben met in de aarde „verborgen schatten", maar het bezit van zo'n schat kan, zo meent de brave Derk, nooit geluk brengen..... Trouwens, zo filosofeert hij, „de geleerden" zeggen dat er op sommige plaatsen goud zit in het zand van de Veluwe. Misschien hebben die kabouters dáár iets mee te maken. Frank van Vloten van het Ronde Huis liet niet voor niets zo veel graven op zijn terrein.... Ho

Note 1943, §10, fol. 298*, add: Derk Tabak, 67 years old (see Note 1939, fol. 48a) says he heard from his grandfather that gnomes can stay in a certain area for a long period of time, but in fact - "easy and really slowly going"- migrate from south to north. Where they come from and where they are going, Derk doesn't know. They choose for their stay and their trek as much silent nature reserves, says Derk -like he does "himself"- "woods and moors," areas where as little noisy modern people come. From family stories, Derk Tabak knows his grandmother -passed away before he was born- saw gnomes regularly, such in the surroundings of Vierhouten, the Vierhouterforest and Hendrik Mouwenveld.

Before he heard these stories about his grandmother, he had seen gnomes himself but never told that to his relations. He says he had seen gnomes multiple times since his 19th or 20th birthday, in total "maybe twenty or thirty times". He saw them in the vicinity of Ossenkolk, on Saxenheim, at the Witte Klap, in the surroundings of the Round House and in the Belvédère forest (see appendix II: "Nunspeet"). He doesn't like to talk about it, people might think "you're bonkers"... There is, according to him, not much to talk about. You ride or walk in such a surrounding and then, suddenly, you see such a fellow, fifty or sixty centimeters tall, stand or walk around..., sometimes fuzzy and vague, sometimes clear and sharp. They all look alike, but you can spot some differences. Some gnomes have a beard, "most of them do." They have quite long hair and a pointy hat, not too high and some sort of keel, around which a leather belt is worn. Wide pants are stuck in half high boots. Everything "very simple".... They don't wear bright colours and sometimes it seems like those colours – Brown, bronze green, grey and vague red"- change. Sometimes they come forth from a vague, misty image, from a "mist-spot", from a "cloud", sometimes they disappear into that as well. Derk Tabak says to be startled when he sees a gnome, he considers it "frightening," he does look, but walks or rides on. Those are things you don't want to mix with as a human, these are "enigma's from God" or "maybe from the Devil"... Derk always had the impression the gnomes did not see him. He never attempted to draw the attention of such a gnome, he "would not dare." He says to have "heard or read" that these gnomes have something to do with "hidden treasures" in the earth, but possessing such a treasure can, as good Derek says, never bring you any luck... However, he philosophizes, "scientists" say that there is gold in the sands of De Veluwe. Maybe those gnomes have something to do with that. Frank van Vloten of the Round House wouldn't have dug in so many places for nothing.... **H.**

Aant. 1946, fol. 38 v, bylage I. De „notities" van de heer Jan ter Horst zyn onduidelyk door het ontbreken van „het verhaal". Dit „verhaal" komt van de wed. Sarah Halberstadt, zie F2. Ik heb getracht er enig verband in te brengen.   JHWE.

De ouders van „Roosie" (Roosje Porcelein), van Nederlandse nationaliteit, hebben zich omstreeks 1920 in Duitsland gevestigd en woonden laatstelyk te Neuenhaus. Vader Porcelein had in het verleden „met de voddekar gelopen", maar handelde later, al voor hy naar Duitsland vertrok in „antiquiteiten en curiosa", heel bescheiden en „met veel gezjouw en weinig winst", zonder „mazzel en broge". Het gezin „leefde op de rand van armoei", maar „met zn drieën __ „Roosie" was enig kind__ vormde men un „degelyk en gezellig, hecht gezinnetje", dat in de eigen omgeving gunstig werd beoordeeld en vrienden had __ook niet-joodse. Hun geluk werd echter verstoord door het sterk groeiende en zo zeer by de Duitse volksaard passende national-socialisme.

Op grond van deze ernstige dreiging besloten de ouders Porcelein in 1939 __naar Jan ter Horst in 1938__ hun „oogappel", „Roosie", te doen „onderduiken" in „het veilige Nederland", en wel by

— kennissen —

12.

„kennissen van kennissen" op een boerdery in de omgeving van Borne. Aan hun Duitse relaties vertelden zy dat „Roosie" „in geringe mate" lydende was aan tuberculose en deshalve was opgenomen in een sanatorium te Hellendoorn. Afgezien van haar joods zyn was er namelyk voor „Roosie" nog een andere bedreigende factor in het barbaarse Duitsland: het meisje bleek sinds haar kleuterjaren in sterke mate „achterlyk" te zyn, „onnozel", psychisch gestoord. De lichamelyke ontwikkeling was vry normaal verlopen, „Roosie" was „een knap meisje". Maar twintig jaar oud te Borne aangekomen, sprak en gedroeg zy zich in veel opzichten „als een kind van tien". Zo speelde zy nog met poppen. Zy had het normale onderwys nooit kunnen volgen en kon lezen noch schryven. Zy deed zich in het kinderloze boerengezin te Borne kennen als een „zeer lief en aanhankelyk" meisje, „gehoorzaam en gewillig" en „op haar manier plichtsgetrouw". Huishoudelyk werk „lag haar wel" en „deed zy keurig", maar „je moest haar alles, van A tot Z, opdragen". Het kind was „strikt eerlyk", „fantaseerde nooit".

Het Bornse gezin had verwanten die in de omgeving van Tilligte woonden, eveneens „kleine boeren". Men ging by hen vaak op bezoek, per rywiel, en „Roosie" ging dan altyd mee, „zy hield veel van die oom en tante in Tilligte". Men fietste altyd de zelfde route:

van Borne naar Weerselo, in de richting Reutum langs de zuidzyde van het kanaal Almelo-Nordhorn, zo tot de weg van Denekamp, en vervolgens naar „de oom en tante in de omgeving van Tilligte.

Toen „Roosie" die route genoegzaam had leren kennen, gebeurde het in toenemende mate dat zy alleen naar Tilligte __waar zy graag by de oom en tante kwam, ook omdat daar nog kleine kinderen waren__ mocht gaan. Zy bleef daar dan één of twee nachten slapen en fietste dan veelal alleen weer terug naar Borne.

Nadat zulks enige keren was gebeurd, vertelde „Roosie", weer thuis gekomen „vermaakt, verbaasd en lacherig" een „vreemd verhaal". Wanneer zy langs het kanaal fietste __zuidzyde__ was daar op een bepaalde plaats aan de overzyde een „vriendelyk, oud, en heel klein kereltje", dat „zo'n meter of tien met haar mee huppelde", dan bleef staan, „huppelpasjes maakte", „net alsof hy danste" en vervolgens „almaar naar de grond voor zyn voeten wees". Op een

— gegeven —

101

13.

gegeven ogenblik was „het kereltje dan ineens weg".... „Oom en
Tante" begrepen dat verhaal niet goed, „kregen schrik en wantrouwen"
en „dachten aan heel andere dingen"! Zo geviel het dat men „Roosie"
zowel vanuit Borne als vanuit Tilligte — door haar onopgemerkt —
volgde, teneinde „eens te zien wat dat dan wel was met die ouwe
kérel".... De begeleiders zagen dan herhaaldelijk vanaf een
veilige afstand dat „Roosie" steeds omtrent een bepaald punt aan
het Kanaal remde en een tiental meters zeer langzaam doorreed.
Dan bleef zij staan, starend naar de overzijde, vriendelijk
lachend en vrolijk zwaaiend.... Tenslotte reed zij dan weer door,
vaak nog enkele keren omziend. Echter: aan de overzijde van het
kanaal zagen deze waarnemers nooit iets byzonders en zeker
geen „oude kerel". —

„Roosie", door „oom en Tante" uit Borne en uit Tilligte by
herhaling nader ondervraagd, lachte by het noemen van „een
oude kerel" daar aan het kanaal. Er was daar, zo zei het meisje,
„een heel klein ventje met een baard", waarby zij de hoogte aanwees
„tot halfweg haar dy". Dat ventje droeg een rode muts met een punt,
„op en om zyn hoofd", alleen zin gezicht stak daar uit. Verder
droeg hy „gekleurde werkkleren"..., en „zag er wel een beetje
gek uit", „eigenlyk lollig", „of hy uit de poppenkast kwam".... „Het
kereltje „huppelde", aldus „Roosie", daar aan de overkant van het
kanaal „een klein eindje met haar mee", „hy kon niet zo snel
vooruit komen met zin kleine beentjes" en „bleef dan dansend staan",
zwaaiend met zin armen" en „naar de grond voor zin voeten
„wyzend". Dan „verdween hy", „zomaar", „hoe en waar naar toe"
wist „Roosie" niet te vertellen. Hy „was dan gewoon weg", en zy
„fietste weer door", „altyd met een bly gevoel". —

Het verhaal van „Roosie" wyzigde zich nimmer, zo zegt
mevr. S. Halberstadt. Wanneer men het meisje tegensprak of zei:
„zoiets kán toch niet", „dat bestaat niet", dan word zy boos en
„eindigde het in een huilparty". — „Roosie" sprak vloeiend en
accentloos Duits, en even vloeiend Nederlands, zy had een
Twents-Duits accent. De woorden „kabouter" of „Heinzel-
mannchen" bleek zy niet te kennen, evenmin de normale kinderverhalen over kabouters. De „ooms en Tantes" van „Roosie"
kenden wel „oude verhalen", „over witte wieven en zo", maar
over het geloof aan „echte kabouters" zegden zy nog nooit gehoord
te hebben, „dat's toch ook Flauwekul"! Zy verboden „Roosie"

— meermalen —

14.

meermalen „over zulke gekke dingen te praten", maar dat sorteerde
weinig effect, hoe volgzaam en gehoorzaam het meisje overigens
dan ook was. —
Ten tijde van de Duitse bezetting wisten de ouders van „Roosie" nog
naar Nederland te vluchten, waar zy, samen met „hun oogappel" door de Duitsers werden „opgepakt en afgevoerd"; wellicht
achtte het „Herrenvolk" hen medeplichtig aan de internationale
plutocratische samenzwering tegen „das ewige deutsche Wesen".
zy keerden niet terug....

Note 1946, fol. 38a, appendix I. The "Notes" of Mister Jan ter Horst are unclear because "the story" is missing. This "story" comes from the widow Sarah Halberstadt, see F2. I have attempted to bring some connection to it.- JHWE.

The parents of "Roosie" (Roosje Porcelein), of Dutch nationality, had settled around 1920 in Germany and their last known abode was in Neuenhaus. Father Porcelein walked "the rag wagon" but traded, long before he departed to Germany, in "antiquities and curiosities," very modest and "with a lot of carrying around and little profit, without "luck and broge". The family "lived on the edge of poverty," but the three of them – "Roosie" was an only child- formed a "daily and cosy family", also favoured in their own surroundings and had friends -also non-Jewish. Their luck was disrupted by the stark growth of national socialism, which suited the Germans quite well.

Based on these serious threats, the parents Porcelein decided in 1939 -according to Jan ter Horst in 1938- to send the "apple of their eyes", "Roosie", into hiding in "the Safe Netherlands", with "acquaintances of acquaintances" on a farm in the neighbourhood of Borne. Their German relations were told that "Roosie" was "more or less" suffering from tuberculosis and for that matter was admitted to a sanatorium in Hellendoorn. Not only was "Roosie" jewish, which was a threatening factor in itself, the barbaric Germans might take offense to the fact that she was considered strongly "retarded" since her infancy, "silly," mentally disturbed. Her bodily development was quite normal, "Roosie" was "a pretty girl". But twenty years old when she arrived in Borne, she spoke and behaved in many aspects as "a ten-year-old". She still played with dolls. She never could follow normal education so she could neither read or write. In the childless farmers-family in Borne, she was known as "a very sweet and affectionate" girl, "obedient and willing" and "in her way dutifully." "She liked" doing the household and "did everything nice and neat" but "you had to tell her from A to Z." The child was "brutally honest" and "never fantasized".-

The Bornish family had relatives living in the surroundings of Tilligte, "small farmers" as well. They often visited, by bicycle, and "Roosie" always went along, "she loved the uncle and aunt in Tilligte very much." They always rode the same route: from Borne to Weerselo, *in the direction Reutum along the south side of the Canal Almelo-Nordhorn, on to the road to Denekamp, and therafter "to the uncle and aunt in the surroundings of Tilligte.*

When "Roosie" learned the way very well, it could occur that she would go to Tilligte alone – "She loved going to the uncle and aunt, especially because they had small children." She stayed there for one or two nights and rode by herself back to Borne.

After this happened on some occasions, "Roosie" told "a strange story", "entertained, amazed and laughing". When she rode along the Canal -south side- she saw on the other side on a particular place a "friendly, old, very small fellow," who "hopped along for about ten meters", then he stood still, "made hopping steps", "like he was dancing" and "kept pointing at the soil under his feet". On a certain moment "the fellow suddenly disappeared".... "Uncle and aunt" did not understand the story, "got scared and suspicious" and "thought about very different things"! And so it happened that they followed "Roosie" as well from Borne as from Tilligte -which she didn't notice- in order "to see what was the matter with the old geezer".... The escorts saw repeatedly from a safe distance that "Roosie" stopped on a certain point along the Canal and rode slowly for about a dozen meters. Then she stopped, stared at the opposite side, friendly laughing and waving.... After a while she rode on, looking behind her on many occasions. However: on the opposite side of the canal these observers saw nothing special in particular, and certainly not "an old geezer".-

"Roosie, repeatedly questioned by "uncle and aunt" from Borne and from Tilligte, laughed when she heard about "an old geezer" at the Canal. There was, so she said, "a very small fellow with a beard," and she pointed at the height "to halfway her thigh". This fellow wore a red cap with a point, "on and around his head", only his face stuck out. Further he wore "coloured working clothes"..., and "looked a little silly," "actually funny," "like he came from a Punch and Judy show".... The fellow "hopped", according to "Roosie", on the opposite side of the Canal "along with her", "he was unable to run so fast with his short legs" and "stood there dancing", "waving with his arms" and "pointing at the soil before his feet". Then "he just disappeared," "how and where to, "Roosie" could not tell". He "was just gone," and she "rode on", "always feeling happy".-

The story of "Roosie" never changed, so said Mrs. S. Halberstadt. When one contradicted the girl or said: "such cannot be," "that does not exist" she got angry and it ended with "her crying".- "Roosie" spoke fluent German without an accent, and fluent Dutch, be it with a Twentish-German accent. The words "kabouter" or "Heinzelmännchen"[24] were unknown to her, as were the common children's stories about gnomes. The "uncles and aunts" of "Roosie" knew the "old tales," "about white women and such", but a belief in "real gnomes" was fairly unknown to them, "it is hogwash anyway"! They forbade "Roosie" on multiple occasions "to talk about these crazy things," but to little avail, how docile and obedient the girl however was.-

During the German occupation the parents of "Roosie" managed to escape to The Netherlands, where they were still apprehended by the Germans, together with "the apple of their eyes", "rounded up and taken away"; apparently the "Herrenvolk" thought them to be complicit of the international plutocratic conspiracy against "das ewige deutsche Wesen" [the eternal German spirit]. They never returned.... **S.**

The road Roosie Porcelein rode from Borne to Tilligte on the South Side of the Canal Almelo Nordnorn (Photograph Wilmar Taal)

24. Dutch and German for "gnome".

From the bank of the Canal Almelo Nordhorn, looking into the direction of Tilligte. Around the years preceding World War II, the roads might have looked very different. The Hunenborg is located on the left side of the viewer. (Photograph Wilmar Taal)

From here we see the opposite side, the north side, of the Canal Almelo Nordhorn, where the dancing gnome must have been standing, waving and pointing to the ground. Approximately from the point where the bush gets thicker (Photograph: Wilmar Taal)

Bij Aant. 1946, §1ª, fol. 57: Er is een geloofwaardig gerucht — geheel los staande van de "waarnemingen van Roosje Porcelein en de personen die daarmee te maken hadden — dat "tegen het einde van de bezetting", "een paar maanden voor de bevrijding", aan de noordzijde van het kanaal van Almelo naar Nordhorn, tussen de weg van Oldenzaal naar Ootmarsum en de weg van Tilligte naar Denekamp, "een centimeter of tien onder het maaiveld", Toevallig "een antieke, zwaar gouden armband" werd gevonden. De vinder deed terzake van deze vondst geen aangifte bij de politie en zou het sieraad te Deventer hebben verkocht. — Hoe gemakkelijk is het te denken dat "het kereltje van Roosje Porcelein" de aandacht trachtte te vestigen op deze "verborgen schat" wanneer hij ten aanzien van haar "danste" en "almaar naar de grond voor zijn voeten wees".... De plaats zou kunnen kloppen! — Hꜱ

At Note 1946, §1a, fol. 57: There is a credible rumour — not connected to the "observations of Roosje Porcelein and the persons involved- that "around the end of the occupation" at the north side of the canal from Almelo to Nordhorn, between the road from Oldenzaal to Ootmarsum and the road from Tilligte to Denekamp, "about ten centimeters below ground level", "an antique, heavy golden bracelet" accidentally was found. The finder never reported his find to the police and apparently sold the jewel in Deventer.-

How easy it is to think that "the fellow of Roosje Porcelein" tried to draw attention to this "hidden treasure" when he "danced" for her and "pointed at the ground below his feet".... It could be the place!- **H.**

Bij Aant. 1948, §3, fol. 326: Zie Aant. 1938, fol. 27: Wed. G.A. Gröbe-Krabbenbos. — Het contact met deze vrouw kwam tot stand via aanwijzingen, verstrekt door mej. Dr. H.E. Heimans te Almelo. — De "weduwe Gröbe", "hippendina", gaf met kennelijke tegenzin toe op haar vent-tochten per rijwiel vaak kabouters te zien. Zij vertelde o.m. — spontaan — dat deze kabouters met belangstelling en genoegen luisteren naar het blazen op de midwinterhoorn. Zij bewegen zich dan wel in de richting van dat geluid en blijven, nabij gekomen, staan luisteren, soms — zo zegt zij te hebben gezien — , met twee of drie bij elkaar". — Vooral in de omgeving van Hezinge, tot nabij de molens van Frans en van Bels, en tot Mander zou zij zulks bij herhaling hebben waargenomen. Hꜱ

Toevoegen: F4. De "weduwe Gröbe", "hippendina", 54 jaar oud ('38), handelt op zeer kleine schaal en zich per rijwiel verplaatsend, in textiel, in lappen met kleine weeffouten, z.g.n. "kilo-goed". Haar areaal ligt ten noorden van de lijn Geesteren-Ootmarsum, zulks tot aan de Duitse grens. — Eꜱ

At Note 1948, §3, fol. 326: See Note 1938, fol. 27: the widow G.A. Gröbe-Krabbenbos.- Contact with this woman was established by Miss Dr. H.E. Heimans from Almelo.- The "widow Gröbe", "Lappendina", reluctantly admitted that she saw gnomes during her ventures by bicycle. She told, more or less -spontaneously- that these gnomes listen with attention and pleasure to the blowing on the midwinterhorn. They move into the direction of the sound and keep, once nearer, still and listen, sometimes -as she said to have seen- "with two or three together".- Especially in the surroundings of Hezinge, up to near the mills of Frans and Bels, and from Mander she repeatedly observed this. **H.**

Add: F4. The "widow Gröbe," "Lappendina", 54 years old ('38) trades on a very small scale in textiles, rags with mistakes in the weaving, so-called "kilo-goods", by bicycle. Her working terrain is north of the line Geesteren-Ootmarsum up to the German border.- **E.**

(Opposite) At Note 1938, §4, fol. 29. "The widow Gerritdina Albertha Gröben-Krabbenbos", &c.-

[circles] = after quite vague indications -Lappendina cannot read maps!- the stretch of land in where the woman should have observed gnomes. See §5. S.

At §4: The woman's name is Gröbe, not Gröben. JHWE.

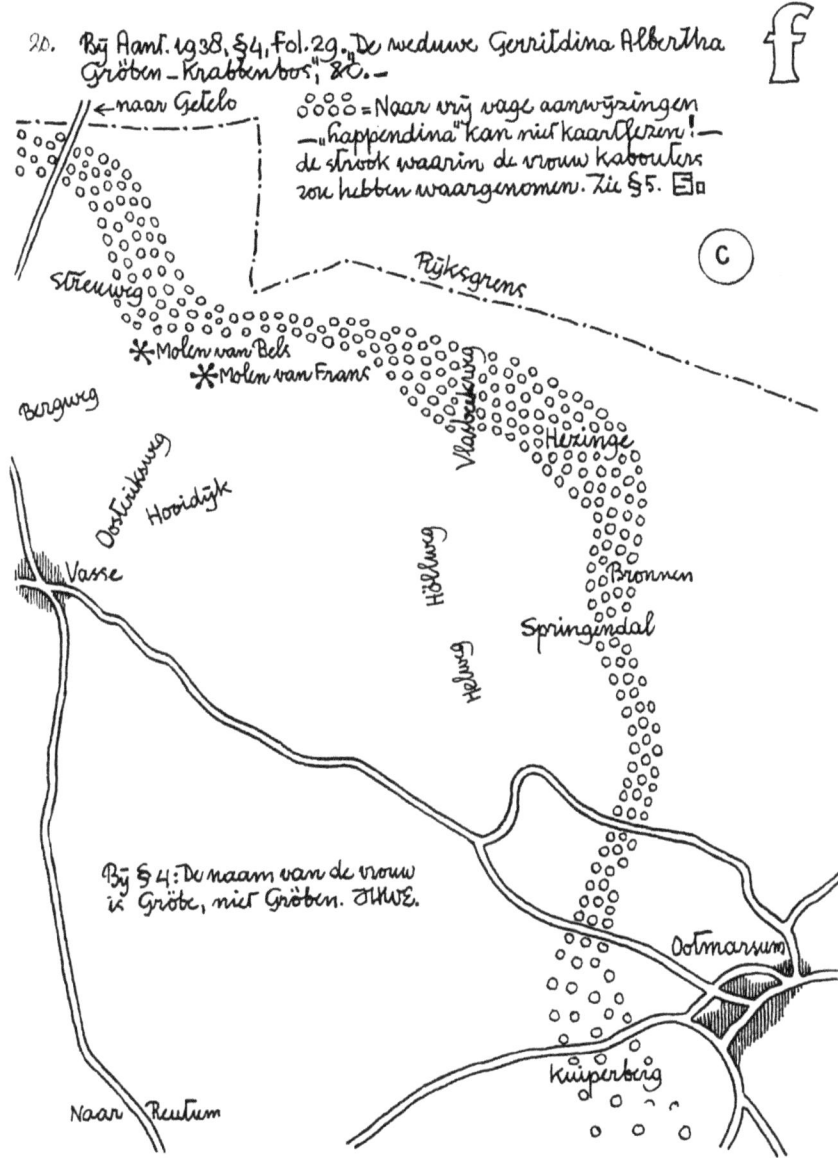

20. Bij Aant. 1938, §4, Fol. 29., De weduwe Gerritdina Albertha Gröben - Krabbenbos, &c. —

←naar Getelo

○○○ = Naar vrij vage aanwijzingen
—„happendina" kan niet kaartlezen! —
de strook waarin de vrouw kabouters
zou hebben waargenomen. Zie §5.

Rijksgrens

streuweg

✳Molen van Bels
✳Molen van Frans

Bergweg

Oosteriksweg
Hooidijk

Vasse

Vlashoukweg

Herzinge

Höllweg

Helweg

Bronnen

Springindal

Bij §4: De naam van de vrouw
is Gröbe, niet Gröben. JHWE.

Ootmarsum

Kuiperberg

Naar Reutum

Bij Aant. 1949, § 3, fol. 344²: „Wanneer ik de plaats van een in de aarde verborgen schat zó nauwkeurig weet, dat ik er „een kring met een diameter van zes voeten" omheen kan trekken, dan heb ik al die poespas niet nodig: dan ga ik graven en zal ik de schat vinden", zo hield ik Gradus van de Pol voor. Deze echter sprak dat heftig en met ernstige nadruk tegen. Zelfs dán, zo zegt hij, weten de kabouters — zo zij dat willen — zo'n schat te beschermen en te verbergen, zelfs onzichtbaar te maken. Buitendien zou het ongeluk — in de meest uiteenlopende vormen — U na zo'n onderneming wel eens kunnen achtervolgen. —   JHWE.

Bij Aant. 1949, fol. 344⁵: Gradus van de Pol, 59 jaar (zie ook Aant. 1948, § 7, fol. 322), zegt „sinds zijn volwassenheid" kabouters te zien, „wel tien of twaalf keer per jaar". Hij is invalide, heeft „allerlei rugklachten" en ontvangt een invaliditeitsuitkering waarvan hij als weduwnaar „best kan bestaan". Buitendien handelt hij — dat is zijn

—liefhebberij—

22.

liefhebberij" — in „tweedehands zakhorloges", die hij „opscharrelt en opknapt" en ook wel repareert. Zijn vak was „bakkersknecht", „een votvak".... Na voor zijn werk te zijn afgekeurd verbleef hij een tijdlang, „wel een jaar of zeven", bij „de familie Scholten", woonwagenbewoners, en „trok met hen mee", altijd in het oosten van het land. De laatste jaren verbleef hij vaak „op logementen", voornamelijk te Deventer en te Almelo. Zijn „tweedehands horloges" verkoopt hij voornamelijk aan „boeren en buitenlui", die hij per rijwiel gaat bezoeken. Van de Pol, een genoeglijk, pienter kereltje, zwerft graag en weet kennelijk de schoonheid en de sfeer van de natuurgebieden zéér te waarderen. Hij ontving weinig onderwijs, maar is stellig niet dom. Hij wekt vertrouwen en weet contacten te leggen met zijn medeburgers. Eenvoudig —„wat boers"— gekleed, ziet hij er altijd schoon en fris uit. —
Gradus van de Pol zegt de kabouters te ontmoeten ten noorden van het Kanaal Almelo-Nordhorn en vooral in de streek rondom de bij dat kanaal gelegen Hunenborg, welk gebied hij begrenst door het kanaal te noemen en Albergen, Reutem, de Kuiperberg, Ootmarsum en Tilligte. Die kabouters bestaan, zegt hij, „zo zeker als er een god bestaat", „al dat dan niet de opre- lieve- heer van de vromen zijn".... Hij, Van de Pol, „ziet ze", „klein", „zo'n anderhalve turf hoog", eenvoudig, ouderwets gekleed in een soort „bruinige" —soms „groenige"— „kiel" met „een riem om het middel". Ze dragen een puntmutsje en een wijde broek. De meeste kabouters hebben een „wat wilde", „ruige" baard en vrij lang haren. Hij zag ze wel „op blote voeten", „gekzenoeg ook bij koud weer", maar meestal dragen ze vrij hoge laarsjes, waarin ze dan de pijpen van de broek stoppen. „Alles veel eenvoudiger en soberder dan bij tuinkabouters". „'t Lijken kwieke kereltjes", maar, aldus Gradus, „ze bewegen zich rustig", „een beetje behoedzaam", vaak „staan ze maar wat te kijken" en Van de Pol zegt nimmer een zittende of liggende kabouter te hebben gezien. Soms „verschijnen ze ineens", „als uit het niets", „uit een wazigheid" en „zo verdwijnen ze ook vaak weer" en lijkt het „of er een soort wolkje, een vage plek, achterblijft". Van de Pol zegt nooit dichter bij zo'n kabouter te zijn geweest dan „een meter of tien, vijftien", maar hij „heeft scherpe ogen" en „weet wat hij ziet".... Een poging om in nader contact met zo'n kabouter te komen ondernam hij nimmer, dat „zou hij niet durven". Ze maken, zo vindt Gradus, ook allerminst een vriendelijke

—indruk—

f 24.

indruk, en „wanneer ze toevallig in je richting kijken, dan doen
ze schaterijnig"…. Buitendien, zo meent Van de Pol, zijn het
„een soort geesten", „aardgeesten" en daar „heb je als mens niks
mee te maken", „da's een andere wereld"….
Met andere mensen — of met zn „maats"— spreekt Van de Pol, naar
hij zegt, zelden over zijn oppervlakkige ontmoetingen met die
„stille kereltjes", zn maats „zouden hem niet geloven", „hem voor
gek verklaren" en hem „er mee pesten"…. Met „meneer Reuvekamp"
(mijn zipgever". JHWE.) kreeg hij „een gesprek", doordat deze een
„antiek horloge" van hem kocht, op de achterkant waarvan een
afbeelding van „een tuinkabouter" was aangebracht.— H.

Bij Aant. 1949, fol. 344ᵈ, #: „Geluid maken ze niet: ze spreken
niet en ze roepen niet, en ook wanneer ze lopen hoor je ze
niet".— B.

*At Note 1949, §3, fol. 344a: "When I know the location of a
treasure hidden in the earth so accurately that I can draw a "circle
with a diameter of six feet" around it, I don't need all that fuss: I
will dig and I find the treasure", so I told Gradus van de Pol. He
contradicted me forcefully and with serious emphasis. Even then, he
says, the gnomes know -as they wish- how to protect and hide such a
treasure, even make it invisible. Apart from that, misfortune -in most
diverse shapes- could follow after such an endeavour.- JHWE.*

f *At Note 1949, fol. 344C: Gradus van de Pol, 59 years old
(see also Note 1948, §7, fol. 322) says to see gnomes "since his
adulthood", "about ten to twelve times a year". He is disabled, has
"all sorts of back problems" and receives a disability allowance of
which he "can live very well" as a widower. Apart from that he
trades —"it is his fad"- in "second hand pocketwatches," which he
"scurries and fixes" and even repairs. His occupation was "baker's
hand", "a lousy job"…. After he was rejected for work, he stayed
for a while, "about seven years," with "the family Scholten, caravan
dwellers, and "travelled around with them", always in the eastern
part of the country. The last years he stayed in "lodging houses,"
especially in Deventer and Almelo. His "second hand watches" he
sells to "farmers and outsiders," whom he visits with his bicycle. Van
de Pol, a pleasant, bright fellow, wanders a lot and appreciates the
beauty of nature reserves very much. He never had much education,
but is certainly no fool. He builds trust and knows how to make*

contact with his fellow civilians. Simply dressed — "like a farmer"- he always looks clean and fresh.-

Gradus van de Pol says to meet gnomes north of the Canal Almelo-Nordhorn and especially in a region around the Hunenborg, near that Canal, he establishes the borders of that area by mentioning the Canal and Albergen, Reutem, the Kuiperberg, Ootmarsum and Tilligte. These gnomes exist, he says "as certain as there is a God," "although that won't be the "good-god' of the righteous"…. He, Van de Pol, "sees them," "small", "about one and a half peat high", simply dressed in an old-fashioned way in a somewhat "brownish"- sometimes "greenish"- "keel" with "a belt around the waist". They wear a pointy cap and wide pants. Most gnomes have a "somewhat wild," "rough" beard and fairly long hair. He saw them "barefoot," "strange enough also with cold weather, but most of the time they wear high boots in which the pipes of their pants are tucked. "All much simpler and more sober than with garden-gnomes." "They seem brisk fellows," but, according to Gradus, "they move very easily", "a bit cautiously", often "they are just standing there watching" and Van de Pol says he hasn't seen a gnome sitting or lying around. Sometimes "they suddenly appear," "like they appear from nothing", "from a haze" and "they disappear in the same manner" and it seems "they leave behind a little smoke or a vague spot". Van de Pol says he never approached a gnome closer than "around ten, fifteen meters," but he has "sharp vision" and "knows what he sees"…. He never dared to attempt to contact a gnome, he "would not dare." They appear, according to Gradus, to leave an unfriendly impression, and "when they accidentally look in your direction, they appear grumpy"… Apart from that, says Van de Pol, they are "spirits of some kind," "nature spirits" and "as a human you don't have anything to do with that", "that's another world"….

With other people -or with his "mates"- Van de Pol speaks seldomly about his superficial meetings with these "silent fellows," his mates "would never believe him", "make a fool out of him" and "tease him with it"…. With "mister Reuvekamp" (my "informer." JHWE.) he got "talking" because of an "antique watch" he bought, on which "a garden-gnome" was engraved on the back.- **H.**

At Note 1949, fol. 344d, #: "They make no sound: they don't speak, they don't shout, and they walk around without making noise".- **S.**

Bij §1, Aant 1955, fol. 146d ["Hier en daar ontstaan door de handel nieuwe sporen, de z.g. Hessenwegen", &C. = Ens.]. Toevoegen: "De oude "Hessenweg" te Nunspeet lag, naar ik mij herinner in een natuurgebied dat de naam had een verblijfplaats te zijn van kabouters. De "oude heer Van Dam (zie fol. 110C, §6) wees in de

— Twintiger —

20.

Twintiger jaren aan geïnteresseerden op een strook waarlangs de kabouters op bepaalde tijden naar het noordoosten trokken en waarin zij ook wel verbleven. Deze strook liep deels parallel met die oude Hessenweg, d.w.z., de oude Hessenweg viel deels in die vrij brede strook bos en heide. Zeer verspreid "uit het zuiden" — eigenlijk het zuidwesten?— komend, wordt die stroom kabouters —zo zei de "oude heer Van Dam, en zo zeggen ook andere lieden die ons vertellen kabouters te kunnen zien— smaller: ze "komen daar bijeen" en ze "blijven daar langer", want al die kabouters zijn wel en route, maar op bepaalde plaatsen onderbreken zij hun reis, vaak voor vele jaren".

At §1, Note 1955, fol. 146d ["Here and there new tracks developed through trade, the so-called "Hessenwegen"&c = Enschede]. Add: The old "trade road" in Nunspeet was, as I remember, in a nature reserve known as a place where gnomes reside. The "elderly gentleman Van Dam (see fol. 110C, §6) pointed out to interested parties where gnomes stayed during their trek to the "north-east". This area partially ran parallel with the old "trade road", meaning the old trade road ran through this broad stretch of forest and moor. Very broad, "from the south" – actually south-west?- the gnome migration gets less broad, "converges" and they "stay longer there" because these gnomes are travelling but in some places they interrupt their journey, sometimes for many years", so say "the elderly gentleman Van Dam, and other people who tell us they see gnomes.- **H.**

[Below] m Add to §7, Note 1955, fol. 166*: Annie Gerding, P. 13: "…. an ethereal being, a ghostly apparition from the earth".- They are all masters over matter. They are capable of sinking into the earth, like we can sink ourselves into water. Effortlessly, they move

through the trunk of a tree, or through a stone, or disappear into a rock wall". **O.**

   "When I observe a gnome which passes before a tree, the tree stays visible through the gnome. The gnome I perceive in a different way than the tree. The latter I see with my normal eyes, so to speak!"- **E**

Toevoegen aan §7, Aant. 1955, fol. 166*: Annie Gerding, p.13: „.....een onstoffelijk wezen, een geestverschijning uit de aarde". — „Zij zijn alleen meester over de stof. Zij zijn in staat in de aarde te zakken, zoals wij ons bijvoorbeeld in het water kunnen laten zinken. Moeiteloos bewegen zij zich onder de grond tussen boomwortels door. Zij kunnen door de stam van een boom heen-lopen of door een steen, of in een rotswand verdwijnen." 🔲

„Als ik een kabouter waarneem die voor een boom langs gaat, blijft die boom dóór de kabouter heen zichtbaar. De kabouter neem ik op een andere manier waar dan de boom. Deze laatste zie ik met mijn, laten we zeggen, alledaagse ogen!"— ⊟ₒ

Aant. 1950, §7, fol. 433. Bij Aant. 1949, fol. 370d, §1 :
Mevr. M.A. Beuving-Böckenholt (zie F3*) heeft in de jaren 1935-1942 Sara Themans leren kennen „als buurmeisje". Er „viel niets op het kind aan te merken", een „keurig kind", „altijd even hartelijk en hulpvaardig". Sara volgde mulo-onderwijs en stond bekend als „een vlotte leerling", die met gunstig resultaat haar eindexamen deed en nimmer een klas doubleerde. Na het verlaten der school had zij de wens apothekersassistente te worden, maar het gezinsinkomen van de ouders liet zulk een opleiding niet toe. Zo ging Sara als ver-koopster werken bij een thans niet meer bestaande drogisterij. De vrouw van de eigenaar van deze drogisterij was joods. Sara deed zich daar kennen, zo meent mevr. Beuving (een bejaarde vrouw), als „ijverig en plichtsgetrouw", de „klanten werden graag door haar geholpen"; en het meisje stond in de volksbuurt bekend om haar kennis van „goed helpende huismiddeltjes". — „Ruim een jaar" vóór de bezettingstijd kreeg Sara „omgang" met „Maarten, een saaie jongen" die op een verzekeringskantoor werkte, een „nette vent, maar „met veel verbeelding". Zijn ouders, „rooms-katholiek", kwamen „uit Holland" en hadden „veel bezwaar" tegen de omgang van hun zoon —die „carrière moest maken"— met een „eenvoudig, joods meisje". Het zich ontwikkelende

—nationaal-socialisme—

28.

j nationaal-socialisme en de ongunstige berichten uit Duitsland speelden daarbij ongetwijfeld een rol"; in de buurt, zei men trouwens ook wel dat de mensen _politiek_ zelf niet zuiver op de graat waren"..../ Er waren, zo vertelt mevr. Beuving, in de straat geruchten, dat Sara — die veel buiten de stad fietste en wandelde, "botaniseerde" (ze had "een hele stapel plakboeken met gedroogde planten") —, op haar zwerftochten "aardmannetjes zeigde te zien". Toen zij 16 of 17 jaar oud was sprak zij daar wel over met vriendinnen, ook wel met ouderen die 't van de meisjes hadden gehoord en vragen stelden. Sara vertelde dan dat zij "af en toe", en "op bepaalde plaatsen", "heel kleine mannetjes", "kabouters" zag, die "zich niets van háár aantrokken".... Zij sprak daar "ernstig" over, "zonder ophef", "zelf verbaasd" over hetgeen zij had gezien, en "vroeg dan wel: zien jullie dat dan nooit?" Sprak men haar tegen of zei men "dat zóiets toch niet mogelijk is", dan verweerde zij zich door te zeggen dat "in de natuur zoveel en grotere wonderen voorkomen".... — Sara Themans was, zo meent mevr. Beuving, "geen fantaste", zij was "resoluut" en "in haar doen en laten zakelijk", "recht door zee". Als zij wat vertelde "overdreef zij nooit", noemde "man en paard", "alleen feiten". Alleen "dat met die aardmannetjes", "dat was gek". Mevr. Beuving zegt in die jaren zelf wel eens te hebben getwijfeld en hebben gedacht "zou 't toch waar zijn", "zou dat kunnen?" Er "bestaan toch ook helder-zienden".... Toen het meisje wat ouder werd sprak zij, "wijzer geworden", nog slechts met enkele "vertrouwde vrienden" over haar "zonderlinge ontmoetingen".... — In 1942, zo vertelt mevr. Beuving, is Sara, "samen met haar keurige ouders" door de duitsers weggehaald en sindsdien heeft men "niets meer van of over haar vernomen"....

j Note 1950, §7, fol. 433. At Note 1949, fol. 370d, §1: Mrs. M.A. Beuving-Böckenholt (see F3*) met Sara Themans during the years 1935-1942 as "a girl next door". There "was nothing special about the child," a "neat kid," "always friendly and helpful". Sara followed secondary education and was known as a "bright student," who performed with favourable results in her exams and never failed a class. After leaving school, she had the wish to become a pharmacy assistant, but the family income could not afford such education. Sara started working as a sales clerk with a local drugstore. The wife of the owner of the drugstore was Jewish. Sara was known, so says Mrs. Beuving (an elderly lady), as a "diligent and dutiful" girl, "customers liked being served by her", and the girl was known in the working-class district for her knowledge of "well working house remedies".- "Approximately a year before the occupation, Sara got "involved" with

*"Maarten", "a boring lad" who worked "at an insurance agency", a "neat fellow", but "with a lot of imagination". His parents, "Roman-Catholics," came "from Holland" and objected heavily to the relationship of their son – who "should make a career for himself"- with "a simple Jewish girl". The development of National Socialism and the unfavourable news from Germany certainly played a part; in the neighbourhood it was whispered these people were -politically- "no good".... / There were rumours, according to Mrs. Beuving, on the streets that Sara -who rode her bike outside the city and walked, "botanized" (she had "stacks of scrapbooks with dried plants")- met "goblins" on her wanderings. When she was 16 or 17 years old, she spoke about it with girlfriends, and with adults who heard it from the girls and had questions. Sara told them that "now and then" and "on certain places," she saw "very small fellows," "gnomes," who "did not care about her".... She spoke about it "seriously," "without making a fuss," "surprised" about what she had seen and "asked if we didn't see such things?" When one contradicted her or said to her "that such things aren't possible," she argued that "nature holds so much and bigger mysteries"....- Sara Themans was, so says Mrs. Beuving, "no air monger", she was "strong-minded" and "strict to the facts", "straightforward". When she told something, "she never exaggerated," "called everything by its name", "only facts". Just "the goblins," "which was crazy." Mrs. Beuving says she had doubts over the passing years and thought "could it be possible", "could it be?" There "appear to be clairvoyants".... When the girl was older she spoke, "now wiser" only with "trusted friends" about her "eccentric meetings"....- In 1942, people say, Sara and her "neat parents" were taken away by the Germans and "nothing has been heard from her since".... **H.**

J Bij Aant. 1949, fol. 3709, §1: [op aanwijzing van de heer R. Smit, agent van politie-rechercheur te Almelo] = "M.J.R." —de man wil niet dat "zijn naam voluit" wordt genoemd—, 32 jaar oud en kantoorbediende van beroep, had in de periode 1938-1939 "verkering" met een joods meisje, zulks tegen de zin van de wederzijdse ouders. "M.J.R." is "van huis uit katholiek", maar "doet er niet veel aan", naar hij zegt. — Met deze "verloofde" (Sara Themans: zie §3) maakte hij op "vrije dagen" vaak "uitstapjes op de fiets": het meisje hield zeer veel van "de natuur" en "wist alles van planten en zo". Zij was in die tijd als verkoopster werkzaam in een drogisterij. — De gelieven kwamen "over en weer niet bij elkaar thuis", "dus" was het al spoedig zó, dat tijdens die fietstochten vaak een rustplaats werd gezocht waar hun liefde iets verder kon gaan dan een hand en een zoen..." — In de "nazomer van 1938" had het paar, zo vertelt "M.J.R.", een rustplaats gevonden, "ergens in het Volterbroek". Kort nadat hun —toch "altijd nog bescheiden"— "liefkozingen" waren begonnen, werd het meisje hem "geschrokken" af. Zij bloosde, zegt "M.J.R.", deed nerveus en "schoof verder van hem weg.... Toen hij haar om een verklaring voor dit vreemde gedrag vroeg, zei zij na enig aarzelen: "Jij zult dat niet geloven, maar kijk, daar, een meter of vijf verder zit een kaboutertje naar ons te kijken",..., althans woorden van deze strekking. Hij, zo vertelt "M.J.R.", "voelde zich genomen" en "begreep er niets van". Zij keerden in een ongenoeglijke stemming huiswaarts. In daarop volgende gesprekken toonde het meisje zich "gesloten" en "ontoegankelijk", maar "hield star vol dat zij in bepaalde natuurgebieden af en toe "kabouters zag".... Zijn repliek was dan "dat kabouters niet bestaan", alleen in kinderverhalen", en dat "iemand die denkt kabouters te zien nodig eens naar een zenuwarts diende te gaan,...." Tenslotte spraken zij er niet meer over, want "daar kwam alleen maar ruzie van", maar "'t bleef hem dwars zitten"....

—Totdat—

J 26. Totdat in de zomer van 1939 zich de situatie van 1938 "min of meer herhaalde". Zij waren naar Denekamp geweest, hadden daar 't museum "Natura Docet" bezocht en in een opperbeste stemming weer huiswaarts gaande, zochten zij een rustplaats op het terrein van de Hunenborg aan het Kanaal van Almelo naar Nordhorn. Zij hadden pinda's bij zich en gingen liggen met een opengevouwen krant —"voor de bast"— tussen zich in. Al pinda's etend, vertelt "M.J.R.", lag het meisje "te draaien", zelfs zó, "dat zij de pindaschillen naar de krant gooide", waarover hij een opmerking maakte. Het meisje, zo vertelt "M.J.R.", lag links van hem, en op een gegeven ogenblik drong het tot hem door, dat zij sleeds "met een starre blik" "langs hem heen keek". Toen hij "een paar keer had omgekeken" en in de richting waarin het meisje "staarde niets bijzonders ontdekte, ging "bij hem een lichtje op" en "kon hij zich niet langer inhouden". Hij zei, "geprikkeld": "Nou wil je toch niet beweren dat daar weer van die rotkabouters zijn!" Zij bevestigde echter zijn vermoeden en zei: "Probeer nou ook eens om hen te zien, dáár bij die adelaarsvarens...." Hij "zag natuurlijk niets bijzonders", maar zij "bleef ernstig aandringen" en beschreef een "vaalgekleurde kleine kabouter die zij, zoals zij boos beweerde, tussen die varens zag staan.... — Zo zijn, aldus "M.J.R.", "in een zeer gedrukte stemming opgestapt" en reden "stilzwijgend" en "bokkend" huiswaarts. 's Avonds, zo vertelt "M.J.R.", heeft hij het meisje een brief geschreven en "het uit gemaakt". Hij vreesde "te blijven hangen aan een geestelijk gestoorde vrouw", want "zoiets is toch abnormaal...!"

[Omtrent Sara Themans zijn mij geen nadere bijzonderheden bekend, behoudens dat zij later door de duitsers is afgevoerd en niet is teruggekeerd.... JWE.]

117

j *At Note 1949, fol. 370d, §1: [On directions of mister R. Smit, officer of police – detective in Almelo]²⁵ = "M.J.R."- the man does not want "his name noted in full" -, 32 years old and his occupation is a clerk, was "seeing" a Jewish girl in the years 1938-1939, very much against the wishes of both his and her parents. "M.J.R." is "raised a Catholic" but according to him "not a practising one".- With his "fiancée" (Sara Themans: see §3) he made "trips by bicycle" on his "days off": the girl loved "nature" very much and "knew everything about plants and such". She was working as a salesgirl in a drugstore.- The lovers didn't "come over to each other's houses" and soon it happened that during these rides, they looked for a resting place where their love could go little further than just a hand and a kiss...".- In the "Indian summer of 1938" the couple found, according to "M.J.R.", a resting place "somewhere in the Volterbroek". Shortly after "their modest" caresses had started, the girl got "startled" and pushed him away.... When he asked for an explanation for her strange behaviour, she said after a hesitation: "you will not believe this, but look over there, about five meters away is a gnome watching us"..., be it words of this meaning. He, says "M.J.R.," "thought the girl pulled his leg" and "he didn't understand it one bit." They returned home in an inadequate mood. The conversations that followed the girl appeared "shut down" and "inapproachable" but remained adamant that "she saw, once in a while, gnomes in certain nature reserves".... His reply was "that gnomes don't exist," "only in children's tales", and that "someone who thinks they see gnomes should certainly visit a psychiatrist...." In the end, they never spoke about it anymore, "it only became an argument," but "he didn't feel right about it"... Until the situation of 1938 repeated itself, "more or less", in the summer of 1939. They went to Denekamp and visited the museum "Natura Docet"²⁶*

---

25. Reinder Smit, born 27 January 1903, lived at the Violierstraat 42 and his last known occupation was adjutant of police.

26. This museum still exists, and advertizes being the oldest museum of natural history in The Netherlands. More information can be found here: https://www.wonderryck.nl/natura-docet-wonderryck-twente/natura-docet-wonderryck-twente/

and returned home "in a great mood", so they looked up a resting place on the terrain of the Hunenborg, near the Canal Almelo Nordhorn. They brought peanuts with them and laid down with an unfolded newspaper – "for the shells"- in between them. While eating peanuts, so says "M.J.R.", the girl was "tossing and turning", even so "that she threw the shells next to the newspaper", about which he made a remark. The girl, so tells "M.J.R." was lying left of him and suddenly it dawned on him that she was looking "besides him" with a "rigid look" on her face. When he turned "a couple of times" in the direction in which the girl was "staring" and saw nothing in particular, "he started realizing something" and "he could not hold back anymore." He said, "annoyed": "you are not telling me that there are stinking gnomes again!" She confirmed his suspicions and said: "Try to see him, over there at the common bracken".... He "saw nothing in particular," but she "seriously insisted" and described a "pale-coloured, small gnome" which she saw, as she angrily stated, "in between the bracken"...- They rode, according to "M.J.R.", home in a "very depressed mood", "silent" and "stubborn". At night, so said "M.J.R.", he wrote the girl a letter in which he "ended the relationship". He feared "to be dealing with a mentally disturbed woman," because "this is abnormal...!"-

[Concerning Sara Themans are no further details known, except for the fact that the Germans took her away and she never returned.... JHWE.] **S.**

[Below]: *Add to §2, fol. 141f, Note 1955 [and addressed to mister Y.M. Wagenaar]: The "elderly gentleman Van Dam" was a returning guest during the years 1921-1928 to Nunspeet. [After 1945, I have made some attempts to exactly track down who and what he was, but without positive result.] I remember the man very well, he was living around Rotterdam, where he, around those years, lived on his own money, as people said "a wealthy man," a "rentier." When he was younger, he "dabbled with cereals," with which he – "especially during the mobilization 1914-1918"(?) – "made a scandalous amount of money". Apart from that, he came from "a wealthy family." I doubt if "the elderly gentleman Van Dam" was really that old, he was somewhat older than my father, who was "in his fifties, but barely! Mister Van Dam was not married and, for as far I know, never has been. He was a great admirer of Nunspeet in those years 1921-1928 and of the landscape of De Veluwe. He stayed in Nunspeet many times a year, in the summer, as well in the winter. He stayed repeatedly at the hotel Ittman, or rented a summerhouse, always "with domestic help." Based on what I remember about mister Van Dam, I can say he was a remarkable character, a peculiar, eccentric fellow. Not a tall posture, especially skinny, but he always wore these showy, baggy fitting, grey checkered -sporty?- suits with plus-four, a large "English cap," beautiful red-green "sports stockings" and rather notable brown, high shoes.*

Toevoegen aan §2, fol, 141ᵈ, Aant. 1955 [en t.a.v. de heer Y.M. Wagenaar]:
De „oude heer Van Dam" was in de jaren 1921÷1928 een steeds terug-
kerende gast te Nunspeet. [Na 1945 heb ik nog wel eens pogingen
ondernomen meer precies vast te stellen wie en wat hij was, maar dat
bleef zonder positief resultaat]. Ik herinner mij de man zeer goed.
Hij was woonachtig te Rotterdam, waar hij in die jaren leefde van
zijn geld", een, zo zei men, „rijk man", een „rentenier". Jonger
zijnde had hij „iets van doen met granen", waarmee hij — vooral
tijdens de mobilisatie 1914-1918" (?)— „bar veel geld verdiende",
Buitendien stamde hij „uit een vermogende familie". Of de „oude
heer Van Dam in die jaren inderdaad zó oud was, betwijfel ik
thans: hij was „iets ouder" dan mijn vader, die toen „een vijftiger"
was, maar dat nog maar niet! De heer Van Dam was ongehuwd en,
voor zover ik weet, nooit gehuwd geweest. Hij was in die jaren
1921-1928 kennelijk een groot bewonderaar van Nunspeet, en van
het Veluwse landschap. In Nunspeet logeerde hij veelvuldig, meermalen per jaar, zowel 's zomers als 's winters. Hij verbleef herhaaldelijk in het toenmalige hotel Ittmann, of huurde een zomerhuisje, altijd „met een huishoudelijke hulp". Op grond van hetgeen
ik mij terzake van de heer Van Dam herinner meen ik wel te mogen
zeggen dat hij een byzondere figuur was, een eigenaardige,
excentrieke kerel. Niet al te groot van postuur, en vooral
mager, droeg hij veelal wat opzichtige, slobberig zittende, grijs
geruite —sportieve?— pakken met plus-four, een grote
„engelse pet", fraaie rood-groene „sportkousen" en nogal opval-
lende bruine hoge schoenen. Zijn magere, altijd bruin verbrande gezicht was versierd met een grijze, bijna witte
„engelse snor — een Hitler-snorretje zouden we nu zeggen.
Hij had de allure van een „oud militair", een „gepensionneerd
kolonel", zulks in zijn manier van bewegen en van spreken,
de —beschaafde— moppen die hij graag tapte, enz., enz..—
Hoewel hij daar zelden over sprak, was het bekend, dat hij
„spiritist" was, iets waarover mijn ouders en hun Nunspeetse
relaties zich misprijzend uitlieten. De man was zeer belezen
en, zo geloof ik ook thans nog, zéér belezen. Zijn eruditie werd
door mijn ouders en hun Nunspeetse relaties besproken, geprezen
en bewonderd, maar nog meer door mij! — De heer Van Dam
toonde zich te Nunspeet een verwoed wandelaar. Hij kende die
omgeving „van boom tot boom", hij wist boeiend te vertellen over
de oude geschiedenis en de folklore van dat gebied, en was in
staat —en altijd bereid— over iedere gevonden veldkei, over

— iedere —

32.

iedere zand-, grind- of oerlaag, over iedere plant, struik of boom, over ieder dier, interessante byzonderheden te vertellen. Hy verstond ook de kunst met iedere bewoner van de streek, man of vrouw, rijk of arm, tot gesprekken te komen, en het vertrouwen van die lieden te winnen. — Ik hoorde in Nunspeet tot de weinige uitverkorenen die hem op zijn zwerftochten mochten vergezellen, hetgeen ik op zéér hoge prijs stelde. Ik genoot van die wandeltochten en ik vereerde de heer Van Dam. Maar één onderwerp bracht my ten aanzien van hem altyd in verlegenheid: de kabouters....

Met de vanzelfsprekendheid waarmee de heer Van Dam —vaak op docerende toon— over concrete, "reële" onderwerpen vertelde, sprak hy ook over kabouters, "aardgeesten" die in en om Nunspeet verbleven en die in feite op hun grote reis naar het noorden" dáár "een rustpunt" vonden en "een ontmoetingsplaats", "een rendez-vous". Voor zover ik my herinner was hy van oordeel dat die kabouters kwamen via

de Hoge Veluwe — Hoenderloo — het Spelderholt en het Ugchelse Bos — de Domein Poossen — het Vierhouter Bos — het Hulshorster Zand — Nunspeet — Het Soerel — Tongeren — De Dellen, de Oldebroekse Heide, de Trysberg en zo verder naar het noordoosten. [Zie de kaartschets, bylage II.] De genoemde plaatsen dienen daarby —ik volg hier de theorie van de heer Van Dam!— te worden gezien als een soms kilometers brede strook waarin zich een gering aantal kabouters bevinden, zodat de kans op een ontmoeting met zo'n "aardgeest" nooit groot is. Op de "ontmoetingsplaatsen" zijn "concentraties", daar "hoef je vaak niet te zoeken om kabouters te zien". De heer Van Dam "bezat het vermogen" zulke kabouters te kunnen zien, soms "in wazige omtrekken", "doorzichtig", soms "helder en duidelyk": "altyd rode mutsen, eenvoudige, wat vaalbruine of vaalgroene kleding, bruine laarsjes", "heel gewoon".... Hy sprak daarover op een vanzelfsprekende en tegenspraak uitsluitende toon, en vroeg nooit "geloof je me" of "zie je ze ook?" Hy maakte ook nooit ophef over die waarnemingen. 't Kwam meermalen voor dat hy tydens een wandeling gebiedend zei: "blyf eens staan", "wees stil", en dan bleef staan staren naar een bepaald punt in het terrein.... Na verloop van enige tyd liep hy dan weer door en vervolgde het gesprek. Op myn soms gestelde, bescheiden vraag: "Waren daar weer...?", antwoordde hy dan nuchter en zakelyk, zonder ophef: "Ja, daar liep"....of "Ja, daar stond...."

— Er —

121

83.

Er over „doorpraten" weigerde hij dan, „Als je het vermogen niet
hebt kabouters te zien, kan je er ook niet in geloven"... Ik had
wel eens de indruk dat hij niet over kabouters wilde spreken
wanneer de mogelijkheid bestond dat die kabouters ons konden
beluisteren. In een andere omgeving deed hij dan wel weer mededelingen omtrent „de aardgeesten", die „tot een andere wereld-
sfeer behoorden". Met ze „spreken", zo vertelde hij, „is onmogelijk",
„maar ze kunnen de gedachten van de mens opvangen en be-
grijpen" en „als ze dat willen" kunnen ze ook hun „wensen of
bevelen op de mens overbrengen". ―
Veel wijzer ben ik op het punt van kabouters van de heer van Dam niet
geworden, althans herinner ik mij dat niet. Ik verzweeg hem dat ik
domweg niet in kabouters kón geloven, „zei niet nee en zei geen ja".
In zijn gezelschap was ik overigens overwegend de zwijgende toe-
hoorder, en ik geloof ook niet dat ik ooit een poging heb gedaan
ook iets te zien van zo'n kaboutermannetje. Aan mijn ouders
―of aan anderen― heb ik in die jaren ook nooit iets verteld over
deze „kabouteravonturen"; later bleek mij dat mijn ouders ―en
anderen― er wel van wisten. ― Zie ook §1ᵉ, Aant. 1936, fol. 409. ☐

His skinny, sunburnt brown face was adorned with a grey,
almost white "English moustache" – nowadays we would call it a
Hitler-moustache. He had the allure of "an old military man," a
"retired colonel", expressed in his gestures, his way of speaking, the
-civilized- jokes he loved to tell, etc., etc., ---

Although he seldom spoke about it, it was known he was a
"spiritualist," something my parents and their relations from Nunspeet
spoke ill about. The man was well travelled and, I still believe, very
well-read. His erudite character was spoken about and praised by my
parents and their relations from Nunspeet, but even more by me!- Mister
Van Dam was an avid walker in Nunspeet. He knew the surroundings
"from tree to tree" and told fascinating stories about the old history and
the folklore of that area and was capable -and always willing- to talk
about every found boulder, every sand-, gravel- or primal layer, every
plant, shrubbery or tree, every animal, something interesting. He knew
how to speak with every inhabitant of the area, man or woman, rich
or poor, and to gain these people's trust. I was one of the very few
chosen to accompany him on his wanderings, which I appreciated a lot.
I enjoyed those walks, and I adored mister Van Dam. But one subject
embarrassed me about him: the gnomes....

With the same naturalness, Mister Van Dam spoke -often in a teaching way- about concrete, real subjects, he spoke also about gnomes, "nature spirits," who stayed in and around Nunspeet and who were on their "big journey North" and found "a place to rest" in Nunspeet, a place they "could meet", a "rendez-vous". For as far as I remember, he thought these gnomes came through: De Hoge Veluwe – Hoenderloo – the Spelderholt and the Ugchelse Forest – The Domein forests – the Vierhouter Forest – the Hulshorster Sands – Nunspeet – Het Soerel – Tongeren – De Dellen, the Oldebroekse Moor, the Trijsberg and so on to the northeast. [See the sketched map, appendix II]. The mentioned places serve -I follow the theory of Mister Van Dam here!- to be seen as a stretch of land, miles wide, in which are a small number of gnomes, so the chances of meeting such a "nature spirit" are slim. On these "meeting places" are "concentrations," you "don't have to look hard to find gnomes". Mister Van Dam "had the ability" to see such gnomes, sometimes in "fuzzy outlinings," "transparent", sometimes "bright and clear": "always red caps, simple, pale brown or pale green clothing, brown boots", "very common".…. He spoke about it naturally and tolerated no contradiction, but never asked me "do you believe me" or "do you see them too"? He never made a fuss about these observations. It occurred more than once during these walks he said "stand still" in an authoritative manner, "be quiet" and kept staring at a certain point on the terrain… After a while he continued his walk and the conversation. Sometimes I modestly asked: "were there…. Again?," and he answered soberly and to the point, without making a fuss: "Yes there walked…" or "yes, there stood…"

He refused to "speak more" about it, "if you lack the ability to see gnomes, you cannot believe in them"… I had the impression that he didn't want to talk about gnomes when the possibility existed they could overhear us. In other surroundings, he mentioned "the nature spirits" who "belonged to another dimension." "It is impossible to speak to them," he told me, "but they can see the thoughts of a human and understand them" and "if they want to" they can also transfer their "wishes or commands" to the human.-

I did not become much wiser concerning the gnomes of Mister Van Dam, although I don't remember that. I never told him I simply could not believe in gnomes, "didn't say no and didn't say yes." In his company, I was mostly the silent listener, and I don't believe I ever attempted to also see something of such a gnome. I never told my parents -or to others- about these "gnome-adventures;" later it appeared my parents -and others- knew about it.- See also §1C, Note 1936, fol. 409. **E.**

§5*, toevoegen: De vraag van mej. Anja van Doorn, of ik van „de oude heer Van Doorn" voor 't eerst iets vernam over „echte kabouters", moet ik ontkennend beantwoorden: in of omtrent 1921 kwam ik, eveneens te Nunspeet, in aanraking met een wat wonderlijke oude baas, die —voornamelijk in te boshoek tussen het Groene-laantje, de thans genaamde F.A. Molijnlaan en de Eperweg— contact zegde te hebben met kabouters, die hem zelf adviseerden in financiële aangelegenheden! Zie „Index" ≠ E., Zwakenberg. —

§5*: The question from Miss Anja van Doorn, if I heard about "real gnomes" for the first time from "the elderly gentleman Van Doorn", I had to deny: in or around 1921 I came, also in Nunspeet, in touch with a somewhat wondrous old geezer, who — especially in te Boshoek between the Groenelaantje, currently called the F.A. Molijnlaan and the Eperweg- said to be in contact with gnomes, who even advised him in financial matters! See "Index" ≠ **E.***, Zwakenberg.-*

Aanl. 1946, §1⁹, fol. 239*, ter attentie van de heer (pater) M. J. Reinhoudt: Wat ik omtrent de genoemde Zwakenberg weet is uitsluitend gebaseerd op herinne- ringen uit de jaren 1922 tot, naar ik meen, omtrent 1935. Mijn ouders bezaten in die tijd een zomerhuisje te Nunspeet —de „Gerharda", gelegen aan het Groenelaantje. Woonachtig te Rotterdam, verbleven wij vrij veel te Nunspeet, niet slechts 's zomers, maar in alle jaargetijden, hetgeen met zich meebracht, dat wij in Nunspeet ook regelmatig brandstoffen behoefden. Deze werden dan besteld bij en in persoon geleverd door Zwakenberg, die in het dorp woonde in een klein huisje, gelegen aan de Dorpsstraat, achter het erf van de thans nog bestaande „Roskam". De man

—was—

16.

was familie van de eigenaar (of eigenares?) van de "Roskam".
Zwakenberg —de brandstoffenleverancier— had in die tijd de
naam een "schraper" te zijn, een "potter" en een "duitendief"....
Hij gold als een man die een "armoedige indruk", maar "echt
wel een paar dubbeltjes achter de hand" had. Ik herinner mij hem
als een vrij lange, magere kerel, enigszins gebogen lopend en
gekleed in een —altijd versleten, maar "hele" en "schone"—
pillowse of manchester broek en een blauwe werkkiel, altijd bloots-
hoofds en op klompen. Ik herinner mij niet hem ooit in een regen-,
of winterjas te hebben gezien. Hij had een zéér onverzorgd gebit in
een gezicht dat gemakkelijk lachte, zij het, zo herinner ik mij
altijd op de grens van onderdanigheid en listigheid. De man
kon leuk, zelfs geestig vertellen over "oud Nunspeet" en de
"oudere Nunspeetse bevolking", over "de notabelen" vooral. Zwakenberg was gedurende vele jaren koetsier geweest, "reed voor
de rijkelui". — Zijn brandstoffen bracht hij rond, gestapeld
op een zeer oude, gammele fiets, die hier en daar met ijzer-
draad was gerepareerd en waarmee hij vaak dwars door 't bos
reed, "liever door bos en veld dan over de wegen". Het was voor hem
geen bezwaar voor één bestelling een aantal keren heen en weer
te rijden. 's Mans leeftijd durf ik niet te schatten, hij was "oud",
beduidend ouder dan mijn ouders toen waren. Deze beklaagden
hem wel: "zo'n oude kerel die nog zó met die brandstoffen in de
weer was"....
In de hiervoor genoemde periode ontving mijn vader —toen een
"vijftiger"— in de "Gerharda" wel bezoek van Nunspeetse relaties,
heren, waarmee hij ook wel samenkwam in het toenmalige Hotel
"De Veluwe", nabij het station. Kwam men samen in de "Gerharda",
dan werd daar "een glaasje gedronken", een enkele keer gekaart, en
"zwaar geboomd" over "de liberale politiek". Buitendien waagden
de heren zich in vereniging wel af en toe eens aan een voorzichtig,
niet al te riskant beursgokje. Dáárbij bleek —op welke wijze is
mij nooit gebleken— dat ook "die oude knuppel", Zwakenberg,
"de duitendief" wel op deze wijze gokte! En dat niet alleen! Met
verbazing sprak men er herhaaldelijk over dat Zwakenberg
terzake van deze financiële manipulaties "zo'n goed inzicht"
had, of een "beestachtig geluk" — het "geluk dat met de dommen
is"—, want meermalen behaalde hij winst wanneer de heren "een
veer moesten laten".... —
Wanneer de gelegenheid zich voordeed praatte ik graag met de oude

—Zwakenberg—

17.

Zwakenberg en luisterde met interesse en genoegen naar zijn Nunspeetse verhalen in het dialect van de Noord-Veluwe. Ik kon het zeer goed met hem vinden! Toen ik weer eens had gehoord dat Zwakenberg geld had verdiend aan "een gokje" dat door de heren "veel te riskant" was geacht, vroeg ik de man: "Heb je daar dan verstand van, Zwakenberg?" — "Nee", antwoordde hij, "Dat vertellen de kabouters me", hetgeen ik toen opvatte als een terechtwijzing, vrij vertaald: "Snotneus, bemoei je met je eigen zaken".....

Latere gesprekken deden mij beseffen, dat het antwoord van de oude baas serieus was geweest, en allerlei latere spontane mededelingen van de man — op terzake gestelde rechtstreekse vragen antwoordde hij veelal niet— samenvattend begreep ik wat hij mij duidelijk wilde maken: o.m., maar voornamelijk in het bosgebied dat werd ingesloten door het Groenelaantje, de thans genaamde F.A.Molijnlaan (toen Grote Weg? Er reed nog een stoomtram!), de Eperweg, de toenmalige Waskolkweg en de spoorbaan naar Zwolle, ontmoette en zág hij kabouters. Vroeger nog meer op een terrein, gelegen aan de toenmalige Waskolkweg, maar daar kwam een kamp voor Belgische vluchtelingen —1914-1918—, waardoor de kabouters werden verdreven. Zwakenberg zei ook wel eens kabouters te hebben gezien "achter het Ronde Huis" en "tussen de Witte Klap en de Mijthstee", alsmede op het landgoed Welna": "kleine kereltjes", "met en zonder baard", met "een rode puntmuts" die "ook om hun oren" zat en beneden "vast zat aan een grote kraag". Voor het overige gekleed "in een gewoon werkpak", "een kiel en een brock", soms "bruin" van kleur, "soms groen", en "die kleuren veranderden wel eens terwijl je naar ze keek". Hij zei ze "lang niet altijd even duidelijk" te zien, ze waren "wel eens wazig" en "verdwenen dan meestal zomaar". Soms ook werd zijn aandacht "zomaar" getrokken naar een bepaald punt, en terwijl hij dan keek ontstond daar "uit de wazigte" een kabouter....—

Met die kabouters "praten" was, aldus Zwakenberg, niet mogelijk. Wanneer je "naar ze zwaaide" reageerden ze niet, evenmin wanneer je "goeie morgen" of iets dergelijks naar ze riep. Maar wanneer je "zorgen" had, over iets piekerde, en daaraan dácht wanneer je zo'n kabouter zag, dan werd het meestal "klaar in je kop" en dan "zag je ineens voor je hoe je er mee aan moest".... Dat had hij, aldus Zwakenberg, "als jonkman van een jaar of

—vijfentwintig —

18.

*vijfentwintig al door" en hij „is daar altijd wel bij gevaren". De
kabouters hebben niet graag, zo meent hij, dat mensen daar
onderling over praten, zij worden in het algemeen het liefst
„met rust gelaten. Hoe meer „vreemden" —recreanten— Nunspeet
bezoeken en hoe meer zomerhuisjes daar worden gebouwd, hoe
„minder kabouters er zullen overblijven"....*

Aant. 1946, §1d, fol. 239*, t.a.v. de heer (pater) M.J. Reinhoudt:
„Zwakenberg", zie ook Aant. 1940, §8, fol. 79.

Aant. 1946, §1e, fol. 240, t.a.v. mej. Anja van Doorn: Door de mededelingen van de genoemde Zwakenberg werd ik voor 't eerst ge-
confronteerd met iemand die over „echt bestaande kabouters"
sprak, „wezens, fantomen, die hij zág en zag bewegen". Ik weet
wel zeker dat ik daar tevoren nooit iets over had gehoord of gelezen. De ernstige mededelingen van de door mij betrouwbaar
geachte oude man hebben toen veel indruk op mij gemaakt, en
een blijvende belangstelling voor kabouters veroorzaakt. Het was
niet zo dat ik dacht „die oude kerel is psychisch gestoord",
echter ook niet zo dat ik ook maar het flauwste spoor van geloof
bij mijzelf kon ontdekken. Ik heb er toen veel en ernstig over nagedacht en kwam er niet uit, evenmin als thans, nu ik 42 jaar
oud ben....

JHWE, 194?.

Note 1946, §1d, fol. 239, addressed to Mister (father) M.J.
Reinhoudt: What I know of the mentioned Zwakenberg is based on
memories from the year 1922 to, as far as I know, around 1935.
My parents owned, in those days, a vacation home in Nunspeet -the
"Gerharda," located at the Groenelaantje. Living in Rotterdam we
stayed a lot in Nunspeet, not only during summer, but all seasons,
which led to the occasion that we needed fuels in Nunspeet. These
were ordered at and delivered in person by Zwakenberg, who lived
in a small house in the village, located at the Dorpsstraat, behind
the yard of the still-existing "Roskam".[27] The man was related to
the owner (or proprietress) of the "Roskam". Zwakenberg -the fuel
distributor- had the name to be a "moneygrubber", a "moneybags"
and a "turn-penny".... He was the man who made a "poor
impression," but "had some dimes hidden away". I remember him
as a fairly tall, skinny fellow, walking slightly bent and dressed in
a worn down, but "whole" and "clean"- pillowse or Manchester*

---

27. Eldermans refers to a hotel "De Roskam", which actually still exists
today, but is now a restaurant.

pants and a blue working keel, always bareheaded and in clogs. I can't remember seeing him in a raincoat or wintercoat. He had very bad teeth in a face that laughed easily, be it, as I remember, always bordering on subservience and cunning. The man could tell stories, even in a funny way, about "old Nunspeet" and the "elderly Nunspeet population," especially about "the notables". Zwakenberg was a coach driver for many years "drove for the rich people".- The fuels he distributed were piled on a very old, rickety bicycle, repaired here and there with iron wire and which he rode straight through the forest, "rather through the forest and field than over roads." He never complained to ride multiple times for a single order. I could not estimate the man's age, but he was "old," significantly older than my parents were then. They felt sorry for him: "such an old geezer who still was busy with these fuels"....

In the aforementioned years my father -in his fifties then- got visited by his Nunspeet relations, gentlemen with whom he met in the former hotel "De Veluwe", near the station. Did they gather in the "Gerharda," they "had a drink", and on occasion they played cards, and "heavily discussed" "liberal politics". Now and then they waged a not too risky and cautious gamble on the stock market together. It appeared – I never got around how he did it- that "the old bat," Zwakenberg, "the turn-penny" gambled in this way. And not only that! They were surprised and repeatedly discussed that Zwakenberg had "such good insight" concerning these financial manipulations, or perhaps "dumb luck"- the "dumb have all the luck" – because most of the time he gained profit when the gentlemen "lost some".... –

When the occasion arose, I liked talking to the old Zwakenberg and listened with attention and pleasure to his stories about Nunspeet in the dialect of the North Veluwe. I could get along fine with him! When I had heard that Zwakenberg made money from such "a gamble", which the gentlemen considered "too risky", I asked the man: "Do you understand that, Zwakenberg?"- "No", he answered, "the gnomes tell me to", which I interpreted as a reprimand, freely translated: "mind your own business, whipper-snapper"....-

Later conversations made me realize, that the old man's answer was serious, and all kinds of later gleanings of the man -when I asked him straight, he never answered- I understood, summarizing, what he tried to make clear: among other, but mainly in the forest area enclosed by the Groenelaantje, the current F.A. Molijnlaan (back then Grote Weg? There was a steam tram driving!), the Eperweg, then Waskolkweg and the railway track to Zwolle, he met and saw gnomes. In earlier times, even more on a terrain, located near the Waskolkweg, but a camp for Belgian refugees was founded there, -1914-1918-, which drove away the gnomes. Zwakenberg was said to have seen gnomes "behind the Round House" and "between the Witte Klap and the Mythstee," "as well on estate Welna": "small fellows", "with and without beard", with "a red pointy hat" which was "also worn around the ears" and "attached to a collar below". For the further part, they were dressed "in a simple working suit," "a keel and pants", sometimes coloured "brown", "sometimes green", and "those colours changed while you looked at them". He said he "could not always see them clearly," they were "sometimes blurred" and "suddenly disappeared." Sometimes his attention was drawn to a certain point, and while he was watching, "from a haziness," a gnome appeared there.....-

It was impossible to "talk" to these gnomes, said Zwakenberg. When you "waved at them" they did not respond, nor when you shouted "good morning" or something similar to them. But when you had "worries," or brooded on something and you thought of that while seeing a gnome, you suddenly became "clear in the head" and then "you saw how you had to deal with it".... "As a young man of twenty-five years old," Zwakenberg had that figured out and "always lived by that". The gnomes do not like, so he thinks, that people talk about that among each other, they would rather be left alone. The more "strangers" -holidaymakers- visit Nunspeet and more summer homes are built there, the "less gnomes will remain".... **S.**

Note 1946, §1d, fol. 239*, addressed to Mister (father) M.J. Reinhoudt: "Zwakenberg", see also Note 1940, §8, fol. 79. **E.**

Note 1946, §1e, fol. 240, addressed to Miss Anja van Doorn: through the gleanings of mentioned Zwakenberg, I was confronted for the first time with someone who spoke about "real existing gnomes", "beings, phantoms, which he saw and saw moving". I know for certain I never heard or read something about that before. The serious gleanings of the old man I considered reliable, made a deep impression on me, and a remaining interest for gnomes. It wasn't like I thought "the old fellow is mentally disturbed," but I couldn't find the faintest shred of belief in myself. I have thought long and hard about it and couldn't figure it out, nor now, when I'm 42 years old.... JHWE.[28]

Bij Aant. 1938, §2, fol. 392ᵃ — T.a.v. de heer S.W. van der Gaag: **b**

Het is mij bekend dat de heer B.G. Hulsker — "Bernard" — geen "schoon strafregister" had. Hij werd twee keer veroordeeld tot een onvoorwaardelijke geldboete, zulks terzake van het onbevoegd uitoefenen van de geneeskunst, en één keer tot een onvoorwaardelijke gevangenisstraf, zulks terzake van abortus. Het is allerminst mijn bedoeling deze delicten goed te praten, maar 't moet mij toch van het hart, dat de ernst van het gebeurde niet byzonder groot was en de man bij zijn euvele daden kennelijk werd gedreven door medelijden — Winstbejag bleek niet, integendeel, by de gepleegde abortus vergoedde hij het "slachtoffer" de door haar gemaakte reis- en verblijfkosten! Dat deze veroordelingen 's mans "verbale betrouwbaarheid" "per definitie" aantasten, vermag ik niet te zien. Bernard Hulsker — inmiddels overleden — stond in zijn omgeving — inbegrepen het kruideniersmilieu en de kruidenhandel — bekend als een vriendelijke, openhartige kerel, "eerlijk als goud", gul en hulpvaardig. Over zijn "ervaringen met kabouters" sprak hij zelden en dan nog uitsluitend met die enkele personen waarvan hij wist dat zij geïnteresseerd waren. Zelf had ik — ondanks een goede introductie — aanvankelijk vrij veel moeite hem op het thema kabouters te krijgen. ▣ᵃ

Of ik 's mans "kabouterverhalen" "voetstoots geloof" doet m.i. weinig terzake. Ik moet bekennen dat ik — helaas! — nooit één "echte kabouter" zag en het bestaan en rondtrekken van zulke wezens ernstig in twijfel trek.... JHWE.

Aant. 1938, §2, fol. 392ᶜ, bij #: Mij intrigeert vooral hoe Bernard Hulsker, indien hij zijn verhalen fantaseerde, zo precies de plaatsen wist te noemen waar ook anderen die "vreemde ontmoetingen" zegden te hebben gehad. JHWE.

At Note 1938, §2, fol. 392a- Addressed to Mister S.W. van der Gaag: **b**

I am aware that Mister B.G. Hulsker –"Bernard"- had "a

---

28. The year 1946 behind Eldermans' signature "JHWE" is in the handwriting of Bob Richel.

criminal record." He was convicted twice with an unconditional fine, for practising unqualified medicine, and one time to unconditional imprisonment for practising abortion. It is not my place to explain away his crimes, but I have to admit that the event was not very serious and the man was apparently driven by pity when performing his ill deeds. He didn't do it for profit, on the contrary, for the performed abortion he paid the "victim" her travel and accommodation costs! I can't see that these convictions affect his "verbal trustworthiness" "by definition." Bernard Hulsker -currently deceased- was known in his surroundings – with inclusion of the grocery- and herb trade- as a friendly, open-hearted fellow, "honest", generous and helpful. About his "experiences with gnomes" he seldomly spoke and then only with people he knew were interested. I had – in spite of a good introduction- initially a hard time to get him on to the theme of gnomes. **E.**

If I believe the man's "gnome stories" unquestioningly, is, in my opinion, of little relevance. I have to admit that I – regrettably- never saw one "real gnome" and seriously doubt the migration of such beings…. JHWE.

Note 1938, §2, fol. 392C, at #: What intrigues me is how Bernard Hulsker , if he imagined all his stories, could name the places precisely where others had these "strange encounters". JHWE.

Simon Fraterman – see Note 1941, fol. 417d, F4- passed away in 1942 at the age of 86. He was a skipper merchant, later planter and merchant in North East Indonesia, and during many years a "rentier." Fraterman (meetings with him occurred namely around 1938) became known as an eager secretive, impatient, rectilinear and conceited man, who surprised his surroundings by making unbelievable stories come true, to provide evidence for them.... He told among other to have regular meetings with gnomes, "as often as he desired," such in De Peel, in eastern Twente and on the North Veluwe. About the nature of these meetings he was very reluctant, "the gnomes do not like it when they are talked about...." Fraterman "a born vagrant" (and certainly peculiar!) travelled a lot, mostly without or with very little baggage. Up to a high age he still walked or rode through the nature reserves of The Netherlands and Belgium. His knowledge of folklore, folk customs in those areas was immense. In his stories, Fraterman often said: "I, as an occultist"...., &c.- **E.**

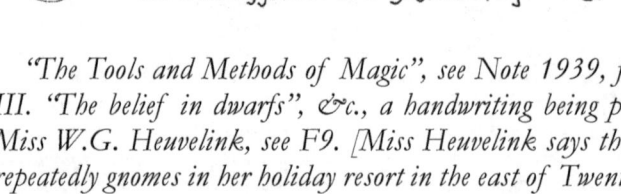

"The Tools and Methods of Magic", see Note 1939, fol. 245d/ III. "The belief in dwarfs", &c., a handwriting being property of Miss W.G. Heuvelink, see F9. [Miss Heuvelink says that she saw repeatedly gnomes in her holiday resort in the east of Twente, however she never got contact with them. She made attempts, among others, by magical means, which were touted to her in southern Ireland. Means and prescriptions, so complicated, that she never was able to follow them completely, and never was able to gain the prescribed ingredients. See Note 1939, fol. 246.] **E.**

CHAPTER FOUR

MISCELLANEOUS WRITINGS CONCERNING GNOMES

In this final chapter, we will take a look at a large number of entries in Eldermans' gnome writings that are neither 'meat or potatoes'! Some of these entries are either funny, or serious but most of them do not fit the categories stated in *The Gnome Manuscript, The Gnome Grimoire* or the categories in the previous chapters of this book. It does show us that Eldermans was a versatile collector - he collected practically everything that had something to do with gnomes. A good example is the garden gnome, which we have seen in the previous chapters. Another example is the following photograph:

It is an advertisement for a brand of coffee, in which we see a gnome running away with a pack of coffee, smiling, because he has stolen the best coffee around. "When you taste it, you buy it", it says in the advertisement. It proves that Eldermans had an overall interest in gnomes and not only the magic used to manipulate gnomes. This chapter will really show that he went to great lengths to collect everything that dealt with the Little People, from advertisements to newspaper clippings.

At Note 1948, fol. 8I: "a remarkable sign, consisting of the connection of two Yr-runes" = see under: the dying and ending life". The connection to gnomes is completely unclear to me (JHWE.). **H.**

Throughout his life, Eldermans was very interested in runes, although he favoured the Germanic runes, which were never used for lingual purposes but for more magical ones – this being contrary to Nordic or English runes, which were used as language and were chiseled into rock or carved into wood.

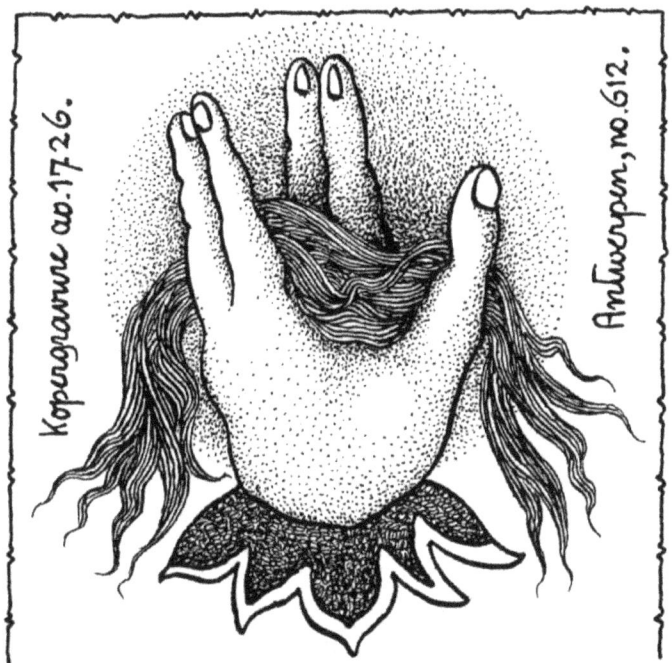

Copperplate anno 1726, Antwerp, no. 612.
After Prosper van Eyck, see Note 1941, III/fol. 330C, "nature spirits" ["attract or repel"?]. Further correspondence was interrupted due to circumstances of war. **H**.

There is a silent joke inside this drawing. The gesture the hand makes, Eldermans may have seen in a book by Charles Poncé titled *Kabbalah* (published 1976), in which a hand is shown making the same gesture and with the same cuff [29], only Eldermans added more 'colour' to it. The

---

29. Charles Poncé, *Kabbalah. Achtergrond en essentie*, Deventer, 1976, pp 8

pun is in the gesture, which resembles the gesture made by Mister Spock from Star Trek, along with the spoken words: "Live Long and Prosper" and then the justification starts about Prosper van Eyck. It may just be coincidence, but I cannot shake off the impression that Eldermans would have appreciated such a pun.

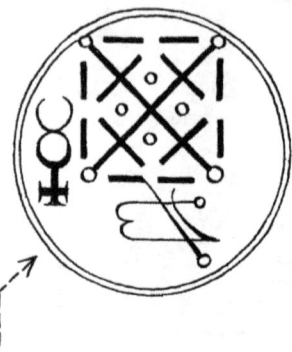

8	38	39	5	4	62	63	1	220
49	15	14	32	53	11	10	36	220
41	23	22	44	48	19	13	45	255
32	34	38	29	25	35	39	28	260
40	25	27	37	36	30	31	33	259
17	47	46	20	21	43	42	24	260
9	55	34	12	13	31	50	16	220
64	2	3	61	50	8	7	37	232

260 239 223 240 250 239 255 220

Aant. 1939, fol. 461E: „Op deze rangschikking van 64 getallen baseert Pierre Duvivier — sprekende over een „magisch vierkant" — zijn verwarde theorie. Het komt mij voor, dat hij een slechte rekenmeester is: wellicht heeft hij zijn wijsheid elders geleend en lijdt zijn plagiaat aan slordigheid. De kabouters, — indien ze bestaan — zullen hem wel door hebben. JHWE." — Ter verbetering: documentatie § 38/1939 [„Kabbala"].

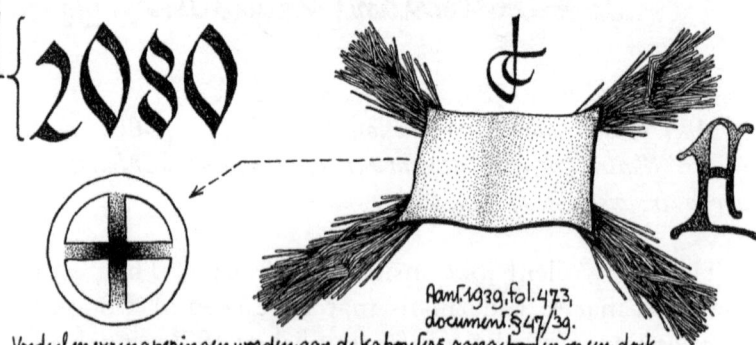

Aant. 1939, fol. 473, document § 47/39.

„Voedsel en versnaperingen worden aan de kabouters aangeboden op een doekje van zuiverlinnen, gelegd op een kruis van strohalmen;" [„Schmidtke", no. N. 604].

Note 1939, fol. 461E: *"Pierre Duvivier based his confused theory on the arrangement of these 64 numbers -speaking of a "magic*

136

square"-. It appears to me he is bad at maths: apparently, he borrowed his wisdom elsewhere and his plagiarism suffers from sloppiness. The gnomes -if they exist- may be on to him. JHWE"- In correction: documentation §38/1939 ["Kabbalah"]. **H.**

Note 1939, fol. 473, documentation §47/'39. "Food and refreshments are offered to the gnomes on a cloth of pure linen, laid on a cross of straws", ["Schmidtke", no. 604].

In the Cabbalah, numbers are very important, as the Hebrew alphabet doesn't only represent a letter but also a numerical value. Magic squares are often found in *grimoires* based on Cabbalistic knowledge, like the Book of *Abra-Melin* or *The Greater Key of Solomon*. Magic squares are also made with letters, like the well-known "Sator-formula". To make this example a 'magic square' the product of each line, horizontally and vertically, and sometimes even diagonally, should be the same. Eldermans emphasizes that this is not the case: the products are different in each line and the horizontal line does not correspond with the vertical line. Eldermans is right in his assessment that this is bad maths.

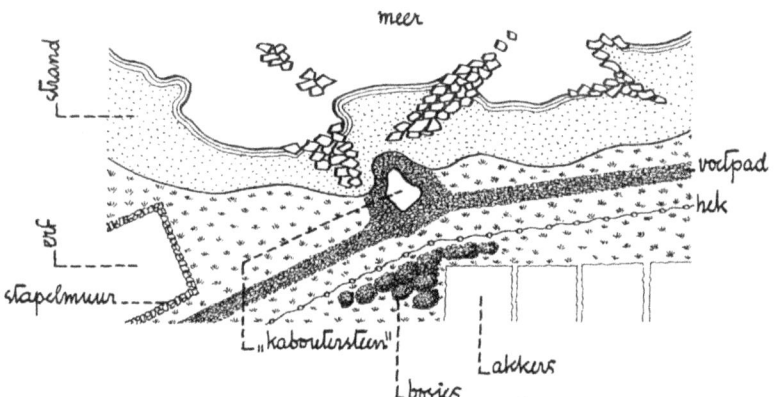

At Note 1938, fol. 2B, addition II: detail from the at)32 added map. The gnomes were observed manifold in the years 1931-1937 around and very close to the "gnomestone", and also between the stone and the nearby bushes". See the documentation §1-DD/1938, "The Singing Kettle", F5.- **H.**

About the above-mentioned observations, a report was written in December 1937 by "Rev. Colin Houghton", see the handwriting "Ex Libris M.d.B.", no. 527. **E.**

The map contains several Dutch words which will appear incomprehensible to the English reader, so here is a translation for all of these words. On the left we see strand (beach), erf (courtyard), *stapelmuur* (piled wall). In the centre, is the word *meer* (lake), "*kaboutersteen*" (gnomestone), *bosjes* (bushes) and *akkers* (fields). To the right we see *hek* (fence) and *voetpad* (trail). The map has no reference, besides a 'report' by reverend Colin Houghton, which suggests this map represents an area in Great Britain or Ireland. *The Singing Kettle* is a little more enigmatic. It could refer to a company of musicians who had perform children's songs since 1979. It could also refer to a short story by Enid Blyton, in which a goblin is mentioned. It is not clear which *Singing Kettle* Eldermans means...

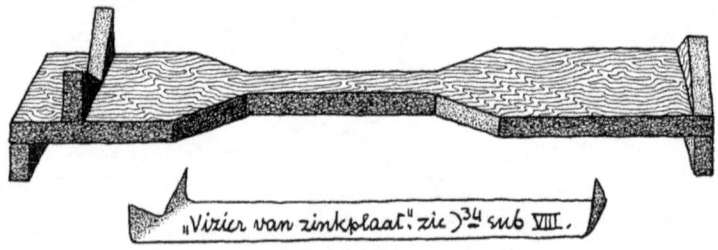

"Visier van zinkplaat", zie)³⁴ sub VIII.

Bij Aant 1938, fol. 3ᴮ en)³⁴/1938, "Gnomes", &c.- [W.O. Nuallain]. Aanvulling no. 8 [The megalithic Tombs of Eire, zie ook fol. 3ᴰ.

"Visor of zinc plate", see)34 sub VIII.

At Note 1938, fol. 3B and)34/1938, "gnomes", &c.- [W.O. Nuallain]. Addition no. 8 [The megalithic tombs of Eire, see also fol. 3D. H.

The visor and the megalithic tombs of Ireland might have something in common, as there is always a spot or stone which is connected to the Sun. Even in Stonehenge, there is the so-called *heel stone* which seems to act like the visor depicted above: the sun rises above this stone around June 21st. Who W.O. Nuallain had been, isn't known.

Bij Aant. 1938, fol. 18 II (En aanvulling): Naar de mededelingen van „vrouw S.F.d.B": un „rond driepootje", un „halve el" hoog, gemaakt van eikenhout. Het wordt geplaatst op „un stil plekske", waar „alles kan worden overzien". Zie de documentatie §12-EE/1938. E.

Toevoegen aan Aant. 1938, fol. 18 IV: „Gnomes", „An example of the solitary fairy is the leprechaun, the fairy shoemaker, whose hoards of gold ar much coveted by mortals". — Het daar bedoelde verhaal (F8) komt voor in „Ancient Legends of Ireland", Lady Wilde, 1887. — O.

Aant. 1938, fol. 19: („vrouw S.F.d.B."), Kabouters verkiezen voor hun gereedschap en andere zaken inlands eikenhout en hebben vaak een afkeer van ijzer. Ijzer kunnen ze moeilijk onzichtbaar maken, lood in het geheel niet. — H.

At Note 1938, fol. 18II (in addition): After the gleanings of "lady S.F.d.B.": a "round tripod", a "half ell" high, made of oak wood. It is placed on "a silent spot", where "everything can be overseen". See the documentation §12-EE/1938. **E.**

Add to Note 1938, fol. 18IV: "Gnomes", "An example of the solitary fairy is the leprechaun, the fairy shoemaker, whose hoards of gold ar [sic] much coveted by mortals".- The mentioned story (F8) is found in "Ancient Legends of Ireland", Lady Wilde, 1887.- **O.**

Note 1938, fol. 19: ("Lady S.F.d.B."), Gnomes choose for their tools and other affairs inland oak wood and are repulsed by iron. Iron is hard for them to make invisible, lead not at all.- **H.**

Although we have had a paragraph about things built by gnomes, this entry differs quite a bit. It explains in more detail, why gnomes are attracted to inland oak wood and why these objects need to be made from oak. The middle entry is, again, strange. The citation resembles a topic in the *Encyclopedia of Magic & Superstition* but Eldermans refers to Francesca Esperanza Wilde, who wrote *Ancient Legends*,

Mystic Charms and Superstitions of Ireland (Boston, 1887) in which we read a chapter on the Leprehaun (minus the "c"). The citation is not from the work of Lady Wilde, but she is very informing about the nature and behaviour of the leprechaun, one of the most fascinating fairies in the international kingdom of Little People. The brief nature of Eldermans' entry doesn't do the leprechaun justice. Information like 'keep your eyes on the leprechaun or you will lose the gold', because the leprechaun has the ability to vanish without a trace, might have been welcome to the reader of his manuscript.

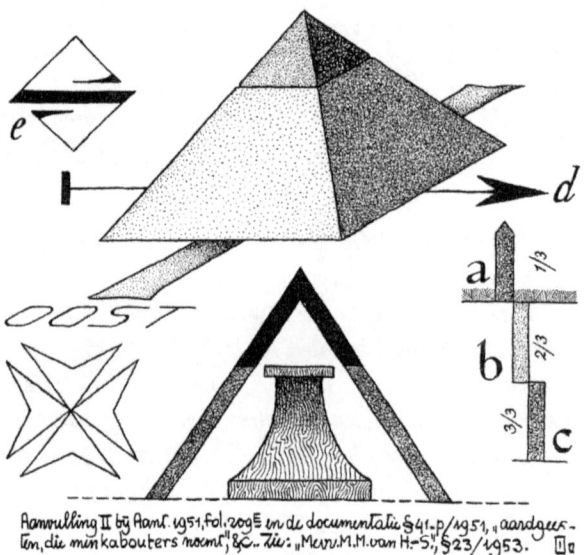

Aanvulling II bij Aant. 1951, fol. 209E en de documentatie §41-p/1951, "aardgeesten, die min kabouters noemt", &c.. Zie: "Mevr. M.M. van H.-S.", §23/1953.

*Addition II at Note 1951, fol. 209E and the documentation §41-p/1951, "nature spirits, one calls gnomes", &c.. See: "Mrs. M.M. van H. – S.", §23/1953. **O.***

Above is another entry about a pyramid. It does not make clear though, exactly what Eldermans wants to get across with this entry. The Templar Croix Pattée and the pyramid might suggest a connection to Freemasonry but that has no reference to the Little People.

South – North.

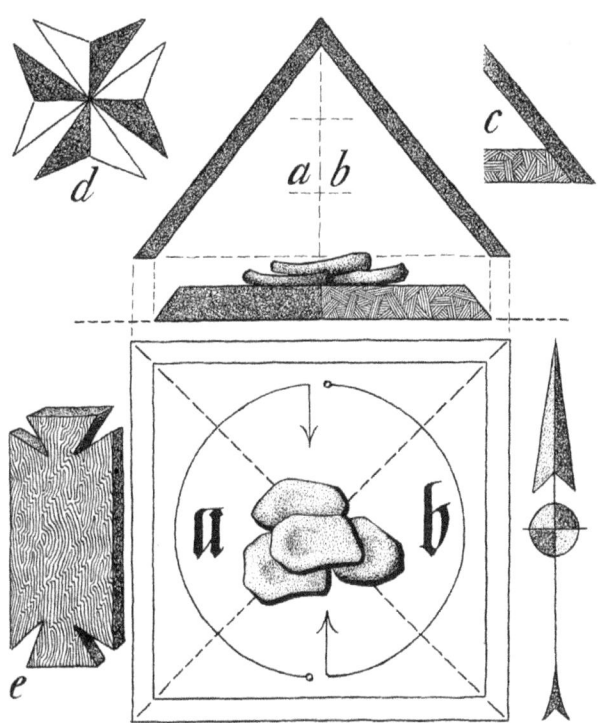

zie Aant. 1951, fol. 212ᵈ [id. doc. §41-p/1951, „aardgeesten, die men kabouters
noemt", &c.] Over de experimenten van mevr. M.M. van Haeren-Slichtenhorst
zijn slechts weinig gegevens beschikbaar. Zie ook §23/1953 („Klabouters").

*See Note 1951, fol. 212H [idem documentation §41-p/1951, "nature spirits one calls gnomes", &c.] About the experiments of Mrs. M.M. van Haeren-Slichtenhorst are little data available. See also §23/1953 ("gnomes"). **H.***

Presumably the drawing represents the experiment of Mrs. Van Haeren, whose name was abbreviated in a previous entry. Why does Eldermans abbreviate her name in one entry, and write it in full in this one? The experiment appears to involve some stacked pebbles in a pyramid, though what the purpose of these pebbles might be for, is not clear. We do know about fairy-stones, pebbles stacked upon another, which are often found in forests or near creeks but these look quite different, so without additional information, it is quite hard to say something pertinent about this entry.

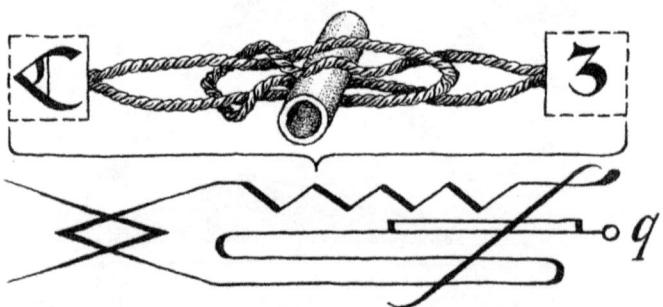

*At Note 1947, fol. 337H: "Gnomes", &c.- documentation §60-f/1947, Murray. **H.***

Eldermans refers to the work of Margaret Murray, whose *Witchcult in Western Europe* (1921) was of great influence on the works of Gerald Gardner and Cecil H. Williamson. He has written a single appendix on 'witches and fairies' but, how this appendix relates to this entry, is unclear. We have a pentacle, a small piece of pipe and rope with the unending knot. Eldermans did not see this in the book by Murray. What is his train of thoughts with this entry?

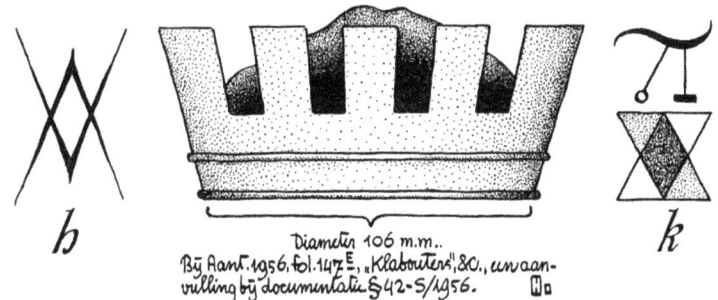

Diameter 106 millimeters. At Note 1956, fol. 147E, "gnomes", &c., an addition at documentation §42-S/1956. **H.**

The crown is quite important in the works of Eldermans, it is a recurring subject in the 'Swiss' Eldermans collection, and in the Cabbalah, the crown "Kether" is the highest of Sephiroth, the first beneath the *En Soph*. The crown is a theme in Eldermans' *sexual magic*, which sometimes also entangles itself into his gnome folklore. The symbols are from *The Greater Key of Solomon*, which might give prevalence to the "Cabbalah"-interpretation…

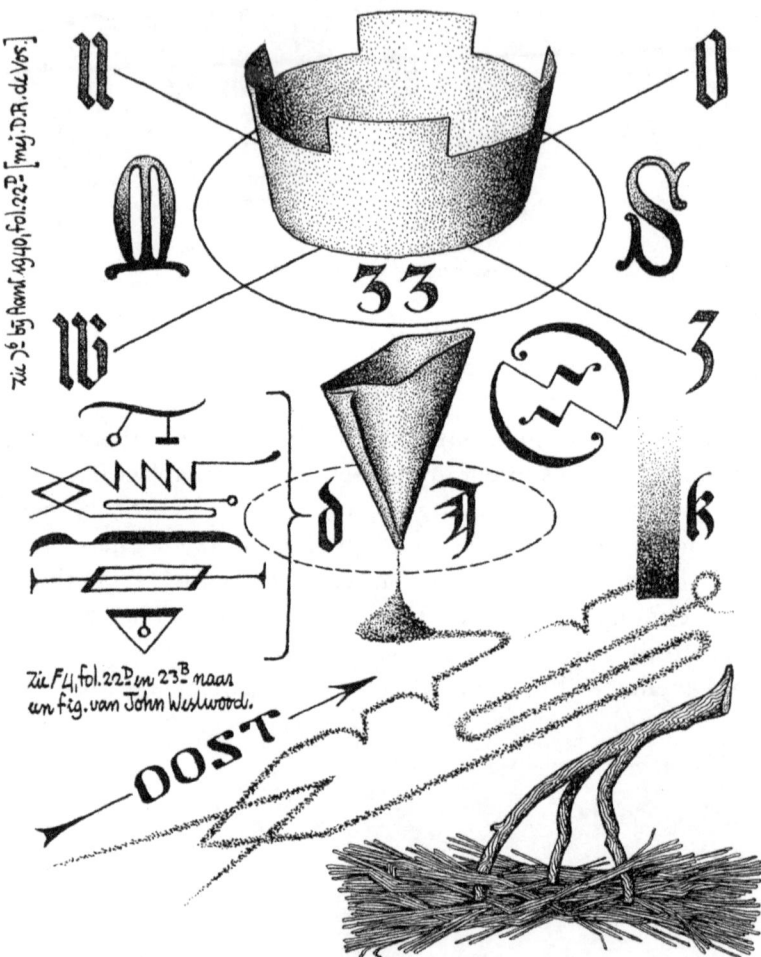

See)6 at Note 1940, fol. 22D [Miss D.R. de Vos.]

See F4, fol. 22D and 23B after a figure by John Westwood.

Addition I at Note 1940, fol. 24C, after the information and sketches of Mrs. W.J.A. Kuypers-Faro. See documentation §9-K/1940 ["Nature spirits", &c..] **H.**

At F5: "Saint Andrew, 30 November. The Saint Andrew-night has magical properties. See for that matter Note 1939, fol. 398H, J.R. Uittien senior. **E.**

Again, we see a crown, this time with the number 33, which has several meanings. It can refer to Freemasonry but it also refers to the age that Jesus was, when he was crucified and then returned from the dead. There are sand-sprinkled figures, there is a straw bush held together with a branch with three twigs. Three twigs refer to masculinity but is also one-eleventh part of 33. The symbols are, in part, from *The Greater Key of Solomon* but, overall, it is another very unclear entry. What does Eldermans want to convey with this drawing?

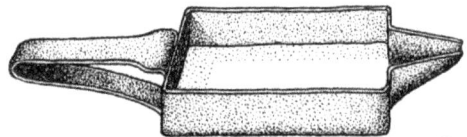

Bij Aant.1950,fol.117B: ["Aardgeesten" e.d.] naar E.O. Stoughton. Recepten: zie Aant. 1950, fol. 203A ["The Modern Attitude"- "Myth or Magic", F5, 6 en 8.]   Eo

At Note 1950, fol. 117B: ["Nature spirits" and such] after E.O. Stoughton. Recipes: see Note 1950, fol. 203A ["The Modern Attitude"- "Myth or Magic", F5, 6 and 8.] **E.**

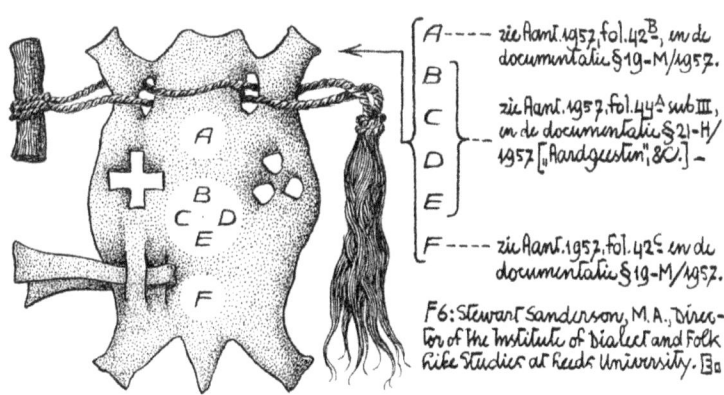

A ---- zie Aant.1957,fol.42B, in de documentatie §19-M/1957.

B
C   zie Aant.1957,fol.44A sub III,
    in de documentatie §21-H/
D   1957 ["Aardgeesten", &C.] -
E

F ---- zie Aant.1957,fol.42C in de documentatie §19-M/1957.

F6: Stewart Sanderson, M.A., Director of the Institute of Dialect and Folk Life Studies at Leeds University. Eo

See Note 1957, fol. 42B, and the documentation §19-M/1957.

See Note 1957, fol. 44A sub III, and the documentation §21-H/1957 ["Nature spirits", &c.]-

See Note 1957, fol. 42C and the documentation §19-M/1957.

F6: Stewart Sanderson M.A., Director of the Institute of Dialect and Folk Life Studies at Leeds University. **E.**

Stewart Forson Sanderson (1924-2016) was a folklorist and linguist who became known for his recordings of dialect. He moved to Leeds University in 1960, where he became the Director of the Institute of Dialect and Folklife Studies in 1964. He became chairman of the School of English in Leeds in the same year and worked on dialect studies, which resulted in *A Dialect Atlas of England* (1987).[30] What this has to do with gnomes, or even pentacles on moleskin, is not clear. Again, we see a discrepancy in Eldermans' justification: his year of reference is 1957 but Stewart Sanderson did not become Director of the Institute of Dialect and Folk Life Studies until 1964... Inquiries made at Leeds University didn't turn up any correspondence sent by Eldermans.

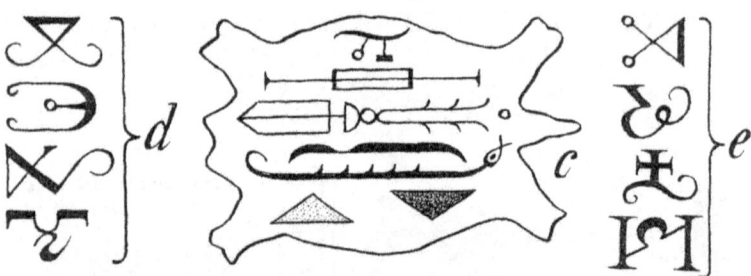

By Aant. 1958, fol. 33^D : zie „Samenvatting" [„Modern Witchcraft", sub XXIV, „Gnomes".] — Totebel : een net, opgehangen aan de vier einden van twee gekruiste halve hoepels. Het net wordt vanuit een schuitje met een over een blok (katrol) lopend touw, dat aan het einde van een over het water schuinstaande paal is bevestigd, in het water neergelaten. JHWE. —

---

30. *David Sanderson, Obituary: Stewart Forson Sanderson, pioneer in studies and recording of folk culture and dialect* on the website https://www.scotsman.com/news/obituaries/obituary-stewart-forson-sanderson-pioneer-in-studies-and-recording-of-folk-culture-and-dialect-1-4284198

At Note 1958, fol. 33D: see "Summary" ["Modern Witchcraft", sub XXIV, "Gnomes".] − Totebel = a fishing net, hung from four ends of two, crossed half hoops. The net is lowered into the water from a boat with a rope running over a pulley attached to a slanted pole hanging over the water. JHWE.- **H.**

There is no exact translation for 'totebel' in English - the word has two meanings in Dutch: a square net which is laid on the bottom of a lake or river, and is used to catch fish, but it also refers to a very untidy woman. It is, once more, an entry without any reference from the text to the drawing: a moleskin with pentacles, which has something to do with gnomes and the title of the book by Gerald Gardner to go into a few lines about a fishing net! Eldermans is very good at raising questions but appears to refuse to answer them.

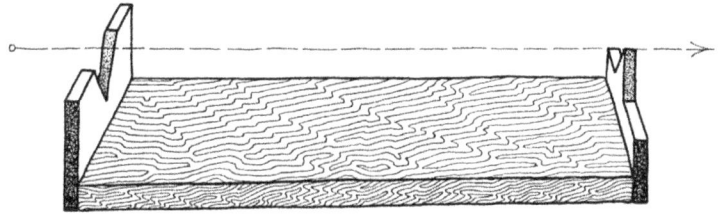

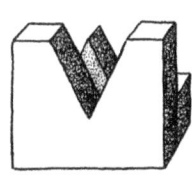

„Duende" en „Gnomo": (Spaans) kaboutermannetje; zie Aant. 1950, fol. 275E, „De Spaanse Schatgraver" (!) [„Criminologische zijpaden", Mr. W.E. van Dusschoten, bijlage IV. ☐o Bij F3: „The Writing call'd Malachim", &c., tabel 4, „Magical alphabets made by combining symbols from the Hebrew, runic and other alphabets, thought to contain power", &c.. Zie Index, nrs. 28, 42, 186 en 204, en Aant. 1952, fol. 61D. ☐o

"Duende" and "Gnomo"= (Spanish) gnome; see Note 1950, fol. 275E, "The Spanish treasure digger"(!) "Criminological side paths", Mr. W.E. van Dusschoten, appendix IV. **E.**

At F3: "The Writing call'd Malachim", &c., table 4, "Magical alphabets made by combining symbols from the Hebrew, runic and other alphabets, thought to contain power", &c.. See Index, numbers 25, 42, 186 and 204, and Note 1952, fol. 61D. **H.**

Here we have another peculiar entry in Eldermans' work. We have a contraption partially made of wood, which is used to look through. The V-shaped opening is the starting point and you must gaze over the triangular shape across the opening but the justification doesn't refer to this contraption - on the contrary. It is about a conman called "the Spanish Treasuredigger" who was active between the years 1889-1948, according to the archives of the Amsterdam police department. How this relates to the *Writing call'd Malachim*, which Eldermans found in Francis Barrett's *The Magus*, in which Barrett says about the alphabet:

> *There is also a writing which they call Malachim, or Melachim, i.e. of angels, or regal; [...]*[31]

The *Writing call'd Malachim* appears to be based on celestial configurations and translated into the Hebrew alphabet. Eldermans speaks of a mixture of Hebrew with runes and other magical symbols, which might contain power and here we see a possible motivation for the creation of his personal talisman to protect him against wounds caused by knives and bullets. Here, two traditions are combined into one talisman: a pentacle from *The Greater Key of Solomon* and runic magic. It might be that Eldermans believed the runic addition to his talisman might strengthen the pentacle from Solomon. But all this doesn't relate in any form to the contraption in the drawing, or the mentioning of the "Spanish Treasure digger". Unless Eldermans suspected the "Spanish Treasure digger" to use combined traditions of magic as well...

---

31. Francis Barrett, *The Magus part two*, downloaded from *The Esoteric Library* at www.sacred-magick.com, pp 64

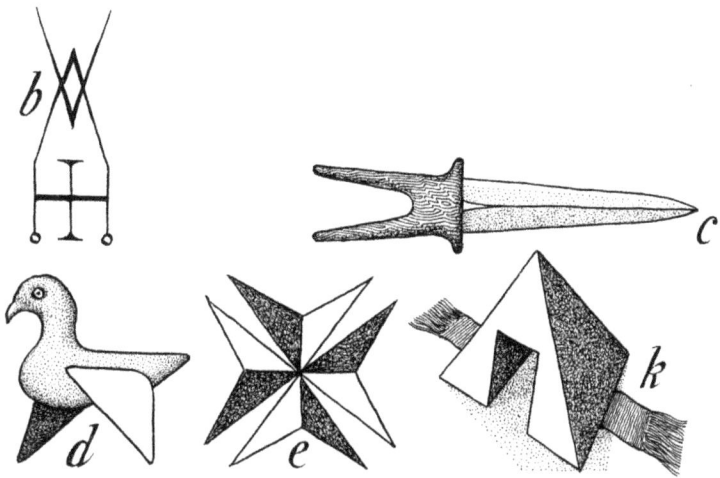

Aanvulling I by Aant .1942, fol.24G: „Aardgeesten" &c., §20-m: „Only three pieces of magical work can be done at each meeting. The witches can work up only so much power at one time, then they must replenish what they have given out", &c.. §21-D: „To know, to dare, to will, to be silent", „This has been the code of the witches", &c.. Zie onder „Gnomes" en)8.

Addition I at Note 1942, fol. 24G: "Nature spirits", &c.. §20-m: "Only three pieces of magical work can be done at each meeting. The witches can work up only so much power at one time, then they must replenish what they have given out", &c.. §21-D: "To know, to dare, to will, to be silent", "this has been the code of the witches", &c.. See under "Gnomes" and)8. **E.**

Although the drawing is a complete mystery on its own, the *code of the witches* was something Eldermans lived by. He didn't wear his heart on his sleeve when meeting other people but most of his family were unaware of his occult interests, to a certain degree, all except for his really close family (his wife, his daughters, granddaughters and, of course, Bob Richel). He didn't actually hide it from people, as some of them still remember 'the strange drawings' hanging throughout the house but Eldermans didn't speak about his fascination with magic and the occult, of his own accord. He did reach out to people who wanted to use magic for a certain purpose to give them advice, or to simply talk them out of it.

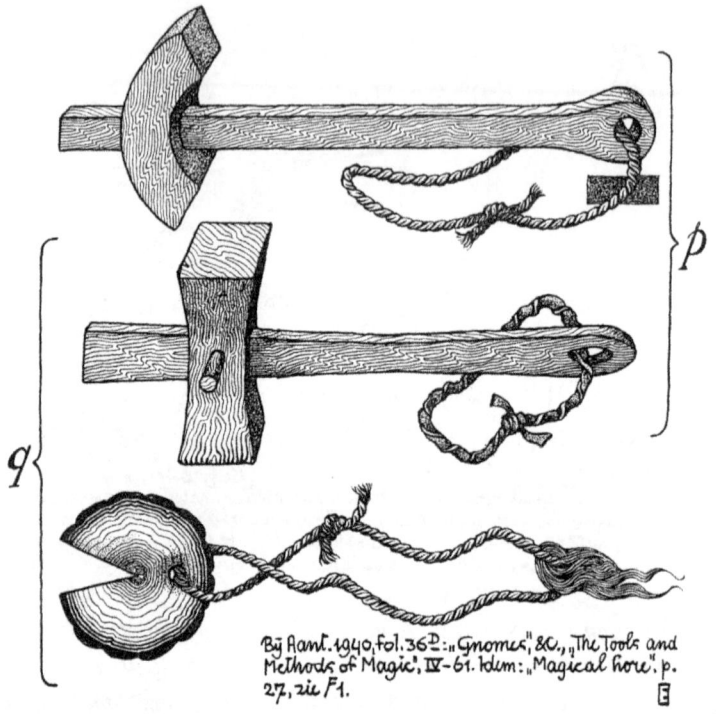

By Rant. 1940, fol. 36ᴰ: „Gnomes", &c., „The Tools and Methods of Magic", IV-61. Idem: „Magical lore". p. 27, zie F1. E

At Note 1940, fol. 35D: "Gnomes", &c., "The tools and Methods of Magic", IV-61. Idem: "Magical Lore", p. 27, see F1. **E.**

The depicted 'tools', made of wood, are perfectly fine to use in rituals concerning gnomes but these are not from *The Tools and Methods of Magic* in the *Encyclopedia of Magic & Superstition*. There is another reference to this book, meaning "*Magical Lore*", which is short for "*Glossary of Magical Lore*", which is nothing more than what it says: a glossary of magical terms which are explained in that chapter. These tools are not found in that chapter, either.

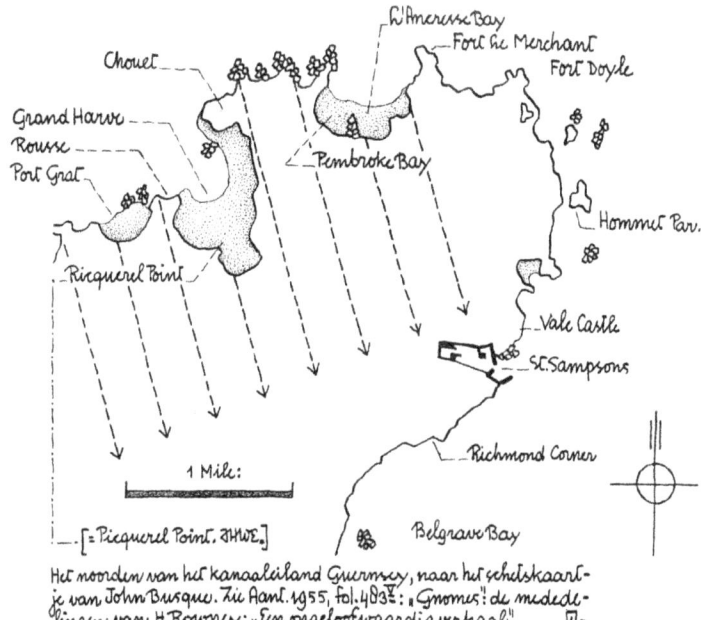

The north of the Channel Island of Guernsey, according to a sketched map by John Busque. See Note 1955, fol. 483V: "Gnomes": the gleanings of H. Rowney: "an incredible story". **O**.

Eldermans and Guernsey have a special relationship, maybe more because Eldermans attempted to invent a gnome-tradition on Guernsey concerning the *Staddle-stones* he had seen all over the island. He connected these mushroom-like stones to a gnome population which used these stones to rest upon or to hide underneath. Matt Harvey B.Sc., Social History Curator at *Culture and Heritage* shined a light on these stones:

> *I've not come across any references in the usual local literature to indicate that they were viewed in any way other than as utilitarian agricultural items.*[32]

---

32. E-mail from Matt Harvey to Peter Hewitt of the Museum of Witchcraft and Magic, dated 31st October 2017

Eldermans dared to challenge this view, forty years prior to this e-mail being sent. But as Harvey said: there is no evidence to support Eldermans' claims. Although there are sources on the internet who claim that these stones have something to do with *witches* on Guernsey, this is as unsubstantiated as it is with the gnomes. There is Fairy mythology on Guernsey, a famous tale is the invasion of the Dark Fairies in 1338, where the men of Guernsey had to go to war with the Fairies, as the fairy men had come to steal the wives of the Guernsey men. But specific *gnome* tales are very hard to find. We have to establish here that Eldermans apparently invented his own gnome-tradition on Guernsey and did not follow local folklore tales.

Tekeningen en schetsen van Otto Schmidtke, zie Aant.1938, fol.200: „Sammlung Schmidtke". - [Idem:„Sammlung für deutsche Volkskunde", §23/1938, met bemerkingen t.a.v.⚡!]

Drawings and sketches of Otto Schmidtke, see Note 1938, fol. 200: "Sammlung Schmidtke".- [Idem: "Sammlung für deutsche Volkskunde", §23/1938, with remarks considering (swastika)!] **H.**

This is the presumed autograph of Otto Schmidtke, which can be found on numerous drawings in the entire Eldermans collection, but most of these "works" are found in the Swiss Eldermans collection in Zürich, where they are kept in the Oskar Schlag collection of the Zentralbibliothek. The objections against the *Sammlung Schmidtke* are explained in *The Silent Listener. The Life and Works of J.H.W. Eldermans* but it appears that Eldermans worked out this invented tradition in quite some detail. For more information, I direct you to the aforementioned publication from my hand.

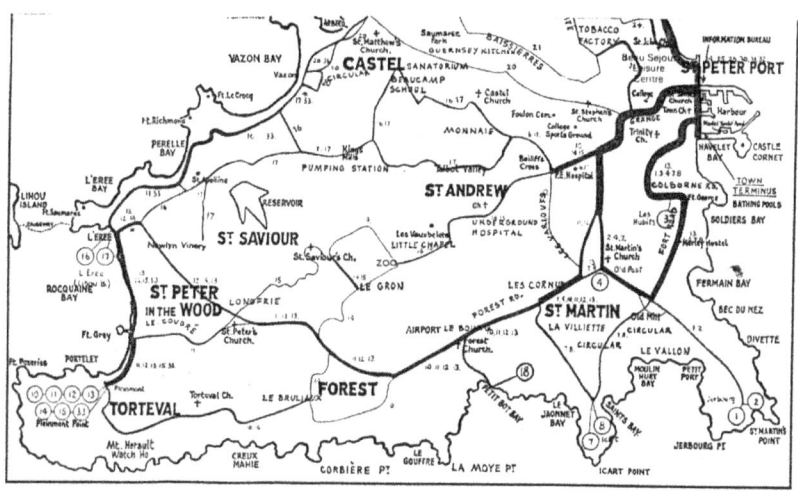

Ter verduidelijking bij Aant. 1938, fol. 10ΙΙ: het zuidelijke deel van Guernsey. Zie de documentatie §5-DD/1938. De als bijlage I bijgevoegde verhalen zijn gevonden in „The world guide to gnomes, fairies, elves, and other little people" = Thomas Keightley, 1789-1872. – Toevoegen aan F2: „Gnomes: dwarfish spirits which live underground and guard buried treasures." – [)28]. – Ⅱ.

In clarification of Note 1938, fol. 10II: the southern part of Guernsey. See the documentation §5-DD/1938. The stories added in appendix I are found in "The World Guide to Gnomes, Fairies, Elves, and other Little People"= Thomas Keightley, 1789-1872.- Add to F2: "Gnomes: dwarfish spirits which live underground and guard buried treasures".-])28].- **O.**

It is not clear what stories by Keightley, Eldermans refers to but Guernsey is not mentioned in *The World Guide to Gnomes, Fairies, Elves and other Little People*. There is a small entry concerning Brittany in France, but in that chapter, Guernsey is not featured. Maybe he refers to stories concerning Brittany and the stories of England, Scotland, Ireland and Wales. But without appendix I, we don't know what it is that Eldermans exactly means.

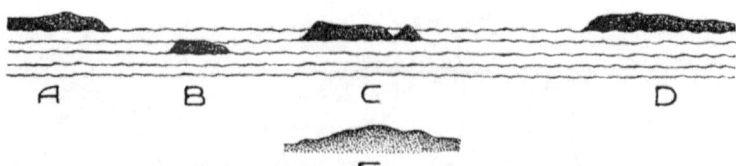

Ter verklaring van Aant. 1954, fol. 433ᴵᴵ: A = Alderney, B = Herm, C = Sark, D = Jersey, E = St. Peter Port. – De „sub VII" genoemde verhalen zijn gevonden in „The World Guide to Gnomes, Fairies, Elves and Other little People" by Thomas Keightley, [New York, originally published in 1880]. §277-BB/1954.   E.

In explanation of Note 1954, fol. 433II: A = Alderney, B = Herm, C = Sark, D = Jersey, E = St. Peter Port.- The stories dubbed "sub VII" are found in "The World Guide to Gnomes, Fairies, Elves and Other Little People" by Thomas Keightley, [New York, originally published in 1880]. §277-BB/1954. **E.**

The drawing refers to the Channel Islands Alderney, Herm, Sark and Jersey, with St. Peter Port being on Guernsey itself. None of the islands are mentioned in Keightley's book.

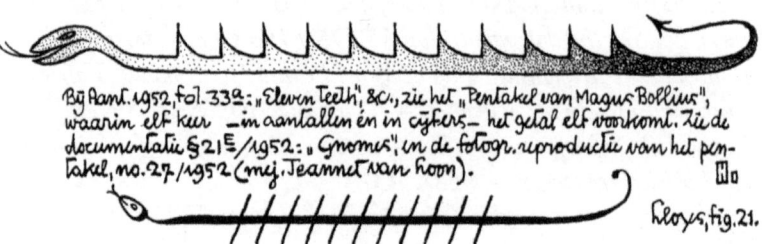

Bij Aant. 1952, fol. 33a: „Eleven Teeth", &c., zie het „Pentakel van Magus Bollius", waarin elf keer _in aantallen én in cijfers_ het getal elf voorkomt. Zie de documentatie §21E/1952: „Gnomes", en de fotogr. reproductie van het pentakel, no. 27/1952 (mej. Jeannet van Loon).   H.

Lloys, fig. 21.

At Note 1952, fol. 33a: "Eleven teeth", &c., see the "Pentacle of Magus Bollius", in which eleven times -in quantities and numbers- the number eleven occurs. See the documentation §21E/1952: "Gnomes", and the photographic reproduction of the pentacle, no. 27/1952 (miss Jeannet van Loon). **H.**
Lloys, figure 12.

The number 11 has no numerological value (as it would equal 2, the number of duality), and the number-magic in Cabbalah would equal eleven to yod and aleph, of which the magical power eludes me. The lower serpent reminds me of the Ogham script, although it does not represent a letter in the Ogham alphabet. Dee Finney of the website, Great Dreams, has another idea about what the number eleven stands for:

> *Number eleven possesses the qualities of intuition, patience, honesty, sensitivity and spirituality, and is idealistic. Others turn to people who are "Eleven" for teaching and inspiration, and are usually uplifted by the experience.*[33]

How this exactly relates to the serpent with the eleven jagged teeth on its back, can be found in the Pentacle of Magus Bollius, a name we already encountered several times. Who Bollius was and where he came from, is not known, as Eldermans does not provide us with any more information. Another typical feature in this entry is the similarity of the name *Jeannet* to the first name of his granddaughter.

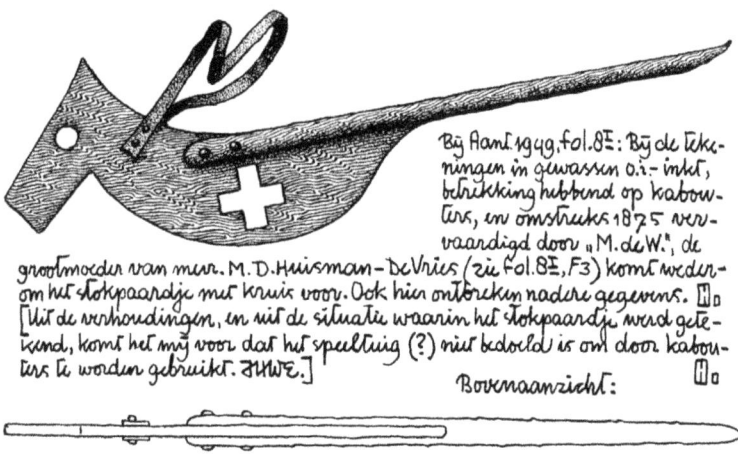

Bij Aant. 1949, fol. 8⁼: Bij de tekeningen in gewassen O.i.-inkt, betrekking hebbend op kabouters, en omstreeks 1875 vervaardigd door „M. de W.", de grootmoeder van mevr. M. D. Huisman-De Vries (zie fol. 8⁼, F3) komt weder om het stokpaardje met kruis voor. Ook hier ontbreken nadere gegevens. ☐ᴅ [Uit de verhoudingen, en uit de situatie waarin het stokpaardje werd getekend, komt het mij voor dat het speeltuig (?) niet bedoeld is om door kabouters te worden gebruikt. ᴢᴛᴡᴇ.] Bovenaanzicht: ☐ᴅ

---

33. Dee Finney, *The Symbolism and Spiritual Significance of the Number 11*, on the website http://www.greatdreams.com/eleven/num11.htm

At Note 1949, fol. 8I: With the drawing in washed East India ink, concerning gnomes and made around 1875 by "M.de W.", the grandmother of Mrs. M.D. Huisman – De Vries (see fol. 8I, F3) shows again the cockhorse with cross. Further information lacks here as well. **H.**

[From the proportions and the situation in which the cockhorse was drawn, it appears to me that the toy (?) was not meant to be used by gnomes. JHWE.] **H.**

Top view:

A horse, and in particular a horse's head is meant to repel evil influences. Most of the time these horse heads are found on structures such as barns. Here it appears to have been combined with the use of the witch's broom: the cockhorse may transport the one riding it to certain places, in order to flee evil. The symbol is christened, hence the cross sawn into the cockhorse - just like crosses are added to roof ornaments, which resemble the head of a horse.

Bij Aant. 1949, Fol. 4ᴵᴵᴵ, toevoegen: "Fugger, 1584: Wenn man an einem Pfal oder Stange den Kopf von einer Stuten aufstäke, so gerät alles dasjenige desto besser was im selben Garten wächst, insonderheit aber vertreibt es die Raupen und Katzen" = ook, zo zegt de molenbaas Gerritsen, de aardgeesten.— (Een aanvulling bij fol. 4ᴵᴵᴵ, sub VI.) **E.**

At Note 1949. Fol. 4III, add: "Fugger, 1584: [from German]: If you place the head of a mare on a stake or pole, then all the better the things grow in the same garden, but especially it drives away caterpillars and cats" = also, so says miller Gerritsen, the nature spirits.- (an addition at fol. 4III, sub VI.) **E.**

As to the name *Fugger*, it is again a mystery. The citation does not yield results, and the name only turns up as the surname of a German merchant's family, of which Ulrich Fugger appeared to be the "Pater Familias". Fugger apparently describes a way to keep cats and caterpillars from your garden, by placing the head of a mare on a stake. According to a certain miller, Mister Gerritsen, it also repels the gnomes, but in other chapters we have seen that gnomes actually *love* the imitated forms of life, or are they simply disgusted that a mare would be beheaded in order to keep the garden free of caterpillars and cats? Do gnomes object against the senseless killing of living beings in order to keep your crops safe? It does not become clear from this entry, however fascinating it sounds.

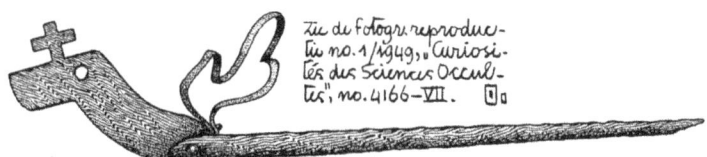

See the photographic reproduction no. 1/1949, "Curiosités des Sciences Occultes', no. 4166-VII. **O.**

Note 1949, fol. 5III: "Cockhorse", appearing on the print no. 39 (around 1797), concerning "gnomes". Lacking further details. The "Horses Head" are similar to the "christened horses heads", as rooftop signs appearing on "haystacks", and such, in Twente. **E.**

At Note 1939, fol. 3, addition no. IV: "Notes" by R.G. Meulenbelt about "Goblins" [East Netherlands]. Idem: [from German] "Book Illumination", sub II. **O.**

Eldermans is quite vague in this entry, although it appears the sketch on the left is illumination work from a book, a knight on a horse, and the connection with the horsehead ornaments from Losser seems apparent, but the connection with "gnomes" or "goblins" is not clear.

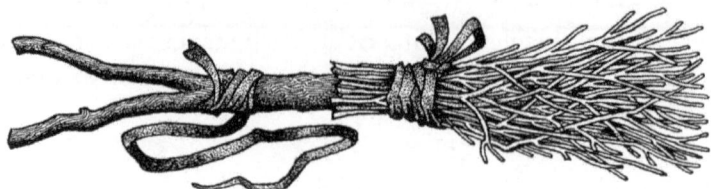

Bij Aanf. 1940, fol. 3 : „Den Beessem", &c.- [„Aardgeesten", sub IV, (1645)].

At Note 1940, fol. 3: "The Broom", &c.- ["nature spirits", sub IV, (1645)] **H**.

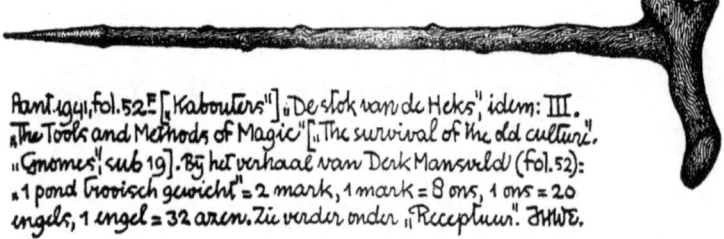

Aant. 1941, fol. 52F [„Kabouters"] „De stok van de Heks", idem: III. „The Tools and Methods of Magic" [„The survival of the old culture". „Gnomes", sub 19]. Bij het verhaal van Derk Mansveld (fol. 52): „1 pond Trooisch gewicht" = 2 mark, 1 mark = 8 ons, 1 ons = 20 engels, 1 engel = 32 azen. Zie verder onder „Recceptuur". JHWE.

Note 1941, fol. 52F ["Gnomes"] "The cane of the Witch", idem: III. "The Tools and Methods of Magic" ["The Survival of the old culture", "Gnomes", sub 19]. With the story of Derk Mansveld (fol. 52): "One pound Trooisch weight"= 2 mark, 1 mark = 8 ounces, 1 ounce = 20 engels, 1 engel = 32 azen. See further under "Recipes". JHWE.

Eldermans is using old Dutch weight measurements here. The 'aas' is a micro-weight which can vary from region to region. It is derived from the old Latin "as" which was both a coin and a weight measurement. In general, the Aas is equal to a milligram, although the Amsterdam Aas weighed 0.048 grams. One started measuring from a pound, which was equivalent to 16 ounces, which equalled 32 lood, 320 engels and resulting in 10240 Aas.[34] One engel was 32 azen. These

---

34. https://nl.wikipedia.org/wiki/Aas_(eenheid)

measurements were used in the recipes where Eldermans refers to in the notes of Derk Mansveld.

Bij Aant. 1957, fol. 6ᵈ, „Aardgeesten", naar mededelingen van „B.G.H.".

At Note 1957, fol. 6III, "Nature spirits", after gleanings of "B.G.H.".-

It is unknown how this relates to nature spirits, but the source certainly does: B.G.H. is none other than Bernard G. Hulsker, an herbalist Eldermans knew from his travels through Twente and whose observations were doubted by Eldermans more than once, although Eldermans did acknowledge that Hulsker might have been on to 'something'. For more information on Bernard Hulsker, I direct you back to the previous chapter, where his case is discussed in detail.

[Below]: At Note 1939, fol. 11, in clarification. See also documentation §8-HH/1939, "The trail of the nature spirits", G.J. ten Bruggecate. **H.**

See also fol. 11III: "Plagiarism", &c.= "The Apostle Thomas exorcises demons. Lektionar Limoges, 10th century.- **E.**

By Aant. 1939, fol. 11, ter verduidelijking. Zie ook de documentatie §Q-HH/1939, "Het spoor der aardgeesten", G.J. ten Bruggecate.
Zie ook fol. 11ᵛᴵ, "Plagiaat", &c. = "Der Apostel Thomas bannt Dämonen. Fiktionar himoges, 10.Th." –

By Aant. 1957, fol. 399ᴵᴵ; idem: documentatie §122-DD/1957, "Aardgeesten", &c. –

At Note 1957, fol. 399II; idem: documentation §122-DD/1957, "nature spirits", &c.- E.

By Index 1939, no. 19, "Aardgeesten", &c. Mededelingen van Adriana van der Helm. – By de foto, bijlage II: "The continuous knot in the form of a horizontal figure eight represents infinity: magical knot inscribed with the name of Pharaoh Tuthmosis III, dated c. 1450 B.C." – Zie no. 19B: – – – – – →

At Index 1939, no. 19, "nature spirits" &c. Gleanings of Adriana van der Helm.- At the photograph, appendix II: "The continuous knot in the form of a horizontal figure eight represents infinity: magical knot inscribed with the name of Pharaoh Tuthmosis III, dated c. 1450 B.C."= See no. 19B: —→

Again, we see Eldermans combining data from various sources. Although it is categorized as Index 1939, the information in English is certainly from the 1970's, as it is a citation from the Encyclopedia of Magic & Superstition (London, 1974), which can be found on page 39. The photograph in appendix II should come from this book. It is not related in any way to "gnomes" or "nature spirits" but rather to the use of string, in magic:

> *String possesses symbolic qualities closely akin to those of thread. It represents the line of continuity and is used when making a magic circle, and to bind individuals with unbreakable spells. As a medical amulet it is said to afford protection against sterility and death.[35]*

By Index 1946, no.54 in de documentatie §41-MM/1946,"Aardgeesten",&c.. De bovenstaande "strik", omschreven door "Mans Reuvekamp" (zie Aant.1946, fol.61II), komt ook voor op de kopergravure, Sammlung Schmidtke, cat.1912, no.S-29-VI.

At Index 1946, no. 54 and the documentation §41-MM/1946, "nature spirits", &c.. The upper "noose" described by "Mans Reuvekamp" (see Note 1946, fol. 61II), also appears on the copperplate, Sammlung Schmidtke, catalogue 1912, no. S-29-VI. **O.**

---

35. N.N. *Encyclopedia of Magic & Superstition*, London, 1974, pp 39

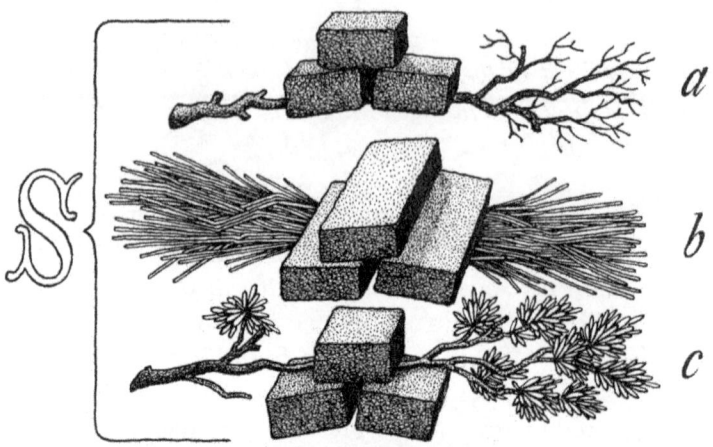

a

b

c

By Index 1940, no. 4, „The Tools and Methods of Magic" c. II, p. 291: ter vergelijking bij de mededelingen van Johan Plechelmus Belterman : zie Aant. 1940, fol. 345½. [„Magische Receptuur", nrs. 14, 19 en 22.] Zie Ms. no. 19 = 1654, „Aard-geesten", „Over een dwaas bijgeloof", Ds. A.J. van der Helm. — H.

At Index 1940, no. 4, "The Tools and Methods of Magic", c. II, p. 291: in comparison of the gleanings by Johan Plechelmus Belterman: see Note 1940, fol. 345I ["Magic recipes", numbers 14, 19 and 22]. See Manuscripts no. 19 = 1654, "nature spirits", "about a foolish superstition", reverend A.J. van der Helm.- **H.**

Again, *The Tools and Methods of Magic* are mentioned in one of Eldermans' entries but none of the depicted branches, or straw with three stones, are in this chapter. The reference to page 291 is again mysterious, as the *Encyclopedia of Magic & Superstition* barely has only two hundred and fifty pages. It is not clear what Eldermans found in *The Tools and Methods of Magic*, which relates to the gleanings of Belterman or the foolish superstition of Van der Helm…

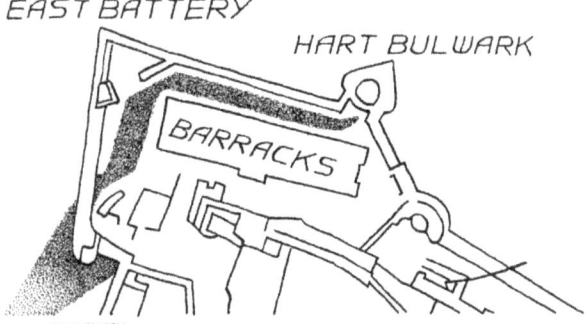

EAST BATTERY

HART BULWARK

BARRACKS

= „Het Terrein waar de kleine wezens, vermoedelijk aardgeesten, werden gezien, zulks in de jaren 1911- 1913, veelal in de schemerige uren van de vroege morgen", &c., (Richard Topley, zie Aant. 1949, fol. 459 F, sub III.   H.

[coloured box] = *"The Terrain where the small beings, presumably nature spirits, were seen, such during the years 1911-1913, mostly during the hours of dusk in the early morning", &c., (Richard Topley, see Note 1949, fol. 459F, sub III.* **H.**

This appears to be a floorplan of Castle Cornet in St. Peter's Port in Guernsey. See the photograph below:

Cornet Castle on Guernsey. The structure below right appears to be what Eldermans sketched. (Photograph Museums.gov)

Once again, there is no known folklore mentioning gnomes or fairies in the Bulwark of Cornet Castle on Guernsey. Although Eldermans said the locals didn't discuss their beliefs in gnomes with 'outsiders', it doesn't take away the feeling that he is inventing tradition here. Why would they tell us about the fairy invasion from the fourteenth century, but nothing about the gnomes seen there today?

• Ian Ballantine …..,,Kabouters staan met hun manier van leven en werken model voor een maatschappij waarin de Amerikaanse jeugd van vandaag gelooft"...

dere verstandige onderaardse wezens.

Van Poortvliet's Kabouters heeft hij in Amerika al 1,2 miljoen exemplaren verkocht. Om met de Nederlandse verkoop te kunnen wedijveren zouden er echter 8 miljoen exemplaren moeten worden verspreid. Ian ziet geen enkele reden om zich daar zorgen over te maken.

Talenten

,,Kabouters staan met hun manier van leven en werken model voor een maatschappij waarin de jongeren van vandaag geloven. De kleine wezens hebben vele talenten die ze niet alleen willen gebruiken voor commerciële doeleinden. Ze weven, bakken potten, bewerken metaal en hout, genezen door middel van planten, kruiden en acupunctuur. Ze zijn lief voor dieren en wonen gezellig in weinig energie verspillende huisjes onder de grond".

Wat de kabouters ons leren is volgens Ian de harde werkelijkheid van de toekomst. ,,Daarom gelooft de Amerikaanse college-jeugd in kabouters. Ze gebruikt haar hersens en fantasie op zeer doeltreffende wijze. De eenvoudige en werkelijk belangrijke waarden in het leven wil ze in ere herstellen".

Hoewel Ian moeilijk tot de Amerikaanse jongeren gerekend kan worden hebben de kabouters op hem ook een grote aantrekkingskracht. ,,Omdat ze zo uitgebalanceerd zijn, niet alleen als individu maar ook hun totale cultuur".

Kabouters leren ons harde werkelijkheid van de toekomst

door Madeleine Boerma

BUSSUM, vrijdag
Het Kabouterboek van onze tekenaar Rien Poortvliet maakt meer indruk op de Amerikaanse jongeren dan de energietoespraken van president Carter, de lange rijen wachtenden voor benzinepompen of een dreigende verhoging van de energieprijzen.

Dit is de mening van de kleine 63-jarige Ian Ballantine, die met z'n iets voorovergebogen houding en ondeugend pret-gezicht zo uit het Kabouterboek lijkt weggelopen. Als adviseur van een Amerikaanse uitgeverij die hij eens zelf oprichtte reist Ian de wereld rond op zoek naar kabouters en an-

Aanvulling VII [24-8-1979] bij Index 1956, no.472-B, ,,Kabouters", &c, E ¤

Addition VII [24 August 1979] at Index 1956, no. 472-B, "Gnomes", &c. **E.**

A Newspaper clipping, from the newspaper *Telegraaf*, published on page 5 in between articles of protest against the Dutch government concerning choices in traffic and social services, is the article about Ian Ballantine and his view on gnomes. The Article is mostly about Rien Poortvliet's *the Gnome* (1976). Here is a translation:

[Next to the picture] *Ian Ballantine ….,, The way of life of gnomes is a model for a society in which the American youth believes"…*

Gnomes teach us the harsh reality of the future by Madeleine Boerma.

Bussum, Friday. The Gnomebook by our artist Rien Poortvliet impresses the American youth better than the addresses to energy by President Carter, the long rows of people waiting at the gas station or the imminent raise of the energy-prices.

This is the opinion of the small, 63-year-old Ian Ballantine, who appears to have walked away from a gnome-book with his bent-over posture and mischievous fun-face. As an advisor to an American publishing company which he founded himself, and travels the world in search for gnomes and other subterranean beings.

Of Poortvliet's Gnomes he sold 1,2 million copies in America. To compete with the Dutch sales, he should spread 8 million copies. Ian sees no reason to worry himself with that.

Talents. "The society of gnomes, their lives and works, is a model for a society that the youth believe in. The small creatures have many talents which they don't want to use for commerce alone. They weave, bake pottery, work metals and wood, heal through the means of herbs and acupuncture. They are kind to animals and live cosily in a little-energy spending abode under the ground".

What the gnomes can teach us according to Ian is the harsh reality of the future. "That is why the American college-youth believes in gnomes. They use their brains and imagination in a very effective way. The simple and really important values in life should be restored".

It is hard to count Ian in with the American youth, but gnomes have a great attraction to him. "Because they are so balanced, not only as an individual, but in their entire culture".

The grim future portrayed in this article did not, in hindsight, come true, although there is a need for alternative energy sources nearly forty years on from when this newspaper article was published. There is a big lobby for clean energy sources, such as wind, water and solar energy but there are also many people opposed to the way these types of energy are generated, as these mostly demand methods which change the look of our horizon completely. Large wind-turbines are seen in various landscapes which people consider "ugly", or large fields of solar panels which spoil our sights of the green pastures. The gnomes might well have applauded these forms of energy generation - they don't fill the atmosphere with carbon dioxide and help to counter global warming. Perhaps, we need to have acceptance of the situation, as it helps to meet our energy-demands but obviously, we do not know how people will look back on these alternative energy sources in, say, a hundred years.

GNOMES: add to §7, Note 1940, sub 122-IV: fig. 2 to 8 ["The plant in folk life"= F2, 1916] E.
At §2, Note 1940, sub 126-IV, [From French: "Mythology of plants", p. 89, fig. 61]. **E.**

The Plant in Folk Life appears to be an article by B.P. van der Voo, originally published in 1902 in the Dutch guide to Language and literary science. The same author also published an article about magic plants in *De Tijdspiegel*, in which he describes the four-leaf clover as a plant that allows you to *see dwarfs and elves and to distinguish witches in church.*[36] It is not strange that Eldermans refers to this particular author. *La Mythologie des Plantes* by Angelo de Gubernatis was published in Paris in 1882 but in this book, there is no mention of fairies, gnomes or other little people.

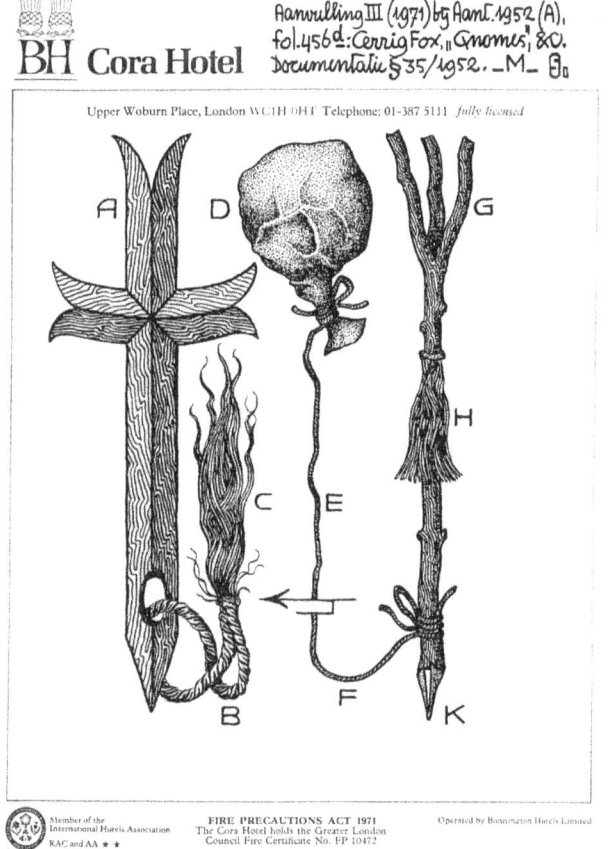

Addition III (1971) at Note 1952 (A), fol. 456d: Cerrig Fox, "Gnomes", &c. Documentation §35/1952. _M_ S.

---

36. B.P. van der Voo, *Tooverplanten. Een studie over vergelijkende mythologie*, in *De Tijdspiegel, editon 69*, 1912, pp 26

The Cora Hotel, formerly located at Upper Woburn Place in London, was an important destination of Eldermans and there are a number of sketches in his collection, which had been made on the headed, hotel paper itself. The Cora Hotel doesn't exist anymore, although the building must have been a sight to see:

> *The General design was adhered to and the five houses, comprising the Cora Hotel, in Upper Woburn Place show only minor variations. Here the order is Corinthian (known as the Tivoli order) with the centre house having four columns and the house on each side four pilasters. The windows on the first floor of the end houses have cornices on brackets, and the windows of the ground floor are arched.*[37]

The most important question remains as to whether Eldermans came to London to consult a collection in the British Library (apparently a collection at the British Museum, around that time), as a number of collections consisted of important occult scriptures (take the Collection Sloane, for example). It could indeed be possible that Eldermans went to London, with those collections in mind.

Zie onder Amgueddfa Genedlaethol Cymru (National Museum of Wales) no. XIV, by Rant 1952, A, fol. 45 B°. ("The Tools and Methods of Magic," c., Gnomen"). Index no. 174, 178, 219 en 278, [a gnome's nocturnal revels, 80:]. Idem:, The Elfin Oak, F6. Bo

---

37. http://www.british-history.ac.uk/survey-london/vol21/pt3/pp103-104

See under "Amgueddfa Genedlaethol Gymru (National Museum of Wales) no. XIV, at Note 1952, A, Fol. 458e. ("The Tools and Methods of Magic", c. "Gnomes"). Index numbers 171, 178, 219 and 278, ["Gnome's nocturnal revels", &c.]. Idem: "The Elfin Oak", F6. **E.**

Again, there is no mention in *The Tools and Methods of Magic* of gnomes, although there is a small entry about wands and staffs. The staff depicted above is not in the chapter. The Elfin Oak is in Kensington Gardens and is sculpted and painted to make it look as if gnomes are living in its bark. The tree is dead and caged to protect the artwork. It had been carved in 1911, by Ivor Innes. While staying at the Cora Hotel, it is quite possible that Eldermans would have visited the Elfin Oak and that in his collection, there would have been photographs of the carvings. In the current personal collections of family members of Eldermans, there are no photographs known of the Elfin Oak, which means that if there had been, they must have been destroyed after his passing.

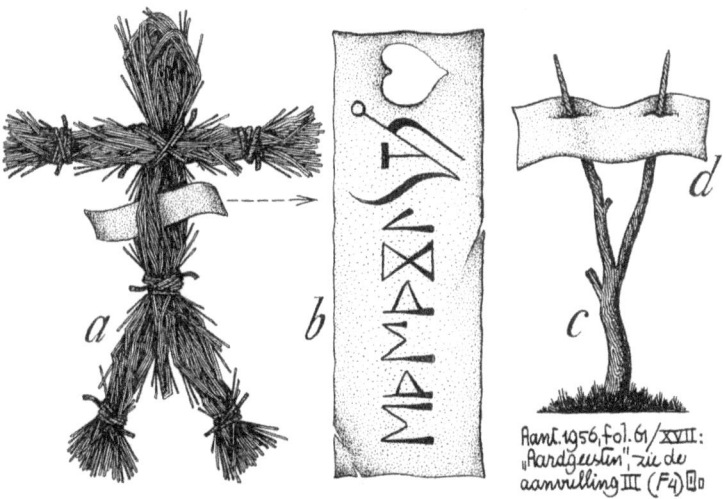

Note 1956, fol. 61/XVII: "Nature spirits", see the addition III (F4) **O.**

Aant. 1957, fol. 411d : De „schijf hout, opgehangen aan een nestel van schapenleer" [M.F. Heegemans, zie Fig. 7] heeft niets van doen met kabouters [Mr. G.J. ter Kuile Sen.], maar met het „afkloppen" van onheil op „ongekleurd (naturel) kops hout". JHWE.

Note 1957, fol. 411d: The "disk of wood" hung from a cord of sheep leather" [M.F. Heegemans, see figure 7] has nothing to do with gnomes [Mr. G.J. ter Kuile Senior] but with "knocking" on "uncoloured (natural) head wood" to ward off evil". JHWE.

[Below] Documentation §42/1952, date of the note: "14 August 1943" (swastika), detail "S"; see however: "The band bearing the inscription forms the cord from which the hammer hangs", Note 1952, fol. 144f, "Deceit", &c.- **H.**

Documentation §42/1952, F4: The connection with gnomes, and such, does not become clear. Hammarström lacks delivering any proof. "Fragments of parchment with runes"??- **S.**

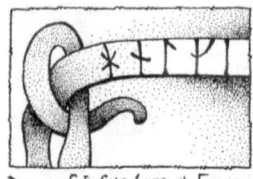

Documentatie § 42/1952, datum van de aantekening: „14-8-1943"(⊕), detail „S"; zie echter: „The band bearing the inscription forms the cord from which the hammer hangs", Aant. 1952, fol. 144ᶠ, „Bedrog", &c.—

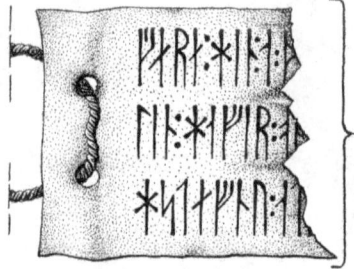

Documentatie §42/1952, F4: Het verband met kabouters, o.d., blijkt niet evident. Hammarström laat na enig bewijs te leveren. „Fragmenten perkament met runen"??.—

Apparently, Eldermans found some parchments and amulets which he suspected to be of national socialist origins. A hammer hanging from a cord might suggest it to be Thor's hammer *Mjölnir*, which is currently a popular symbol with neo-nazis. This was also adhered to by the German SS in the years 1933-1945. In the Wewelsburg museum's collection about the terror of the SS, there are a few examples of Thor's hammer worn as an amulet.

Thor's hammer used as a national socialist amulet. To the left we see two buttons depicting a Norwegian Drakkar, a viking dragon boat with Vikings standing at the bow. (Photograph Wilmar Taal)

Ter vergelijking bij §1C, Aant. 1955, sub 78-III, naar Bror Stjerna, eind 19e eeuw. Zie de „Mededelingen van mevr. Derkje Mulder – Vis" =)12. ⊟o

Bij §3, Aant. 1955, sub 80C-III, toevoegen: W. Jenkyn Thomas, The Welsh Fairy Book, London, 1907. ⊟o

In comparison with §1C, Note 1955, sub 78-III, after Bror Stjerna, end of the 19th century. See the "Gleanings of Mrs. Derkje Mulder – Vis"=)12. **S.**

At §3, Note 1955, sub 80C-III, add: W. Jenkyn Thomas, The Welsh Fairy Book, London, 1907. **E.**

Eldermans mentions Bror Stjerna, but Bror means brother in Swedish. There is a Bror Stjerna who lived in the United States as a Swedish immigrant. However, it could mean that Bror does indeed mean 'brother' and Eldermans thought this to be the first name of his 'witness'. *The Welsh Fairy Book* by William Jenkyn Thomas (1870-1959) is still available and can even be downloaded online.

Bij §4, Aant. 1958, sub 137d-III: „Ancient Legends of Ireland" (1887) is geschreven door Jane Francesca Wilde, zich vaak noemend „Spiranza", echtgenote van sir William, oudheidkundige, oorspecialist en publicist, de moeder van Oscar Wilde". Zie nader:)E. **E.**

At §4, Note 1958, sub 137d: "Ancient Legends of Ireland" (1887) is written by Jane Francesca Wilde, who called herself "Spiranza", wife of Sir William, historian, ear specialist and publicist, the mother of Oscar Wilde". See more:)7. **E.**

ARABITA

Bij Aant. 1948, fol. 42E [„Aardgeesten", &c..]: „Aanwezig dienen te zijn drie messen: één met een punt en een wit handvat, één in de vorm van een antieke dolk, en één met een zwart handvat waarvan het lemmer de vorm van een zeis heeft." Zie de documentatie §17-S/1948 [mij. Pie van der Vaart]: „Kabouters". **E.**
Idem: „Figures des instruments de l'Art", „Faucille", zie Aant. 1948, fol. 43B. **H.**

At Note 1948, fol. 42E ["Nature spirits", &c..]: "Three knives need to be present: one with a point and a white hilt, one in the shape of an antique dagger and one with a black hilt, of which the blade is shaped as a scythe". See documentation §17-S/1948 [miss Pie van der Vaart]: "Gnomes". **E.**
Idem: "Figures des instruments de l'Art", "Faucille", see Note 1948, fol. 43B. **H.**

This entry originates from *The Greater Key of Solomon* - the preparation of the sword. These symbols and the word *Arabita* need to be engraved on the blade at six o'clock in the morning using the piercer of 'The Art'. The *Figures des instruments de l'Art* is also from the same book -

Faucille represents the scythe-shaped blade.[38] According to the text in *The Greater Key of Solomon*, this has nothing to do with gnomes.

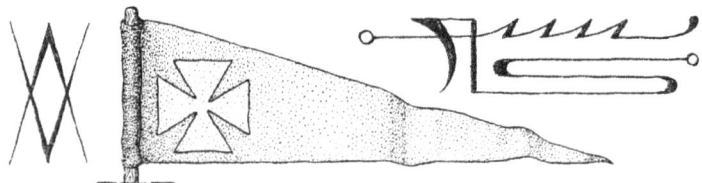

Bÿ Aanf.1948,fol.44ᴮ in documentatie §18-w/1948 [„Gnomes"].

At Note 1948,, fol. 44B and documentation §18-w/1948 ["Gnomes"].

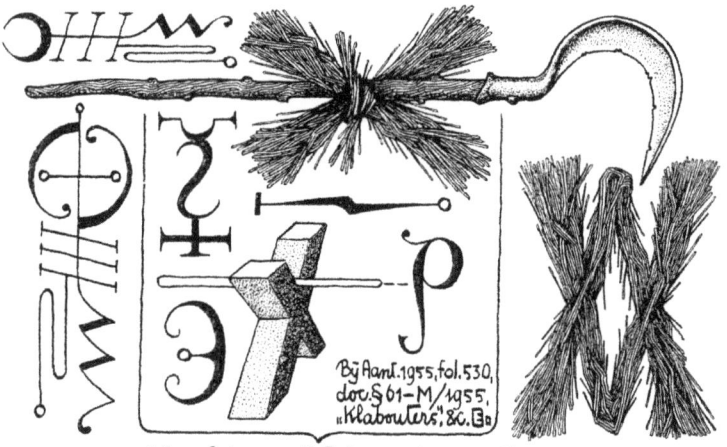

Bÿ Aanf.1955,fol.530, doc.§61-M/1955, „Klabouters". &c.Eⁿ

Zie Aanf.1955,fol.531ᶜ, documentatie §62-R/1955, Société des Traditions Populaires, IX- p.615, „Gnomes", &c. — Collectie M.F.Molenaar, fol.531ᶜ, F6. Bⁿ

At Note 1955, fol. 530, documentation §61-M/1955, "Gnomes", &c. **E.**

See Note 1955, fol. 531C, documentation §62-R/1955, Société des Traditions Populaires, IX- p. 615, "Gnomes", &c.- Collection M.F. Molenaar, fol. 531C, F6. **S.**

---

38. Rabbi Salomon, De Sleutels van Salomo, Amsterdam, 1954, pp 26-27

Here we have another example of Eldermans combining various magical traditions. The pentacles appear to come from ceremonial magic but the crossed straw sheaves appear to originate from folk magic from the Twente region. In this entry, Eldermans uses an older Dutch word for gnomes: klabouters, which has an additional letter 'L' in the word, instead of kabouter. The version with the additional L was popular in the Southern part of The Netherlands, next to Alverman or Hetseman. The name also appeared in Twente and De Veluwe, but not as frequently as in De Peel.

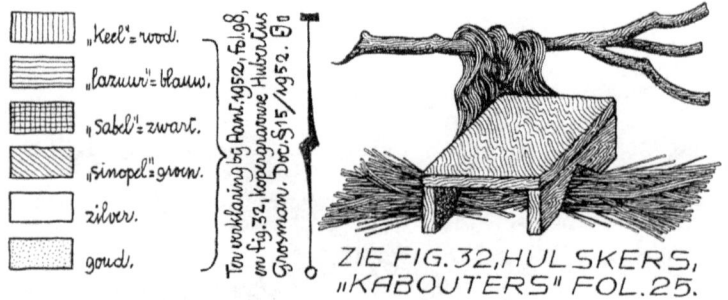

ZIE FIG. 32, HULSKERS, "KABOUTERS" FOL. 25.

In clarification at Note 1952, fol. 98 and fig. 32, copperplate Hubertus Grosman. Documentation §15/1952. **S.**
See figure 32, Hulskers, "Gnomes", fol. 25.

Next to the drawing, we see a key of six boxes with various shadings, which refer to *colours*. We see, "Keel" which equals *red*. "Lazuur" is *blue*. "Sabel" is *black*. "Sinopel" is *green*. The final two are *silver* and *gold*. What these boxes actually refer to, is unknown. The depiction is about folk magic concerning gnomes: the three-twigged branch, the strand of hair and the sheaf of straw under the table, which appears to *repel* gnomes.

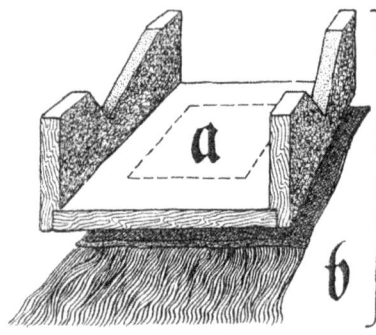

At Note 1952, fol. 103F: documentation §29-m/1952.- "A History of Witchcraft: Gnomes. III"- Add to F4: Henry Hubert, "The rise of the Celts"- London, 1934. (see H-no. 188) **H.**
At F5: "The ancients credited the Druids with metaphysical speculations, of which all trace has vanished. I should say, rather, that the Druids - judges, physicians, directors of consciences, and poets as they were – were moral observers and psychologists". **E.**
"The Tools and Methods of Magic"= c. VII, p. 568, fig. 209, anno 1665. **H.**

How the sketch relates to the text, is unclear. Although the text relates more to the purported magic of the Druids (a stance which is being challenged more and more in recent years and which, surprisingly, is supported by Eldermans), there appears to be no relationship with the wooden object seen in the depiction.

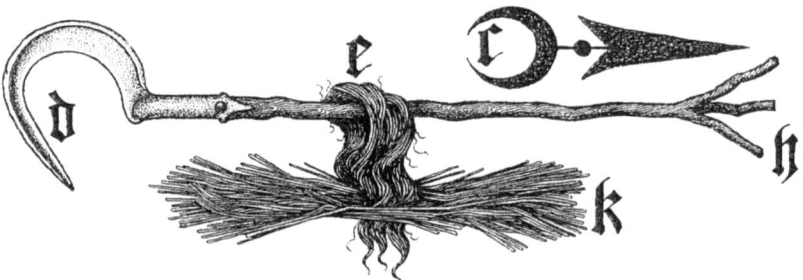

At Note 1952, fol. 109d, documentation §35-VI/1953, "Gnomes".- The copperplate anno 1722 is property of mrs. W. Hofmans – Sanders; see the photographic reproduction no. 48/1952.- At fol. 109d, f3: "Horned God on the Gundestrup Cauldron, elevating the Torque (Mémoires de la Soc. Des Antiquaires de France, 1913". **E.**

The name of the owner of the copperplate, is suspect. Her surname is contrived out of two people who had notably made an impression on Eldermans: Greet Hofmans and Maxine Sanders. Greet Hofmans was a psychic who had some influence over Queen Juliana of The Netherlands and which led to what is called the Hofmans-affair, as the Dutch government and Prince Bernard were opposed to the psychic and her influence over state affairs. Maxine Sanders is the wife of Alex Sanders, the so-called *King of the Witches*. How all of this relates to the Gundestrup Cauldron is unclear, although Cernunnos is certainly seen lifting a torque.

Bij §2b, Aanf. 1960, sub 126-III, F2: „In de brief van de apostel Paulus aan de Filippenzen 2:10 is sprake van ,..... dergenen die in de hemel en die op de aarde en die onder de aarde zijn;" zie)2. 🅐₀

Bij §2c: „Filippenzen, (II-11): .... opdat op het hooren van den naam van Jezus de knieën gebogen worden van alwie in de hemelen, op de aarde en onder de aarde zijn, &c." – 🅑₀

At §2b, Note 1960, sub 126-III, F2: "In the letter of the apostle Paul to the Phillipians 2:10 it has been said: "…. Those who are in heaven and on the earth and those who are under the earth", see)2. **A.**

At §2C: Phillipians, (II-11): …. So that upon hearing the name of Jesus the knees are bent of all who are in the heavens, on earth and under the earth, &c.".- **E.**

This entry originates from the book of Martin Koomen, concerning the letter of the apostle Paul to the Phillippians, written on page 27. Especially in the Irish fairy tradition, this phrase from the Bible was important. As Koomen himself writes: *It doesn't come as a surprise that this phrase has been used in gratitude in the Irish fairy-themes*[39]. Eldermans noted it down and looked up the original citation in the Bible and compared it to the version presented by Koomen. There seemed to be a slight difference.

Toevoegen aan §3ᵉ, Aant. 1960, sub 130-III, de „Mededelingen van mevr. H. R. Hamersveld–Riemersma", bijlage no. 2. Bij F3: „de kleur is groen". E₀

Add to §3I, Note 1960, sub 130-III, the "Gleanings of Mrs. H.R. Hamersveld – Riemersma", appendix no. 2. At F3: "The colour is green". **S.**

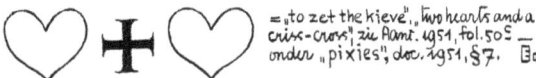

= „to zet the kieve", two hearts and a criss-cross", zie Aant. 1951, fol. 50ᶜ — onder „pixies", doc. 1951, §7. E₀

= "to zet the kieve", "two hearts and a criss-cross", see Note 1951, fol. 50C- under "pixies", documentation 1951, §7. **E.**

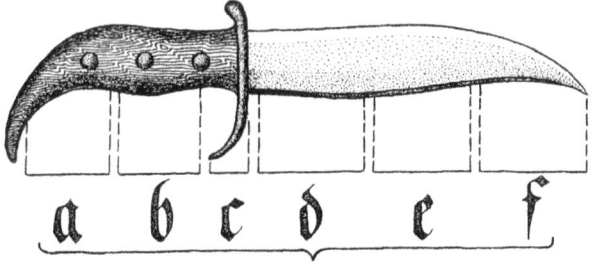

Bij Aant. 1955, fol. 288ᵃ: zie „Athame" (arthame), The magic knife described in The Key of Solomon and other magical textbooks, used for drawing the magic circle", &c.. Documentatie §42-III/1955, „Gnomes"; „de plaatsing van de symbolen". Naar het genoemde handschrift in het bezit van mevr. S.F. Hubert–Van Galen. H₀

---

39. Martin Koomen, *Het Koninkrijk van de nacht. Over dwergen, elfen en andere geesten van aarde, lucht, water en vuur*, Amsterdam, 1978, pp 27

At Note 1955, fol. 288H: see "Athame"(arthame), "The magic knife described in the Key of Solomon and other magical textbooks, used for drawing the magic circle", &c.. Documentation §42-III/1955, "Gnomes"; "The placement of the symbols". After the mentioned handwriting, property of Mrs. S.F. Hubert- van Galen. **H.**

This entry comes from the *Encyclopedia of Magic & Superstition*, to be exact, from the chapter *Glossary of Magical Lore* (pp 229), but the citation is not complete, it continues on in the book:

> *[...] as used by modern witches, it has a black handle and magic symbols on its blade.*[40]

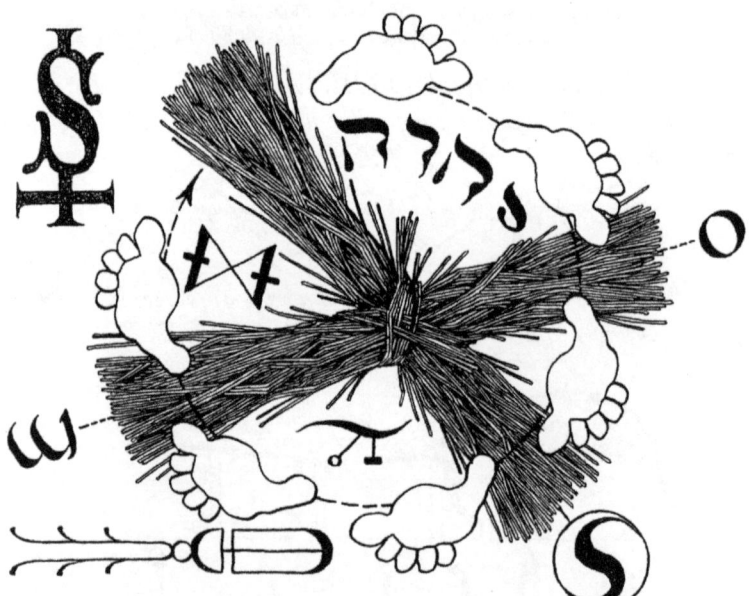

40. N.N. *Encyclopedia of Magic & Superstition*, London, 1974, pp 229

At Note 1955, fol. 288K, "The ritual according to Mrs. Selly F. Hubert-van Galen", &c., see documentation §42-III/1955 ["Gnomes"= fol. 289] "The Unlocked Secret", see F4. Add to F5: J.A. Macculloch, "The Harrowing of Hell", Clark, Edinburgh, 1930.- [As promised the names belonging to the initials "H.v.d.V.", "M.B.", "H.B.W." and "J.K." are not mentioned. JHWE.] **S.**

Here again, we see a mixture of folk magic and ceremonial magic: the sheaf of straw is placed in an East-West direction but the symbols around it are from various magical texts: *The Greater Key of Solomon, the Petit Albert* and the Cabbalah (Tetragrammaton). In what way Mrs. Hubert-van Galen might have 'invented' this ritual, or whether Eldermans constructed this and attributed it to her, is uncertain.

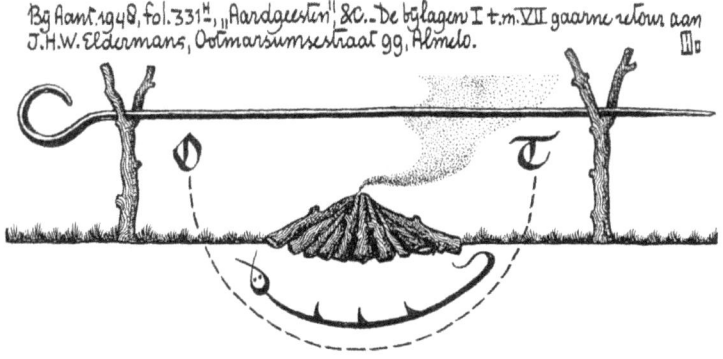

At Note 1948, fol. 331H, "nature spirits", &c.- The appendices I to VII please return to J.H.W. Eldermans, Ootmarsumsestraat 99, Almelo. **H.**

Most of this manuscript was constructed during Eldermans' retirement whilst living in The Hague. Why he would refer during those years, to his time in Almelo, might be explained by Eldermans inventing a gnome tradition in The Netherlands. One could say he copied this from older notes but why maintain an address that you haven't lived at for more than twenty-five years?

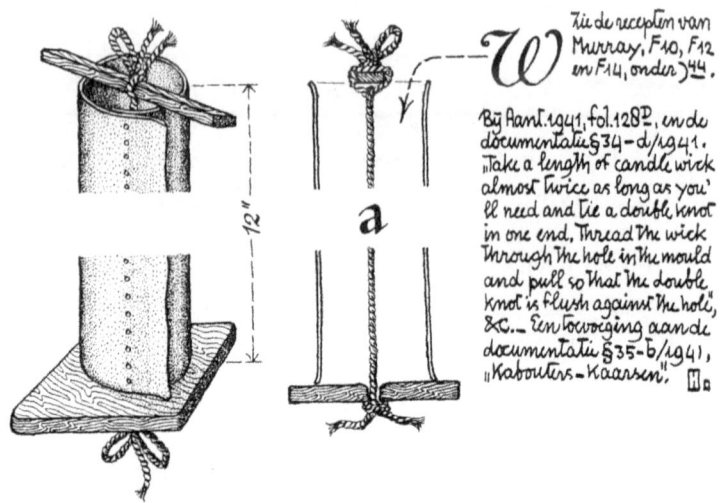

W See the recipes of Murray, F10, F12 and F14 under)44. At Note 1941, fol. 128D, and the documentation §34-d/1941. "Take a length of candle wick almost twice as long as you'll need and tie a double knot in one end. Thread the wick through the hole in the mould and pul,l so that the double knot is flush against the hole", &c.- An addition to the documentation §35-b/1941, "Gnomes-candles". **H.**

At Note 1942, fol. 43E: [Legends, Traditions, Coutumes et Contes du Pays", see F IX]. "Outstanding similarities and undeterminable differences", see §9/1942. **H.**

The title in French is incomplete, it is a book by Zacharie le Rouzic from 1939 and is about Carnac, a town in Brittany, France where enormous rows of standing stones are to be found, stretching over more than a mile. How this relates to the depiction, with the cane and broom and the strange West-East situated, gnome monogram, is unclear. There isn't much known about the alignments of Carnac in regards to gnome folklore.

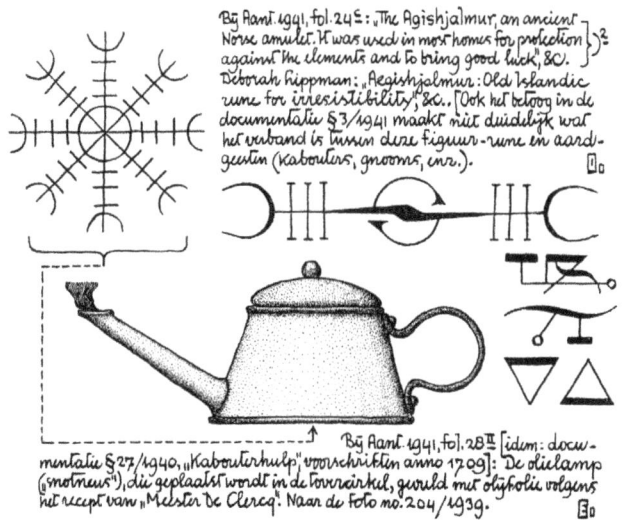

Gnomes, etc… A title page from Eldermans' work.

At Note 1941, fol. 24C: "The Agishjalmur, an ancient Norse amulet. It was used in most homes for protection against the elements and to bring good luck", &c.)2

Deborah Lippman: "Aegishjalmur: Old Islandic rune for irresistibility"&c.. [Also, the argument in the documentation §3/1941 does not make clear what the connection is between this figure-rune and nature spirits (gnomes, goblins, etc.). **O.**

At Note 1941, fol. 28II [Idem: documentation §27/1940, "Gnome help", prescriptions anno 1709]: The oil lamp (snot nose), which is placed in the magic circle, is filled with olive oil according to the recipe of "Master De Clercq". After the photo no. 204/1939. **E.**

Aegishjalmur, the so-called Helm of Awe, used by the dragon Fafnir in the Poetic Edda in the poem *Fáfnismál* - it is in the 30th stanza of the Dutch translation, where it is mentioned as the 'Helm of Terror'.[41] It is not a physical helmet, as some have believed, where the eight prongs pointing in every direction protect the wearer from evil intent, from all directions. And even Eldermans acknowledges that the connection between this symbol and gnomes is unclear, although it could provide protection from *malignant* gnomes. According to the sketch, the symbol needs to be engraved on the bottom of the oil lamp, which isn't advised in *The Greater Key of Solomon*. Eldermans is, apparently, experimenting again with various magical traditions.

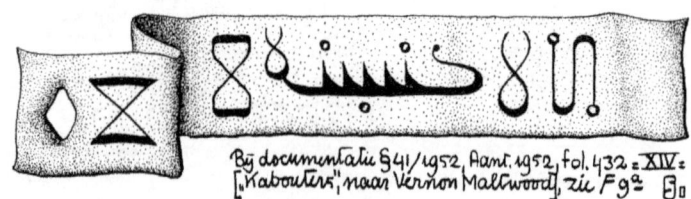

Bij documentatie §41/1952, Aant. 1952, fol. 432 = XIV= ["Kabouters", naar Vernon Maltwood], zie F9a S.

At Documentation §41/1952, Note 1952, fol. 432 = XIV= ["Gnomes", after Vernon Maltwood], see F9a **S.**

---

41. Jan de Vries (transl.) *Edda. Goden- en Heldenliederen uit de Germaanse oudheid*, Deventer, 1978, p. 201

Here we have a pentacle having something to do with gnomes - the serpent is a good indication. Although attributed to Vernon Maltwood, I can't find any reference to him, apart from a Katherine Maltwood but not to someone called 'Vernon'.

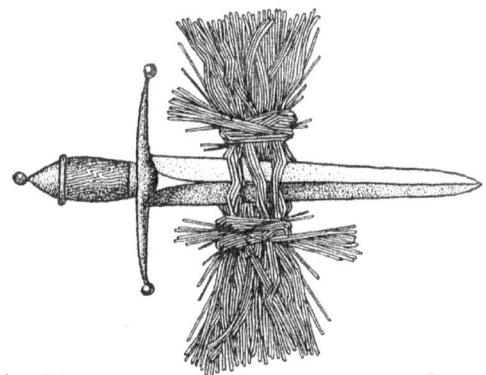

By Aant.1951,fol.207ᴮ [„Witchcraft",&c.,cap.„Gnomes"(ao.1921),fig.37(T.H.),F4]

At Note 1951, fol. 207B ["Witchcraft", &c., cap. "Gnomes" (anno 1921), fig. 37 (T.H.), F4] **H**.

A dagger or athame through a knotted sheaf of straw, referring to witchcraft *and* gnomes, but the interesting part is the initials T.H., which stands for Titia Hoogendoorn, a witch born in Pendang, Indonesia but who lived in The Hague. Strangely enough, there is no record for a Titia Hoogendoorn born in Pendang, in August 1948. However, there might be an explanation: Titia Hoogendoorn could be a pseudonym for someone else but looking for this, is like looking for a needle in a haystack.

By Aant.1951.fol.204ᵘ
F2:15e eeuw. Zie de
documentatie§40•
S/1951,„Gnomes",
naar Sellman.

At Note 1951, fol. 204H F2: 15th Century. See the documentation §40-S/1951, "Gnomes", after Sellman. **H.**

On this, we see a type of gothic lettering, dating back to the fifteenth century, which apparently has something to do with gnomes according to a certain Sellman. What did Eldermans mean by this, why did he include this in his works? Although I have been able to solve some of his mysterious entries, the ones I can't solve are the frustrating ones. I continue to have hope that some of Elderman's work is still out there, which might shine a light on these small, mysterious entries in his manuscript.

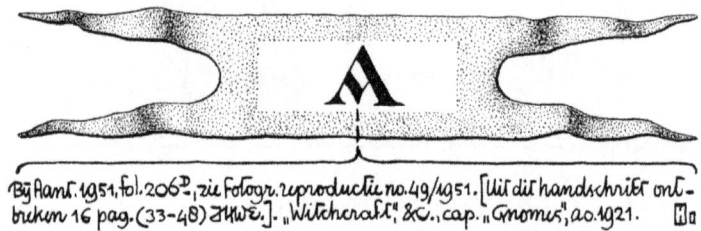

Bij Aanf. 1951, fol. 206ᴮ, zie Fotogr. reproductie no. 49/1951. [Uit dit handschrift ontbreken 16 pag. (33-48) JHWE.]. „Witchcraft", &c., cap. „Gnomes", a.o. 1921.

At Note 1951, fol. 206D, see photographic reproduction no. 49/1951. [From this handwriting 16 pages are missing. (33-48) JHWE.]. "Witchcraft", &c., cap. "Gnomes", anno 1921. H.

On the spot where we see the letter A, a pentacle needs to be drawn, which can, apparently, be found in a photograph. More intriguing, is the mentioning of a handwriting in which sixteen pages are missing, and looking at the numbers, I get the impression that these pages are missing from the Gnome manuscript. Eldermans numbered the pages from 1-33, and then occasionally, a page number turns up but according to this, it might be rewarding to start looking for page 48 - it might turn out to be another invention of tradition... Eldermans creating the handwriting in which sixteen pages are missing...

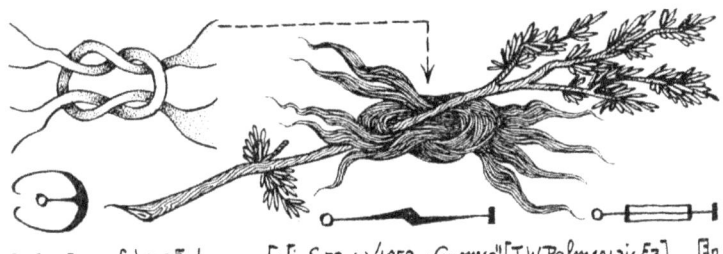

By Aant.1952, fol.172E, documentatie §52-w/1952, "Gnomes" [J.W.Palmer, zie F3]. E

At Note 1952, fol. 172F, documentation §52-w/1952, "Gnomes" [J.W. Palmer, see F3]. **E**.

The strands of hair are tied like the unending knot around a branch, cleared of twigs so the knot could be applied. There are three symbols which appear to come from one of the Grimoires that Eldermans knew about. This entry appears to, again, combine ceremonial magic with natural or folk magic. But to what end? Who is J.W. Palmer? Of course, there are plenty of 'Palmers' in the world but none of the ones I could find, do not appear to have anything to do with gnomes.

[Below] *At Note 1949, fol. 483E: "Magic and gnomes", see documentation §51-II/1949; idem §21/1941: "The Old European Tradition of Ceremonial Magic", cap IV, P. 609.- ["Sammlung für deutsche Volkskunde", Otto Schmidtke, catalogue 1912, no. 420-p.- Add to fol. 483E, F1: "The names, depictions, metals and colours which belong to the various planets", see the photographic reproduction no. 37/1949*. **E**.

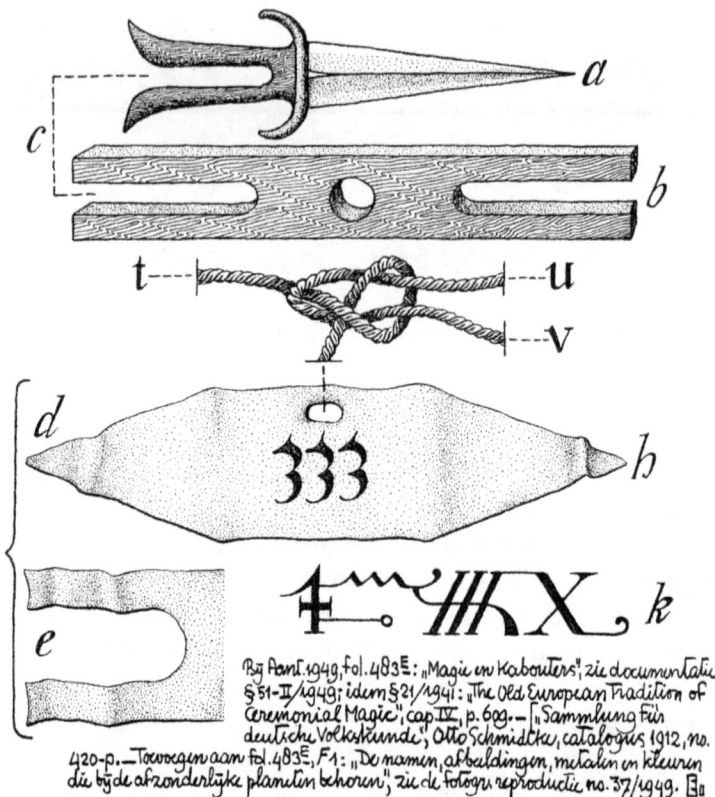

Bij Aant.1949, fol.483ᴱ: „Magie en Kabouters", zie documentatie §81-II/1949; idem §21/1941: „The Old European Tradition of Ceremonial Magic", cap.IX, p.609. — „Sammlung für deutsche Volkskunde", Otto Schmidtke, catalogus 1912, no. 420-p. — Toevoegen aan fol.483ᴱ, F1: „De namen, afbeeldingen, metalen en kleuren die bij de afzonderlijke planeten behoren", zie de fotogr. reproductie no. 37/1949. Bo

Here is a small indication that Eldermans means by *Sammlung Schmidtke* the same as the *Sammlung für deutsche Volkskunde* (Collection of German folklore), which we have seen to be non-existent, as it didn't turn up in the list of the collection of H.M. Montauban van Swijndregt, who apparently sold it to Eldermans in 1929 or 1939, according to Bob Richel. In the papers of Bob Richel, we do find some more information on H.M. Montauban van Swijndregt - he should have been a member of a Rosicrucian Society in Rotterdam and Bob found the home address of Montauban van Swijndregt. These claims, however, could not be verified, and as Montauban van Swijndregt was quite a religious man, membership of the Rosicrucians might have been in conflict with his personal faith. The final list of his collection did not reveal any works concerning folklore, in whatever shape or form. These two collections being one and the same, does shed a new light on the works of Eldermans. There is a certain 'invention of tradition' going on, which I will return to in the final chapter of this book.

[Below] *At Note 1953, fol. 16B ["Various objects"- "There are many examples of similar imitations", &c.- See under "Gnomes"] W. Déchelette, "Gnomes. VI".*

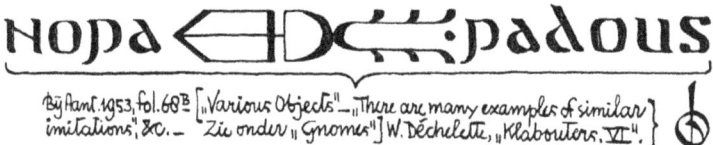

I was able to find a *Manuel* Déchelette who wrote about prehistoric Europe, but not a W. Déchelette. I suspect Eldermans could have made a mistake, as Manuel Déchelette did not write about gnomes. Eldermans did, however, make a connection between Little People and prehistoric monuments based on a drawing in the *Encyclopedia of Magic & Superstition*. It is speculation at best, but it could be the connection between this name and the entry...

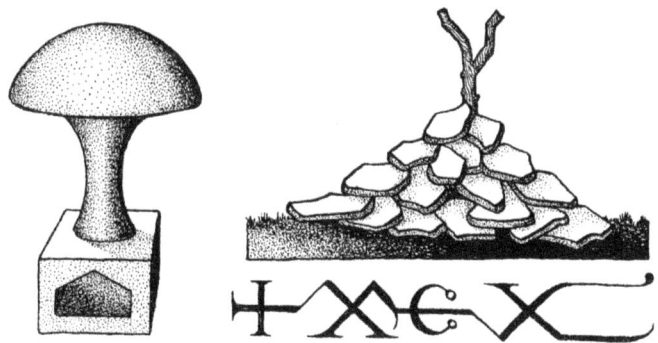

Documentation §22/1942, and Note 1942, fol. 192e: ["The magical reputation of Ammonita muscaria probably arises from its hallucinogenic properties", &c.. See the "addition XIV" at Note 1942, fol. 251 ("Nature spirits"). **H.**

Amanita muscaria is the Linnaean genus and family name for the *fly agaric*, a toadstool which, in The Netherlands, is often connected to gnomes, not as much as a means to see them, but more as the house of a gnome, or something they love to sit on. The red toadstool with white dots, grows towards the end of summer into the autumn and is also said to have been used by witches to make witch's ointment. The hallucinogenic properties of the fly agaric might have been the source of stories about witches who thought they were flying. In ancient shamanic cultures, the fly agaric was very important, such that one a toadstool was worth an entire reindeer! The toxicity of the fly agaric is actually quite overrated. The toadstool isn't poisonous enough to kill you, or even make you sick but it can produce some strange effects. In The Netherlands, the species is protected, which means it may not be damaged, picked or harvested in any way. It is my fair guess that it isn't because the species is endangered (I have no trouble finding fly agarics in the woods during the autumn) but more because it could be used as a cheap substitute for drugs, causing it to become endangered, after all. Harvesting fly agarics can result in a substantial fine, if an offender is caught.

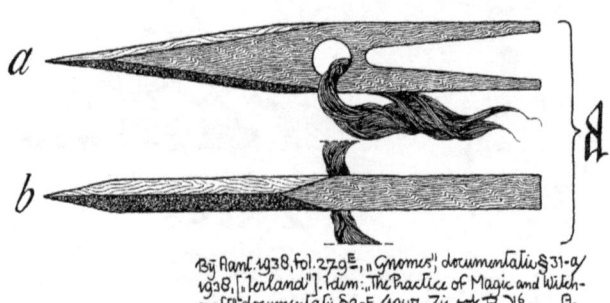

By Aant. 1938, fol. 279ᵉ, „Gnomes", documentatie § 31-g/ 1938, [„Ierland"]. Idem: „The Practice of Magic and Witch- craft", documentatie §2-E/1947. Zie ook ℞. Yᵉ.   Bo

At Note 1938, fol. 279E, "Gnomes", documentation §31-a/1938, ["Ireland"]. Idem: "The Practice of Magic and Witchcraft", documentation §2-E/1947 See also R)16. **S.**

This wooden object could have two uses: it is a representation of a human being, or the wooden object is used to see gnomes in the 'free' field, through the hole. Which representation is right, is certainly up for debate.

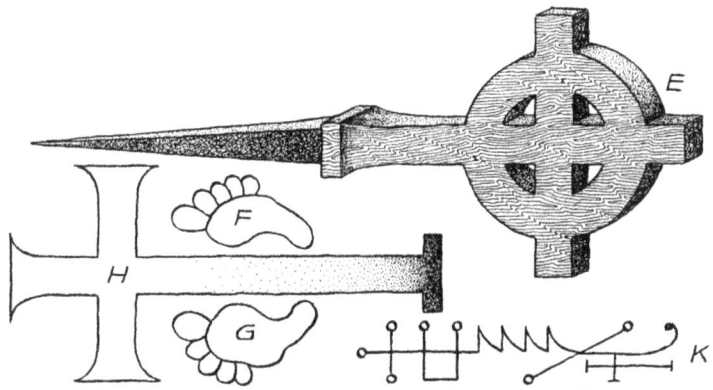

By Aant. 1938. fol. 281ᵈ: „Magic can be seen as the poor man's science. Like science, it is believed to provide the power by which the ordinary human being can exercise some control over the outside world, if he has the knowledge", &c._ Zie F4, 5, 7, 8, 9 en 12: „Gnomes". Aan F14 toevoegen: „Sir Francis Dashwood, leader of the 18ᵗʰ century. Hell Fire Club" = bij foto no. 92/1938. [3]ₒ

At Note 1938, fol. 281d: "Magic can be seen as the poor man's science. Like science, it is believed to provide the power by which the ordinary human being can exercise some control over the outside world, if he has the knowledge", &c.- See F4, 5, 7, 8 and 12: "Gnomes". Add to F14: "Sir Francis Dashwood, leader of the 18th century Hell Fire Club" = at Photo no. 92/1938. **E.**

This is another peculiar entry in the gnome manuscript concerning magic, gnomes and the Hell Fire Club. What these have in common, is up to the reader or interpreter to find out. Is this a citation from Dashwood? Eldermans was fascinated by Francis Dashwood and the Hell Fire Club – it's seen in plenty of his writings and drawings but what has this to do with gnomes? Should we go out on a limb and see a connection between gnomes living under the earth, guarding treasures hidden there by the demon Lucifuge Rofocale, who, in turn, is wrongfully worshipped as the Devil? And thus, reasoning that the Hell Fire Club would be such a worshipping society? Although Eldermans was a fascinating collector of magic paraphernalia, he sometimes made connections only *he* could understand.

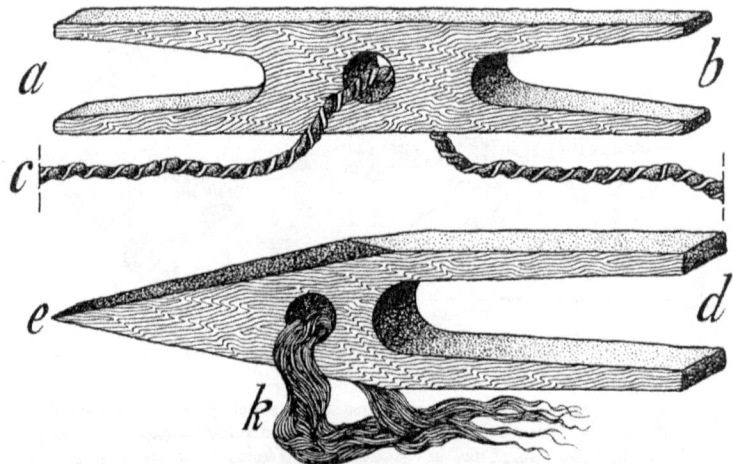

At Note 1947, fol. 14E, the figures 198 and 206, lithography, anno 1904, John Thornton, cap. IV, p. 324 and 326. Idem: "The Practice of Magic and Witchcraft", see the documentation §2-E/1947: "Gnomes". [The use remains unclear!] **H.**

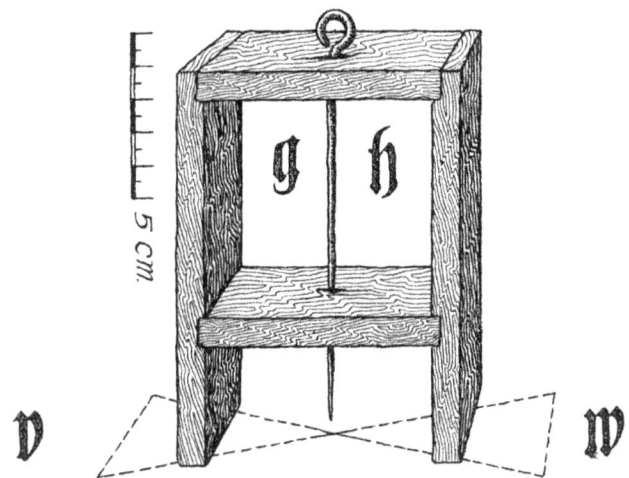

Bij Aant. 1947, fol. 17e, "The Practice of Magic and Witchcraft," documentatie §2-F/1947: "Gnomes". — Detail uit fig. 27 (fotogr. reproductie no. 31/1947): het voorwerp waarvan het gebruik onbekend is. Zie de betreffende correspondentie Mei-Juni 1947. H.

At Note 1947, fol. 17e: "The Practice of Magic and Witchcraft", documentation §2-F/1947: "Gnomes".- Detail from figure 27 (photographic reproduction no. 31/1947): The object of unknown use. See the correspondence regarding this from May-June 1947. **H.**

This object, fairly small if you may believe the measurements, is collected by Eldermans, but he doesn't know what it's used for. Approximately ten centimetres in height, it will be hard to find a practical use for the iron pin in the centre, like being something to fixate an object or something. The use might be not practical, but presumably magical. This construction might be designed to harvest or contain power. How this relates to gnomes is not clear, in the same way Eldermans had no idea what this object was used for.

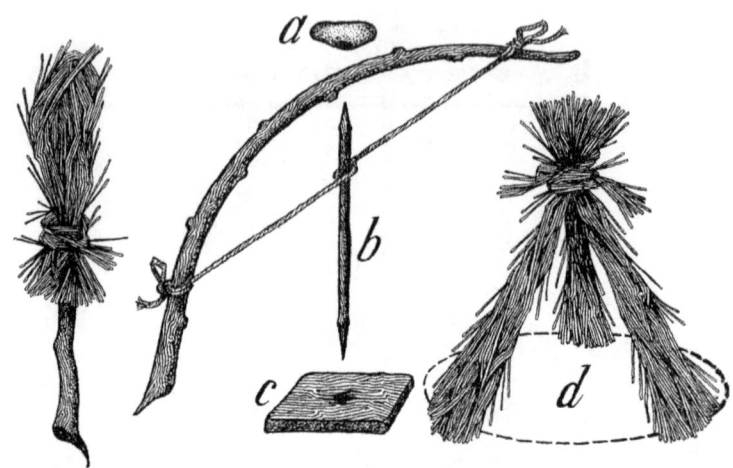

By Rant 1955, fol. 365ᴴ ["The Tools and Methods of Magic", schema III] en documenta-tie §62-m/1955. ["Aardgeesten: Kabouters"=)24 en)26] [W.H.N. Burgerdamme]. ロo

At Note 1955, fol. 365H ["The Tools and Methods of Magic", scheme III] and documentation §62-m/1955. ["Nature spirits: Gnomes"=)24 and)26] [W.H.N. Burgerdamme]. **H.**

In this drawing, we recognize tools to make fire (A-C) and presumably the straw tripod is meant to set alight. How this relates to the broom on the left is unclear. Probably it needs to disperse the smoke coming from the burning tripod, possibly to incense something or someone, or at least take away the smell of humans so that gnomes might not be offended by it. The lack of information provided by Eldermans, causes this drawing to be open for diverse interpretations.

[Below] *At Note 1955, fol. 365H and 366A: "Nature spirits: Gnomes". Gleanings of Geurt van Zeggelen – Moes and H.A. Klinkhamer. See the appendices III and IV (1955)* **E.**

The designs in this drawing are not uncommon for Eldermans. We have already seen the branch with the scythe-type blade (not jagged in this drawing), the branch with the three twigs (masculinity) and the straw cross underneath a cloth with a pile of rocks. Presumably, this is a set-up to attract gnomes, but the real reason why this set-up is constructed, might be in the gleanings of Van Zeggelen – Moes and Klinkhamer…

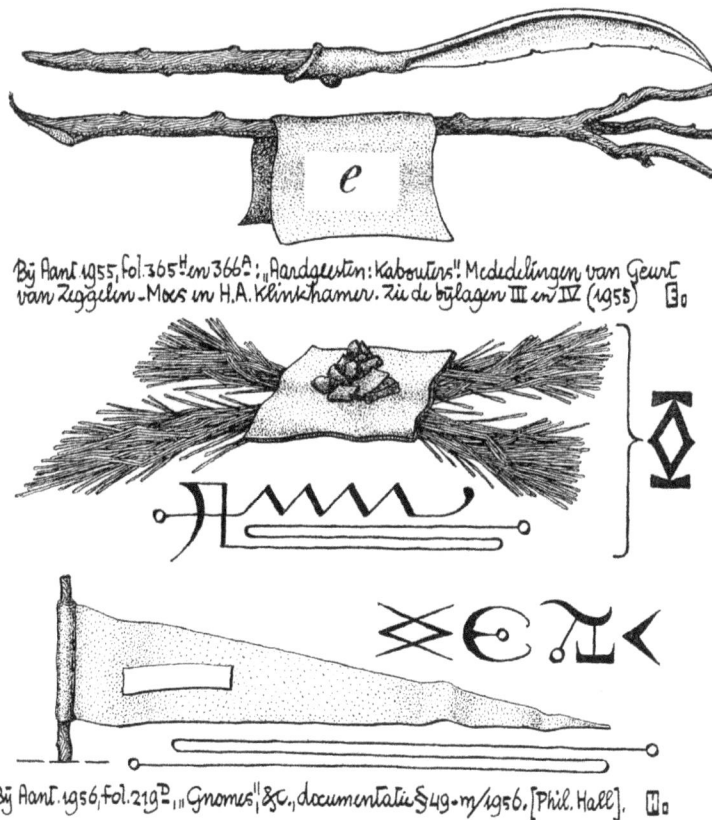

At Note 1956, fol. 219D, "Gnomes", &c., documentation §49-m/1956. [Phil. Hall]. **H.**

A flag to be placed somewhere on the property, presumably with the purpose of attracting gnomes (a sigil for Venus is included, which means it must awaken the emotion of love in the gnome). It is not known who Eldermans means by Phil. Hall.

[Below] *At Note 1956, fol. 220D, documentation §51-p/1956, "Nature spirits", after fig. 117, Geo Walker, see F4. [Idem: "The Survival of the Pagan Gods", see fol. 220E, F2.]* **O**.

The name 'Geo Walker' appears frequently in Eldermans' work, especially in concordance with nature spirits and natural magic. *The Survival of the Pagan Gods. The Mythological Tradition and Its Place in Renaissance Humanism and Art* is a book by Jean Seznec, translated into English by Barbara F. Sessions and originally published in 1953. A new print was published in 1972, which Eldermans may have consulted in the Royal Library or it could be that this book was in his personal collection. The book deals with the downfall of the Gods of Olympus and their resurgence during the Renaissance. How this relates to the drawing, is not clear.

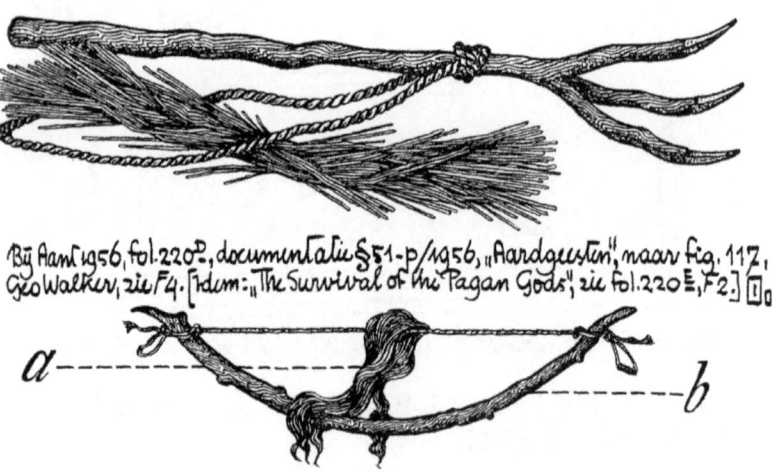

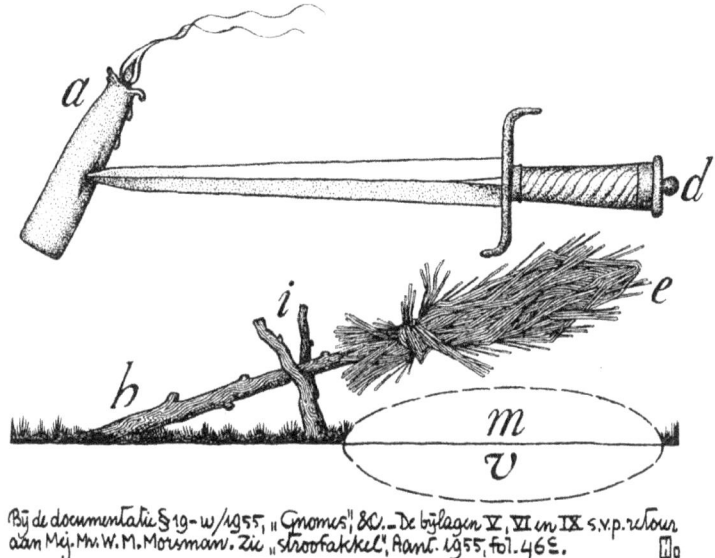

Bij de documentatie §19-w/1955, "Gnomes", &C.- De bijlagen V, VI en IX s.v.p. retour aan Mej. Mv. W. M. Morsman. Zie "stroofakkel", Aant. 1955, fol. 46C. H.

At the documentation §19-w/1955, "Gnomes", &c.- The appendices V, VI and IX please return to miss LL W.M. Morsman. See "straw-torch", Note 1955, fol. 46C. **H.**

The straw torch was quite popular during folk-festivals in Twente, where the torch was carried during dark nights to represent the light, which was thought to return after the 21st December. The candle being pierced by the athame, has something to do with the blessing of the light but again, Eldermans' lack of information does not confirm or deny this interpretation.

Mellie Uyldert in Onkruid,
Tijdschrift voor een natuurlijke
manier van leven :

> Kabouters zien er uit als
> mensen van vlees en bloed, maar ze
> zijn van 'n wat fijner stof gemaakt.
> Zoals wij mensen door de lucht heen
> gaan, zo gaan zij door alle soorten
> materie heen, ze verdwijnen in een
> aarden heuvel of een boomstam of in
> de grond. Wie ze niet zien kan, zou
> per ongeluk op een kabouter kunnen
> gaan zitten, maar dat zou hem niet
> schaden. Op bepaalde tijden van het
> jaar trekken ze ergens heen, dan vol-
> gen ze in lange rijen altijd dezelfde
> weg door het bos en dan zijn de
> vrouwtjes er ook bij, zoals mevrouw
> Gerding in Nunspeet mij vertelde en
> zoals de bevolking daar altijd heeft
> waargenomen. De poezen zag zij met
> de hele rij mee springen.

Toch een vervelend idee : per ongeluk
op een kabouter gaan zitten ...
Kan mevrouw Uyldert (of mevrouw Gerding, of de bevolking van Nunspeet)
niet vragen of ze van te voren "kijk uit!"
of 'Au!" willen roepen ?

Toevoegen aan §4ᵃ, Aant. 1948, fol. 392*, "Kabouters": "Bescheurkalender", Koot & Bie, "Woensdag,
6 Juni 1984.　　　　　　　　　　　　　　　Eₒ

Add to §4a, Note 1948, fol. 392, "Gnomes": "Bescheurkalender"*[42]
Koot & Bie, "Wednesday 6 June 1984. **E.**

---

42. A hard term to translate. "Zich bescheuren" is to laugh out loud, tearing yourself up, however the term "scheuren" is to rip, which exactly what needs to happen here: this page is from a day calendar and every day you need to rip the previous day from the calendar. It is simple wordplay in Dutch, in English it might come down to 'Tear me up calendar'…

This might be one of the strangest entries in Eldermans' gnome works. It is a page from a calendar compiled by two Dutch comedians, Kees van Kooten (Koot) and Wim de Bie (Bie), who had a show on Sunday evening television, in which they tackled actual developments in Dutch society with a biting satire. In this particular joke from 6th June 1984 (being one of the most recent entries in Eldermans' work!), they make fun of Mellie Uyldert, an author on esoteric subjects, who strangely got entangled in Eldermans' work after his passing. Mellie Uyldert was supposed to have provided texts with drawings from Eldermans, in a book thought to be published by the publishing house 'De Driehoek' from Amsterdam. In this joke, an excerpt of Uyldert's writings on gnomes is ridiculed by Koot & Bie. They ridiculed a lot of 'fringe' subjects, as they also made a television item about the thesis of Frits Bom that the Dutch dolmens were built by an 'intelligent race' (not necessarily an extra-terrestrial race but his book reads a lot like the work of Erich von Däniken's *Chariots of the Gods*). The printed part is from the writings of Mellie Uyldert, the handwritten part is the commentary made by Koot & Bie. The text of Uyldert goes as follows:

> *Gnomes look like people of flesh and blood, but they consist of a finer substance. Like we people move through the air, they can go through all kinds of matter, they disappear in an earth hill, or a tree trunk or into the ground. Who can't see them might accidentally sit on a gnome, but it would not hurt him. On certain times, they migrate somewhere and travel in long rows down the same road through the woods and their females are also present, like Mrs. Gerding in Nunspeet told me and like the locals have always observed them. She saw her cats jumping along the parade.*

And this is the commentary made by Koot & Bie:

Mellie Uyldert in Onkruid,[43] magazine for a natural way of life: [...] It appears to be a bothersome idea: to accidentally sit on a gnome... Could Mrs. Uyldert (or Mrs. Gerding, or the locals from Nunspeet) ask if they can shout in advance 'watch out' or 'Ouch'?

Toevoegen aan §3ª, Aant. 1937, fol. 33I: F2. „Lewis Manfield vergeet m.i. dat de handelingen, voorgeschreven in „de Sleutels", vaak zeer ingewikkeld, omslachtig en tijdrovend zijn en buitendien gebonden aan bepaalde tijden, data en plaatsen. De voorgeschreven materialen zijn vaak kostbaar en zeer moeilijk te bekomen. Wil men zich wijden aan deze magische experimenten — bijv. teneinde in contact te komen met een kabouter— dan wordt dat een dagtaak in dient men zich wel haast los te maken van werkkring en familieleven, en dient men vermogend te zijn." (Vertaling mej. A. van Keulen.)   Eo

= *d*

Add to §3a, Note 1937, fol. 33I: F2. "Lewis manfield forgets, in my opinion, that the operations, prescribed in "The Greater Key" often are very complicated, cumbersome and time consuming and next to that bound to certain times, dates and places. The prescribed materials are often valuable and very hard to come by. If one wants to devote himself to these magical experiments — for instance, to get in contact with a gnome - it is a day job in itself and one needs to cut themselves off from work and family, and you need to be wealthy". (Translation miss A. van Keulen.) **E.**

This almost reads as a complaint. Eldermans does have a point. Some of the mentioned ingredients are very hard to obtain, like the blood and fat of a man that has died around 20th July. Obtaining other ingredients is no different: feathers of certain birds, some spices, herbs which do not grow locally - in short, you need to have time, money and possibilities.

---

43. Onkruid translates as weed. It is the title of a Dutch magazine concerned with esoteric subjects.

The pentacle below does *not* come from *The Greater Key of Solomon.*

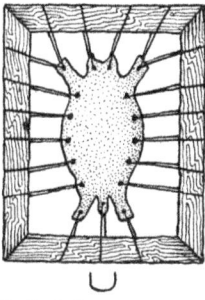

By §1ª, Aant. 1941,
fol. 6Ⅱ, naar Percy
Alfred Bryce, ao. 1904, „Gnomes" [„Moleskin", &c., zie §1b, F3.]

At §1a, Note 1941, fol. 6II, after Percy Alfred Bryce, anno 1904, "Gnomes" ["Moleskin", &c., &c., §1b, F3.] **E.**

Most pentacles concerning the attraction of gnomes have to be drawn on parchment made of moleskin. Moles, being subterranean creatures, might possess properties that appeal to gnomes. In Eldermans' work there are many descriptions of how to prepare the parchment: the mole needs to be killed and the skin stripped under clear, running water, so that the blood mingles with the water. The flesh of the mole needs to be buried where predators cannot get hold of it, and the skin needs to be dried and incensed, this needs to be repeated for a number of days until the parchment is ready to be used.

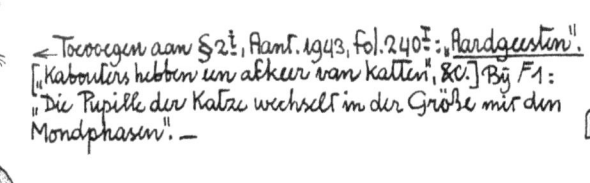

←Toevoegen aan §2ᵗ, Aant. 1943, fol. 240ᵗ: „Aardgeesten".
[„Kabouters hebben een afkeer van katten", &c.] Bij F1:
„Die Pupille der Katze wechselt in der Größe mit den
Mondphasen". —

Add to §2i, Note 1943, fol. 240I: "Nature spirits". [Gnomes have an aversion to cats", &c.] At F1: [From German] "The pupils of a cat change in size with the phases of the Moon".- **A.**

> Ex Libris:
>
> J. H. W. Eldermans.

> Maart 1947, tentoonstelling Deventer. Verzocht wordt alle stukken, gemerkt met het naast-staande ex libris, terug te zenden aan J.H.W. Eldermans, Ootmarsumsestraat 99 te Almelo.
>
> JHWE.

March 1947, Exhibition Deventer. Requested to send all the pieces marked with the ex-libris depicted here to J.H.W. Eldermans, Ootmarsumsestraat 99 in Almelo. JHWE.

The Ex-Libris of Eldermans is still something I hope to see in one of the second-hand books I order online. Eldermans appeared to have collaborated on many exhibitions, although some of the exhibitions he mentioned did not take place (like the ones in the parapsychological institute in Utrecht) but, apparently, some of the exhibitions he mentions did actually take place. It is not known if he contributed drawings or objects to these exhibitions and which exhibition was held in Deventer in 1947, is not something Eldermans thinks as useful to mention.

> Bij §1e: "In een Oudengelse toverspreuk tegen plotselinge pijn (spit?) wordt deze toegeschreven aan een kleine speer die door Asen, alven of heksen afgeschoten wordt."—
>
> Ao

At §1e: "In an ancient English spell against sudden pain (lumbago?) which was attributed to a small spear which was shot by Asen, Alves or witches."- **A.**

This isn't only known in English fairy-lore but also in The Netherlands, where the sudden appearance of lumbago was attributed to elves who shot tiny darts into our backs. The stone arrowheads which could be found in De Veluwe were also attributed to the Little People.

Bij §1d: „De christelijke dichter Sigvat beschrijft in een van zijn verzen een reis naar Zweden die hij in 1018 had gemaakt, en waarbij hij in de bossen van West-Götaland geen slaapplaats had kunnen vinden, omdat iedereen in de streek het alfablot vierde: het offer aan de elfen".— H□

At §1d: "The Christian poet Sigvat describes in one of his verses a journey to Sweden which he made in 1018, in which he could not find a place to sleep in the forests of West-Götaland because everyone in the area was celebrating the Alfablot: the sacrifice to the elves".- **H.**

This entry is taken from the book by Martin Koomen.[44]

1,

Bij Aant. 1936, §3, fol. 21: „Robin's pincushion", het speldekussen van Robin, de goede boskabouter". Zie „Mosgal" = „Slaapgal' = „Bedeguaargal". Zie ook §3a: „galwesp".— E□

At Note 1936, §3, fol. 21: "Robin's pincushion", the pincushion of Robin, the good forest gnome". See "Rose bedeguar gall" = "moss gall" or "Bedguar gall". See also §3a: "gall wasp".- **E.**

Robin's pincushion is an abnormal growth in plants caused by the larvae of the Bedeguar Gall Wasp. In folklore it is believed that Robin Goodfellow is responsible for the strange growths. Robin is a fairy, but does it appear that he might be gnome? In Shakespeare's *A Midsummer Night's Dream*, Robin, or Puck, is responsible for all the mischief, and this growth could be considered a result of fairy mischief...

Aant. 1936, §5, Fol. 31. Over dit onderwerp werd geschreven door Buss, Reinhard J., „The Klabautermann of the northern seas. An analysis of the protective spirit of ships and sailors in the context of popular belief, christian legend and Indo-European mythology." Berkeley, Los Angeles, London 1973. University of California Press (Folklore Studies 25), 138 p.— JHWE.
Bij F8. Er staat: „In dit verband vind ik de naam Klabauterman te weinig opvallend om er een aanwijzing voor directe invloed van onze kabouter *in te zien."* E□

---

44. Martin Koomen, *Het Koninkrijk van de nacht. Over dwergen, elfen en andere geesten van aarde, lucht, water en vuur*, Amsterdam, 1978, p. 44

Note 1936, §5, fol. 31 About the subject was written by Buss, Reinhard J., "The Klabautermann of the northern seas. An analysis of the protective spirit of ships and sailors in the context of popular belief, christian legend and Indo-European mythology". Berkeley, Los Angeles, London 1973. University of California Press (Folklore Studies 25), 138 pages.- JHWE

At F8. It says: "In this context I find the name "Klabouterman" little outstanding to see a clue of direct influence on our gnome". E.

§1, fol. 35 : in plaats van fig. VI; zie: „Uriel", &c. [„Aardgeesten" F8.]

§1, fol. 35: instead of figure VI; see: "Uriel", &c. ["Nature spirits"F8] S.

G 29.

De „Aantekeningen" zijn tot 21-12-1979 voorzien van voetnoten. In de „kaboutersverhalen" t19-t24 zijn de persoonsnamen door mij. M.R. Janssen veranderd. De ware personalia heb ik vermeld in de „Index" = zie onder XVIII. JHWE.

G *Footnotes are added to the "Notes" until 21 December 1979. In the "gnome-stories" t19 to t24 the personal names are changed by Miss M.R. Janssen. The true personal details are mentioned in the "Index"= see under XVIII. JHWE.*

And here we might have found an explanation for the many troubles we encountered when looking for the witnesses of gnomes. Eldermans had someone change their names. This is unfortunate, as we are not able to verify these stories, or to track down surviving family members who might have known something more about it. Apparently, Eldermans made promises to these people to alter their names or even leave them out of his works. Why he would do that in a manuscript which would not be read by outsiders, is unknown. Possibly, he feared that his work might eventually leave the house and he wanted to be on the safe side.

[Below] *Addition no. IX at Index 1949, no. 342-DD: Arnold Jan Scheer, "Panorama", no. 39, 26 September 1980, "Look, there goes a gnome", &c.. A strange report! JHWE*

Arnold Jan Scheer, an advocate for the preservation of the Sinterklaas culture, was very interested in people who saw gnomes. He published a couple of articles in magazines like *Nieuwe Revu* and *Panorama*, but he also had a television show called *Showroom* in which he interviewed Annie Gerding-Le Comte, who mentioned Eldermans in the first minutes of her interview. She might have directed Scheer towards Eldermans, who was interviewed for *Panorama*. This section is the interview with Eldermans and a short description of his research. The text is translated below.

> *Mister Eldermans from The Hague researched gnome-observations his entire life. He is a former investigating officer of the Justice department. He has never seen gnomes or "fairies". His interest concerns the historic and modern gnome-observations of farmers and other inhabitants of rural areas. In 1933, he started registering gnome-observations by drawing them as dots on a map. His current maps point out a migration route which directs, in length, over East-Netherlands. The route goes through North Drenthe, Overijssel across De Veluwe through the Kamper Klippen, de Dellen, 't Eperholt, Tongeren, Wilna, Doornspijker Moor, Forestry Nunspeet, Muncipal forest, the Round House to the Willemsforest, where the migration divides. One half goes to Halfweg, the Elspeter moor, Large Colony, Staverden, Speulder field to the south. The other through the Belvédère forest, Hulshorster sands, Leuvenhorst and Leuvenums forest. Except for old writings, the most important source for Eldermans was a map drawn in 1927 by the then elderly Mister Goudswaard, teacher and guest in Guesthouse Denneheuvel in Nunspeet. Eldermans about his conversations with gnome-observers on De Veluwe, in De Peel, Drenthe and North east Twente: "At night you are talking and*

when there are no others, it follows: Mister, you will not believe this… You see, among each other they know. They know damn well what to hide for the vicar'.

Scheer, however, makes a mistake. He reads the migration maps incorrectly: he sees them from *north to south*, and they should be read from *south to north*.

De heer Eldermans uit Den Haag heeft zijn hele leven onderzoek gedaan naar kabouterwaarnemingen.Hij is oud-opsporingsambtenaar van Justitie. Zelf heeft hij nog nooit kabouters of „fairies" gezien. Zijn belangstelling gaat vooral uit naar historische en hedendaagse kabouterwaarnemingen van boeren of andere platelandsbewoners.

In 1933 begon hij kabouterwaarnemingen te registreren, door ze als stippen op kaarten aan te tekenen. Zijn huidige kaarten wijzen duidelijk op een trekroute in de lengterichting over Oost-Nederland. Zo leidt de route via Noord-Drenthe, Overijssel over de Veluwe via de Kamper Klippen, de Dellen, 't Eperholt, Tongeren, Wilna, Doornspijkse heide, Boswachterij Nunspeet, Gemeentebos, 't Ronde Huis naar het Willemsbos, waar de trek zich splitst. De ene helft gaat dan via Halfweg, de Elspeter Heide, Grote Kolonie, Staverden, Speulder Veld naar het zuiden. De andere via het Belvédèrebos, Hulshorsterzand, Leuvenhorst en Leuvenumsebos.

Behalve oude geschriften was een belangrijke bron voor Eldermans een kaartje dat in 1927 werd getekend door de toen al bejaarde heer Goudswaard, onderwijzer en gast uit Pension Dennpheuvel te Nunspeet.

Eldermans over zijn gesprekken met kabouterwaarnemers op de Veluwe, in de Peel, Drenthe en Noordoost-Twente: „'s Avonds zit je te ouwehoeren en als er geen anderen bij zijn, komt het: meneer zal het niet willen geloven... Kijk, onder mekaar weten ze het wel. Ze weten verdomd goed wat ze voor de dominee moeten verstoppen."

Aanvulling no. IX bij Index 1949, no. 342-DD: Arnold Jan Scheer, Panorama", no. 39, 26 September 1980, „Kijk, daar gaat un kabouter", &c.. Een vreemd verslag! ZijWE.

Toevoegen aan Index 1949, no. 342-FF, sub III: „Pentakels en Talismans voor den Zaterdag, onder invloed van Saturnus": Deze Talismans kunnen ook goede diensten verlenen bij het lokaliseren en het exploiteren van ertsaders en in de bodem verborgen schatten".—

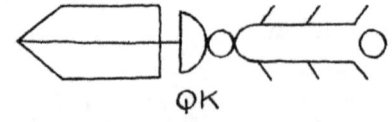

QK

NOPA PADOUS ♄

QL   QM

QN: zie a. „Zegel van Saturnus", b. „Karakteristieken van Saturnus", en c. „Goddelijke Letters van Saturnus".

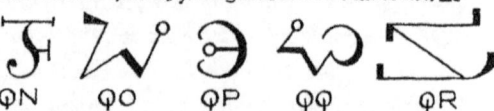

QN   QO   QP   QQ   QR

Aanvulling no. III bij Index 1949, no. 343-BB: „Hoe men zich meester kan maken van schatten, die worden beheerd door de aardgeesten, door het volk kabouters genoemd". = zie de documentatie §268-PP/1948 (mej. E.Sanders).

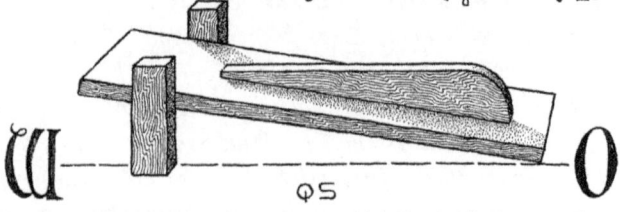

W   QS   O

Bij de documentatie §267-HH/1949, „Gnomes", &c., Paul Williamson.—

CHAPTER FIVE

EPILOGUE

Is this the entire gnome-research by Eldermans? I would be disappointed if it was. We are speaking of more than half a century of fascination with the Little People, and to put that into merely four hundred pages of work is something I personally would not accept. Regarding the sequence numbers on the known manuscripts (5e and 16b) suggests that there is *a lot more* material, somewhere. It might be in a bookcase gathering dust, it could be in a moving box in someone's attic or it could be, God forbid it, destroyed. Regarding the contents, could we call Eldermans a thorough researcher? Let me answer that question at the end of this chapter. Eldermans said on many occasions that he never saw a gnome. The way he writes that down, I get the impression that his inability to see gnomes is one of his greatest regrets, especially when he is of an older age. Although he could be quite sceptical towards certain witnesses and he might have said in 1946, that he could not find a single shred of belief in himself for the Little People, he appeared, in later years, to be milder in his judgment. Once people have finished laughing about gnomes and regard the evidence with attention, they might come to a completely different opinion. Joke Bosman recalled that he only once spoke about gnomes in the context of the town Vaassen, where they were staying for a short holiday. Near Vaassen, was an area which should be looked at more carefully, as gnomes could exist there. Vaassen is quite close to Vierhouten, a place where Eldermans had written about an elderly gentleman who rented a camping house and saw gnomes through a certain window. He was never able to determine where the house once stood.

Vaassen is also not far from Nunspeet and although his parents lost their vacation house "Gerharda" in 1938, it is not strange to think that he went back to Nunspeet, hopeful to see one of those pesky gnomes, one day. He would not. In 1978, when he reached out to Johan Montenberg, the researcher of the Round House stories, he might return to Nunspeet once more. But his ideas concerning gnomes were infectious. In Montenberg's later writings, we see that he starts taking gnomes a bit more seriously, although he still denies believing in them, as we can see in a letter he wrote to the Provincial Archives of Gelderland on 26th June 1990. But, once Montenberg starts to see names like "Aortjeshuus" (the house of Aortje), he mistakes it for "Aardjeshuus" (House of the Earth) and makes a connection with gnomes. Another story of his walks in Nunspeet, is about a man who says about the Round House Area that "if gnomes exist, they live here" and on hearing this, a woman faints. Now we can take this for granted but Montenberg has proven himself to be a man with a rich imagination. When he received photostats of Eldermans' work with the compliments of Bob Richel, he became scared, as he believed Eldermans to be a top official in the Department of Justice and he feared that this would lead certain authority figures to his home. Montenberg already thought his house was 'bugged' by the Dutch Secret Service and he became more paranoid, as he got older. Eldermans might have been responsible for feeding this man's paranoia to great length!

But Montenberg was lucky: Eldermans wasn't known for discussing his occult interests with everyone, not even his own family. Judith van Meel wrote to Jeannet Richel in 2004 that Eldermans once remarked that 'gnomes do exist'. And that's where it ended. For the most time, he kept his gnomes as a pastime, something he loved to read about, he loved to draw and about which he stored a lot of information.

Most of this information is either from grimoires, other books concerned with the folklore of gnomes or even from witnesses who actually saw one of the Little People standing by a tree in a lonesome field. Although he was very interested in gnomes and magic, it appears that he only wanted to read up on gnomes when they were not considered an allegory. I know he read and knew about Eliphas Levi, who actually wrote about gnomes in his *Transcendental Magic, its doctrine and ritual*, but as being spirits of the earth in an allegorical way:

> *It must be borne in mind that the special kingdom of the gnomes is at the north, that of the salamanders at the south, that of the sylphs at the east, and that of the undines at the west. These beings influence the four temperaments of man, that is to say, the gnomes affect the melancholy, salamanders the sanguine, undines the phlegmatic, and sylphs the bilious. Their signs are -the hieroglyphs of the bull for the gnomes, who are commanded with the sword; those of the lion for the salamanders, who are commanded with the bifurcated rod or the magic trident; those of the eagle for the sylphs, who are commanded by the holy pentacles; finally, those of the water-carrier for the undines who are commanded by the cup of libations. Their respective sovereigns are Gob for the gnomes, Djîn for the salamanders, Paralda for the sylphs, and Nicksa for the undines.*[45]

And this isn't the only entry about gnomes in Levi's work. But, in Eldermans' notes, there is *nothing* to be found about Levi's writings. The same goes for Collin de Plancy's *Dictionnaire Infernal*, in which gnomes are a lemma, which is actually explained in detail and often contradicts Eldermans' ideas on gnomes but does not appear in his gnome-notes, although it is quite clear that Eldermans read that book! One explanation could be that he didn't deem it interesting

---

45. Eliphas Levi, *Transcendental magic, its doctrine and ritual*, London, 1896, pp 220-221

enough. Another explanation might be that he didn't really think about it, or that he never actually registered that these authors wrote about gnomes. The last explanation I can come up with, is that he did read it, did write it down but that we do not have access to that part of his gnome writings. We have to deal with the fact that some of his gnome-writings simply have disappeared or are still somewhere in private collections. Considering that the 16b part of the *Gnome manuscript* in the Museum of Witchcraft and Magic are photostats, should lead us to the conviction that *the originals are still out there*.

INVENTION OF TRADITION

One accusation I take seriously and I wish to make my personal responsibility, is the fact that I suspect Eldermans of *inventing tradition*. There are strong indications that Eldermans gave alternate interpretations of certain phenomena he encountered with the purpose of creating a whole new gnome-folklore. This became quite apparent in his interpretation of the Staddle Stones found on Guernsey. He thought them to be hiding places for the Little People, although he was well aware these were used to dry hay on. His idea of how the hay was dried was *wrong*. The Staddle Stones were the foundation of a hayshed, the construction was built on top of these stones, and in the shed, the hay was dried. There was no other use known than a practical one. It would not stop Eldermans to *repeatedly* emphasize his version of affairs. Eldermans based this on a witness who said that these stones turned up in places where no hay was grown. But what Eldermans overlooked, and his witness apparently so, was that these stones, after they lost their practical use, were considered *esthetical ornaments*. Even today, these stones are to be seen on the internet, as garden decorations.

The area in which the evidence is so convincing for an accusation of the *inventing of tradition*, is Twente. Although Eldermans reports many sightings of gnomes nearby the

Canal Almelo-Nordhorn, the nineteenth and twentieth century folklorists do not report that much gnome-activity in Twente. There are a few stories that survived, which tell us how gnomes misbehaved, or were incidentally killed by a farmer but the whole gnome-folklore that Eldermans describes, is fully absent in the works of the folklorists. The problem is that the landscapes in Twente are quite captivating and can be considered 'magical' in nature. Maybe Eldermans thought there was something missing in the local folklore and so he invented his personal gnome folklore, there. The same goes for De Veluwe. There are stories of gnomes living in the hills around Vierhouten and stories of gnomes who actually work for people at night but the many stories Eldermans collected, appear to have been unknown. One might think that these stories had not been collected yet, or the witnesses simply never trusted the folklorists and never told them of their experiences. But, how did Eldermans convince these people to entrust them with one of the biggest secrets of their lives? And there is another problem. In other writings of authors like Arnold Jan Scheer, it is mentioned that Eldermans also collected gnome stories in Drenthe - the province known for the most remains of Bronze Age Dolmens. In the gnome notes of Eldermans, there isn't one single entry that mentions his research in Drenthe. Other provinces where gnome-tales have been noted, like Noord-Brabant and Zeeland, are also missing from his notes. It could be explained that these notes were made but are lost. Another explanation is that Eldermans didn't think of these provinces to be interesting.

Another indication that Eldermans was guilty of *invention of tradition* is the great difference between surviving gnome-tales in De Peel compared to the stories Eldermans had collected. Peel-gnomes were poor, traded their labour for food and stayed far away from villages or cities because they feared the church bells. Eldermans' gnomes didn't actually *fear* the church bells, but loathed the hypocritical ways of Christians. One of these tales described a gnome guarding treasure, which isn't too common in De Peel. A really famous tale is the gnome lamenting the death of the gnome king, Kyria, but it is completely lacking in Eldermans' work. It appeared that Eldermans wanted to develop a gnome mythology for The Netherlands, just as Great Britain and Ireland had a rich 'Little People' folklore. Maybe he thought that was missing from The Netherlands and he decided to change that. But, in doing so, he might well have damaged the gnome folklore, just like Wil Huygen and Rien Poortvliet had done with their books on the gnomes.

Diek Callenbach and Jan Eldermans in a forest, presumably in Nunspeet, according to their ages (they appear young). Photograph courtesy of Gerda and Els van Zuuren.

LACK OF ORIGINAL RESEARCH

When we look back on *The Gnome Manuscript, The Gnome Grimoire* and *The Gnome Compendium* we can safely say that the bulk of the entries Eldermans made, were citations he found in (popular) books. Wil Bosman, his former neighbour, said that Eldermans was 'always busy drawing' and that he read books 'from the Royal Library' in order to 'make his drawings'. We have identified some of the books he consulted in his gnome-notes. The first being the *Encyclopedia of Magic & Superstition*, which was cited on many occasions, and he used chapters from this book to make up his own pseudo-library like *The Tools and Methods of Magic, Glossary of Magical Lore and Spirits of Nature*. He often only cherry-picked the phrases that spoke to him, unwittingly altering the meaning of those phrases. The most interesting feature is that Eldermans took these phrases and attributed them to totally different sources. *The Tools and Methods of Magic* consisted of hundreds of pages, that it becomes a question if he took the title for one of his own manuscripts, that which he consulted as a reference book. But there are other books of which Eldermans consulted pages that never existed in the book. One example is *Curiosités des Sciences Occultes*, where he consulted information on gnomes that isn't even in the book, on pages which do not exist.

Another important source for Eldermans, was the book *Het Koninkrijk van de nacht* by the journalist, Martin Koomen. There are numerous entries of Koomen in Eldermans' work, which might indicate that Eldermans thought the work of Koomen to be of the greatest importance. But sometimes Eldermans forgot to mention his source and I was thrown back to my own memories, as to whether I had seen that particular entry in Koomen's book, or not. Most of the time, my memory did not fail me. Eldermans owes a great deal to Koomen, as Koomen's book actually reads like the blueprint of Eldermans' gnome-research. It isn't too far-fetched to think that Eldermans also read Koomen's previous book,

Het ijzige zaad van de Duivel (the icy seed of the Devil), being a history of witches and demons.

Another important source for Eldermans were the grimoires *The Greater Key of Solomon* and *The Secret Grimoire of Turiel.* These are frequently cited in the works of Eldermans, and the symbol and words *Nopa Padous* appear on many occasions in his work. Although the work of Marius Malchus doesn't refer to gnome, and *Solomon* only has one chapter which concerns itself with gnomes, Eldermans sees more connections to gnomes where others fail to see them. And so, we are treated to pentacles which haven't got anything to do with gnomes, or he sees a connection between the mention of *Kuba Walda* in Koomen's book with a pentacle in *Solomon.* These elements are brought together with the ease of an ignorant man but I refuse to believe that Eldermans was ignorant - I do think he saw connections between magical works that aren't that obvious. What I do think to be a 'wrong-doing' on his part, is attributing gnome-lore to authors who actually never had interest in, or even wrote about, gnomes. And here we touch the subject of *invention of tradition again…*

Opposite: Jan Eldermans in Twente in older age, near a Saxon well and a statue of a white woman.

Left: Jan Eldermans at a fence in Nunspeet. Right: Jan Eldermans on one of the bridges in the Belvédère forest, spanning over a creek. (Photographs courtesy of Jeannet Richel)

AN ACHIEVEMENT IN ITSELF

Although we can criticize the contents of the manuscript, the work is, in itself, more than impressive. Keep in mind that in these books only the entries concerning *gnomes* are used but there are far more entries concerning witchcraft, ceremonial magic and folklore, which have nothing to do with gnomes. In the Swiss collection, there is a 1500-page manuscript written on blotting paper, which has the exact same page lay-out as the gnome-manuscript, in Boscastle. It convinced me that the gnome manuscript was of a *posthumous construct*. Let me elaborate on that. In 1985 and 1986, Bob Richel received his 'heritage' from Diek Eldermans, who was in charge of the destruction of the works of Eldermans and there were a few boxes Bob was allowed to take home with him. Bob himself described in a letter to Graham King (then the owner of the Museum of Witchcraft) how he started to categorize these drawings and works. So, after Eldermans, the works got *re-arranged*. Once you start re-arranging a collection, it loses its original meaning, the purpose the creator had with these works is lost forever. Richel started making several categories based on Eldermans' notes in his works. And so, the gnome manuscripts 16b and 5e came into existence. Whether there are any other works concerning the gnome magic of Eldermans is unknown. I can speculate about how the collection has been dispersed or destroyed but that will not help anyone. Bob sold a lot of the works of Eldermans, so it is very possible that someone may well have bought these pages and still has them in an acid-free box in his, or her, collection. Maybe the owner has passed away, and the drawings ended up in a cardboard box in the attic of one of their heirs, unbeknownst to them of what they have in their homes.

Eldermans took very good care of his work. All is laid out in a neatly fashion, the drawings and the text are in straight lines - he presumably used linear paper underneath his blotting paper, just to make sure that the lay out would be similar. There is an even distance between the lines of text and it is only in his later life, between 1980 and 1984, that his handwriting starts to become a little shaky. It is, however, apparent that the works were made by someone who *cared* for these pages, someone who wanted to make sure that it had a uniform quality to it. Another hypothesis, and that might explain why it is on blotting paper, is that these pages were made from earlier drawings, which he again categorized and reproduced. The older examples were destroyed, and these newer drawings were the ones he wanted to leave behind, in one way or another. He still took care that the names of people who didn't wanted to be mentioned and were still unrecognizable. As we saw, he was someone who had taken care of the altering of names or adding pseudonyms. It looks like he acted very much on purpose. There had to be a voice in the back of his mind that was telling him to leave the world a small heritage - his drawings, his words, his objects and his own *inner world*.

The achievement does not stop with the pages on blotting paper. He left behind a massive collection of *drawings*, all made on quality paper and patiently coloured with ecoline ink. By using a spirit burner, he could dry the drawing quite quickly (ecoline means working wet in wet, which always messes up the colours), so he could apply a new layer of ink. In that manner, Eldermans worked very methodically. He had his own drawing board, which he constructed himself, he had his mixing trays, his pencils and his brushes which he used to apply the ecoline with instead of a dip pen. Although the drawings are more on the subject of Ceremonial magic, or his fabled Rueff method and sado-masochistic sexual magic, there are some drawings in which his fascination for the 'Little People' surfaces. One such drawing is the personal property of Jeannet Richel, his granddaughter; the other one is in the collection of the Museum of Witchcraft and Magic. The gnome figure in this work is something Jeannet and Martine Richel remember coming from a children's book but they, unfortunately, can't recall which one. It is quite possible that Eldermans was a master in copying drawings and various styles - even to the point of making the originals look better in his own drawings. This is one of the rare occasions he used colour in a drawing concerning a gnome.

In this drawing, we see a lot of symbolism. There is the Hebrew letter resembling mem or sammekh, or it could be pseudo-Hebrew, as far as we know. Next to this letter is the Tetragrammaton, in mirror image (it should be yod, he, vow, he and yet it is the other way around: he, vow, he, yod), which might refer to the *underground* nature of the gnomes and their connection to a darker magic. The drawing also refers heavily to *The Greater Key of Solomon*. The gnome itself holds a pendulum, which might refer to the art of dowsing. There are two six-pointed stars, of which the right one consists of two triangles, which could refer to the credo of Hermes Trismegistus: *as above, so below*. And vice versa, *as below, so above*. Heaven and earth are one, so all what lives on the earth or in the earth can also be found in the heavenly spheres. And that is what I think is missing in Eldermans' work: it is all very superficial, there is very little contemplation in his work: where do these gnomes come from, what is their purpose, why do they ignore humans who see them, why do they reveal themselves if no one is allowed to see them, why do only certain people have the *ability* to see gnomes, why do *these* people have that ability (is it something in the water, in the soil, in the environment or is it in the genes?).

The greatest achievement of Eldermans is that he *documented* everything that he found out but he never went further than documenting. He never asked *himself* questions which he tried to answer through means of research. There could be various reasons why he didn't. Maybe he didn't know how to contemplate these questions. Maybe it didn't interest him enough to start pondering about what he read or what he saw. Was he simply looking for *similarities* and expecting to prove the existence of gnomes through comparison? Or, which I think is one possibility, that might need some research: he simply *couldn't* discuss these subjects with someone he considered his intellectual equal. Someone who could give him feedback, who could make him think about what he discovered, who would challenge him in a positive way for a journey on a more philosophical path than that of the documentalist. It is also very well possible he thought such a person did not exist. He was alone with all his knowledge on the subject and he did not believe there was one person out there, who could understand him. He was alone in a world of people who were only bothered with what to cook for dinner, how to pay the newspaper subscription and what would be on the television that night. That there might be no one who could reach his intellectual level. He was always alone with the books he selected, the paper, the pen and the ink…

As he thought it was supposed to be.

ACKNOWLEDGMENTS

Publishing three books in a row is a monstrous undertaking and it was never meant to be a trilogy. Only the perseverance of Jan Eldermans and the enormity of his collection has made it possible that these three books on gnomes have become a reality.

In general, I want to thank Peter Hewitt for thinking alongside me, about how this book should come into existence. I refuse to take credit for that - I just took the advice and worked with it. I must say that I am very pleased with how the result turned out.

These books could not have been possible without my wonderful publishers, Jane Cox and Gemma Gary. Their publications are actually small works of art in themselves and deserve to be read by a large audience. I have to say that I am proud to be a member of the Troy family once more.

Special gratitude should be awarded to Graham King, as without his knowledge on the subject and his perseverance, this collection might well have been lost. It's his achievement that the Richel-Eldermans collection is available for admiring eyes and that it has been saved for prosperity.

Also, to Simon Costin, Judith Hewitt and the wonderful staff of the Museum of Witchcraft and Magic in Boscastle. Your work on presenting information on magic (or magick), giving people an unbiased view of a lore that could possibly be older than written history, is remarkable and I can't praise you enough for your perseverance with the people close by, who do not appreciate what you are doing, even though they sell wonderful ice-cream!

I owe much gratitude to Hans van Maanen of Skepter magazine, who always is willing to buy one of my articles, which has made my research into the Eldermans-collection possible.

I owe Nanda Stumphius a great debt, indeed, for her help in tracking down historical people in Almelo, in the Stadsarchief Almelo. She has been an amazing help in identifying various people from Eldermans' works.

Last, but not least, I owe great gratitude to Jeannet (1955-2020) and Martine Richel, for being such help where and when they could and for allowing me to delve deep into the world of both their grandfather and father. I am very happy to now start working on the research for the book about Bob Richel.

But probably, the most gratitude should go to my lovely wife, Natascha, who has had to endure yet another run of months in which I was glued to my laptop, walking from the table to the bookcase, flipping frantically through a tome of magical lore. You, Shana and Dylan are the guiding lights of my life. Alright, Shamus (2008-2018) and Hedwig can get some credit, too, as long as they don't bite and claw.

These books were only possible with the aid of much coffee, chocolate, assorted nuts, cola zero, gallons of water, tea, yoghurt, bananas, dates, YouTube, Facebook, the occasional take-out, pepper crisps, liquorice and some music in the background - be it Wagner, Mercyful Fate or 16 Horsepower.

This is the job I love; this is what I do best and I hope to continue doing it for a long time.

ILLUSTRATIONS

The Richel-Eldermans collection, Museum of Witchcraft and Magic, Boscastle, United Kingdom

Personal collection Jeannet Richel

Personal collection Gerda and Els van Zuuren

Personal photographic collection Wilmar Taal

Museums.gov.

BIBLIOGRAPHY

Barrett, Francis, *The Magus part two*, internetdownload

Froud, Brian & Alan Lee, *De Elfen*, Bussum 1979

Keightley, Thomas, *The world guide to Gnomes, Fairies, Elves and Other Little People*, New York, 1978

Koomen, Martin, *Het Koninkrijk van de nacht. Over dwergen, elfen en andere geesten van aarde, lucht, water en vuur*, Amsterdam, 1978

Kuile, Mr. G.J. ter, *Twentsche Eigenheimers. Historische Schetsen*, Almelo, 1936

Lenihan, Maurice, *Limerick, its History and Antiquities; Ecclesiastical, Civil and Military, from the Earliest Ages*, Dublin, 1884

Levi, Eliphas, *Transcendental Magic, its Doctrine and Rituals*, London, 1896

N.N., *Encyclopedia of Magic & Superstition*, London, 1974

Noppen, Frans van, *J.H.W. Eldermans in Nunspeet*, Nunspeet, 2015

Poncé, Charles, *Kabbalah. Achtergrond en Essentie*, Deventer, 1976

Salomon, Rabbi, *De Sleutels van Salomo*, Amsterdam 1954

Scheer, Arnold Jan, *Kijk! Daar gaat een kabouter in Panorama 39*, 26 September 1980

Smyth, Frank, *Modern witchcraft. The fascinating story of the rebirth of paganism and magic*, London, 1970

Voo, B.P. van der, Tooverplanten. *Een studie over vergelijkende mythologie in De Tijdspiegel 69*, 1912

Vries, Jan de, Edda. *Goden- en heldenliederen uit de Germaanse oudheid*, Deventer, 1978

CONSULTED WEBSITES

https://web.archive.org/web/20080413013430/http://www.geocities.com/twentschgenootschap/geveltekens.htm
https://www.wonderryck.nl/natura-docet-wonderryck-twente/natura-docet-wonderryck-twente/

David Sanderson, Obituary: Stewart Forson Sanderson, pioneer in studies and recording of folk culture and dialect on the website https://www.scotsman.com/news/obituaries/obituary-stewart-forson-sanderson-pioneer-in-studies-and-recording-of-folk-culture-and-dialect-1-4284198

Dee Finney, The Symbolism and Spiritual Significance of the Number 11, on the website http://www.greatdreams.com/eleven/num11.htm

https://nl.wikipedia.org/wiki/Aas_(eenheid)

http://www.british-history.ac.uk/survey-london/vol21/pt3/pp103-104

Lightning Source UK Ltd.
Milton Keynes UK
UKHW011856171122
412372UK00002B/3